SAINT PAUL THE PHARISEE

Jewish Apostle to All Nations

V. REV. DR. STEPHEN DE YOUNG

ANCIENT FAITH PUBLISHING

CHESTERTON, INDIANA

Saint Paul the Pharisee: Jewish Apostle to All Nations
Copyright © 2024 Stephen De Young

Published by:
Ancient Faith Publishing
A Division of Ancient Faith Ministries
1050 Broadway, Suite 6
Chesterton, IN 46304

Cover Icon of Saint Paul by the hand of Shayne Swenson
Cover design by Samuel Heble

ISBN: 978-1-955890-70-0

Library of Congress Control Number: 2024944022

Contents

SAINT PAUL'S EPISTLES

An Interpretive Translation

Saul of Tarsus

The historical person of Saul of Tarsus is the necessary starting point to understand not only the saint but also his writings preserved by the Church in the New Testament. Saul was a man—a man formed by a particular culture in a particular time and place, with a particular education. He operated, during his entire life, within the Roman Jewish world. Yet his letters, or epistles, have long since ceased being communications from a person to communities he had helped found or was seeking to advise. Instead, they have become theological treatises for abstract arguments disconnected from any historical reality. Discussions of the Book of Romans, for example, now enter the realm of speculation over the potential logical order of various decrees in the mind of God—not any actual concerns of Christians, both Jewish and former pagans, in the capital city of the Roman Empire.

Saul of Tarsus lived in the first century AD and spent the vast majority of his life in the Eastern Roman Empire. As a Jewish man who inherited Roman citizenship from his father, he occupied a liminal position in Roman society. Jewish religion, in all its manifold forms, never fit neatly within the religious and cultural milieu of Roman civilization. This reality led to the general oppression of the Jewish people as noncitizens and to occasional outbreaks within St. Paul's lifetime of more significant forms of persecution. Near the time of his martyrdom, these tensions erupted into open Jewish revolt, leading to the destruction of the temple in Jerusalem and a brutal, systemic de-judification project throughout Palestine.

Nevertheless, St. Paul's citizenship exempted him from any number of the indignities suffered by his people. Yet Paul was never a Roman collaborator, nor did he remain long a member or supporter of the violent resistance groups that proliferated during his lifetime. He sought to lead a Jewish way of life and of being in the world despite the external pressures of Rome. As communities formed surrounding his preaching, he led and advised them to adopt the same tack—living out quiet lives in pious simplicity that would let the authorities safely ignore them.

Saint Paul considered himself a Pharisee throughout his life; even Christianity as a label referred to one of many Judaisms extant in the period.[1] His encounters with, and commissioning by, the resurrected Jesus of Nazareth caused Paul to identify Him with a particular understanding of the Jewish Messiah. The coming of the Messiah, then, caused Paul to see his life and the lives of the other apostles as standing at the inauguration of a new epoch—an epoch in which he had been called to play a particular role in the working out of the salvation of the world. He sought, more than anything, to faithfully answer this call with his life.

Organization of the Book

This book consists of three elements, two of which have been blended together. First, it is a survey of the life of St. Paul as recorded in the Holy Scriptures and interpreted within the Holy Tradition of the Orthodox Church. Second, the book contains surveys of the writings of St. Paul preserved within the New Testament. These two elements

---

1 Judaism in the first century was not a single, unified religion. The religious lives of Jewish people in various places within the Roman Empire and beyond took on a variety of forms. Christianity and Rabbinic Judaism are both forms of first-century Judaism that have survived to the present day.

have been comingled in this presentation for a purpose: Proper interpretation of St. Paul's epistles requires them to be understood within
the historical milieu in which they were composed. His writings are,
therefore, here framed within St. Paul's life and work to facilitate this
contextual understanding.

The third element of this book is an interpretive translation of St.
Paul's epistles. In truth, all translation represents an interpretation,
but the level of interpretation applied here is unapologetic. I make no
pretense of objectivity. The translations in this book are not intended
for devotional reading, much less liturgical use. Rather, they are
intended to convey the meaning of the original text in a form that, as
much as possible, mimics the mode of reception of the original texts
as letters. To this end, I have included no chapter or verse numberings,
and I have freely added explanatory phrases when necessary to convey
meaning. Though these translations are intended to be utilized in tandem with the discussions of the epistles in the relevant chapters, they
are not inserted between them. The translations are at the end of the
text so that they will not disrupt its flow. In many cases, the overview
of St. Paul's epistles given in the main text will help the reader understand choices made and expressions in the interpretive translations.

Old, New, and Even Newer Perspectives on St. Paul

The Protestant Reformation not only brought about but, in many
ways, consisted of a radical reinterpretation of the epistles of St. Paul.
This sixteenth-century mode of interpretation, now known somewhat
ironically as the "old perspective on Paul," has more recently fallen out
of vogue even in Protestant circles, which are arguably dependent on
it. A number of scholars from a Protestant background, beginning in
the latter half of the twentieth century, formed what they called the
"new perspective on Paul." They focused on questioning certain basic
distinctions of the Protestant Reformation based on a renewed knowledge of the facts on the ground in first-century Palestinian Judaism.
As this move to get beyond Reformation-era approaches to reading

and understanding St. Paul has gained strength and confidence, it has become common to refer to these views as the "original perspective on Paul."

The new ("original") perspective represented a movement to overcome a stereotyped, ahistorical reading of St. Paul's writings that had become Protestant orthodoxy—with any deviation from that ahistorical approach risking the label of "heresy." It was not long before various "post-new perspective" movements began that were more comfortable abandoning entirely what is ultimately Martin Luther's reading of Paul for a more contextual understanding. These movements have culminated in an approach called "Paul within Judaism." This view of Paul as writing within Judaism rather than participating in the founding of a new religion—or even being the founder of Christianity himself—has opened new vistas of interpretation. This movement has included not only Christian and secular scholars from a variety of backgrounds but also a number of prominent Jewish scholars.

Authorship Questions

Modern scholars typically contest Paul's authorship of some of the epistles attributed to him. Philippians, Colossians, Ephesians, and what are called the Pastoral Epistles, 1 and 2 Timothy and Titus, are generally considered to be later compositions under Paul's name. The Epistle to the Hebrews has raised questions about its authorship since the patristic era. All these texts are treated in this book as being Pauline in content and in authorship.

Pauline authorship represents a spectrum; it is not a single idea. None of St. Paul's epistles were written by him in the sense that he picked up a writing implement and a parchment or papyrus and wrote them down longhand. He dictated all his epistles to an *amanuensis*, or secretary. That writer, sometimes identified in the text, would make necessary grammatical and stylistic corrections and then read the result back to Paul. The apostle would make any further corrections or changes he deemed necessary; then, the secretary would be responsible for taking the letter to its destination, reading it to the recipients, and answering their questions.

If this is the closest relationship between Paul and one of his epistles at one end of the spectrum, then the Epistle to the Hebrews and Paul's sermons, as recorded in the Acts of the Apostles, are on the opposite end. These texts represent St. Paul's teaching as summarized, arranged, and recorded by another person.[2] In between these two poles are several epistles that identify, along with Paul, a coauthor: St. Timothy. When texts identify themselves in ways that suggest these varied relationships with the author, a more responsible scholarly approach would be to accept these identifications rather than reject authorship by Paul entirely, unless it were to become absolutely necessary.

Positive arguments that epistles other than Hebrews—in many ways a special case—are not Pauline remain unconvincing. The strongest and broadest arguments are based on differences in vocabulary and occasionally in literary style. In both cases, but particularly in style, the difference in secretarial writers, indicated by the texts themselves, is an adequate explanation alone. Further, however, the "seven uncontested epistles" of St. Paul are a relatively small amount of text. Even if Paul himself had handwritten these texts, they would not constitute an adequate sample to make firm conclusions about the authorship of a different text, let alone one with a stated coauthor.

Using Fresh Language

Throughout this book, I have deliberately eschewed certain language. This language is certainly acceptable and has become the usual language of the Church. However, familiar terminology can sometimes be misleading. By using the word *Messiah* instead of *Christ*,

---

2   Likely St. Luke in all cases. This will be discussed further in Chapter 16, "Epistle to the Hebrews."

community instead of *church*, or *Torah* instead of *law*, I hope to unsettle commonly held notions and help the reader reassess Paul in his historical context, rather than project the experience of present-day Christians into the past.

In addition to the interpretive translations of St. Paul's epistles, all other translations contained within this book are my own. The particular intent of this book—to move past layers of accretion and read St. Paul in his original context, to see his life in its historical contours—requires moving away from the now stereotyped language found in standard English translations. Theological meanings that have developed over centuries are quickly, even unconsciously, read into familiar terms. For these reasons, translations in the present text will deliberately break with convention in many places.

The overall intent of this work is to allow people to encounter St. Paul the Apostle, the rabbi from Tarsus, the founder of Christian communities throughout the Roman world. Through this encounter, by coming to know the actual, existing Paul, his works can finally be understood as they were written. These are letters written and sermons preached by a real man to groups of real people facing real situations in life. The ongoing importance and, indeed, the scriptural quality of his epistles lie precisely in the way in which he met the issues and challenges of his day as well as how that particularity informs the equally particular situations faced by Christians in the present.

CHAPTER ONE

Tarsus and Early Life

Tarsus, at the turn of the era, was one of the most historically important and prominent cities in the Roman Empire. The city was already ancient, built on a human settlement that stretched back well into prehistory. By the Luwian and Hittite periods in the early second millennium BC, Tarsus was already one of the most prominent cities in Cilicia and all of Asia Minor, today's Turkey. Cilicia would later be governed by a satrap of the Persian Empire, before becoming a Greek and later a Roman province. Cilicia includes the southeastern coast of Asia, with Tarsus at the curve between Asia Minor and the Levant, just above modern Syria. Historically, and in the early first century AD, Tarsus was at the intersection of the Near Eastern Semitic world and the Greek.

The Religious World of Tarsus

Tarsus was a pagan city. As a Hittite city, her patron god was Shanta, later Sandas in Greek transliteration. The name of this god seems to be derived from the Luwian word for "anger" or "wrath." He is generally depicted waging war with a bow and arrow and is therefore considered to be primarily a god of victory in battle. Sandas was also appeased to prevent the spread of plague, likely related to his depiction as a god of wrath. Traditions regarding Sandas probably share in traditions surrounding the god Resheph in the Levant and in certain early traditions surrounding the god Apollo.[3]

Sandas is a rare god whose cult managed to continue through radically different cultural periods, never being fully assimilated into the pantheons of Tarsus's conquerors. From the earliest sources, it seems that Sandas was likely the founder of some stage of the settlement of Tarsus or an early ruler, but his name is otherwise lost to the Neolithic, preliterate period. Under Greek influence, Herakles came to be identified as the founder of the city, though this suggests a possible failed attempt to assimilate Herakles and Sandas together. The Persians referred to Sandas in imperial Aramaic as the "Baal of Tarsus." At least in Tarsus, Sandas ended up occupying a place in Greek cosmology as a titan, the earliest tier of gods later overthrown by the Olympians.

The most prominent temples in Tarsus in the first century AD were dedicated to Sandas, with attached shrines to Hercules, where he would be worshiped alongside Sandas as a hero. The blood of sacrifices offered to Sandas was then taken and offered to Hercules by pouring it into the ground. Both Sandas and Hercules featured prominently in an annual festival that seems to have adopted a form of the ritual of the funeral pyre of Herakles practiced elsewhere in Asia Minor. The feasts and sacrifices offered at Tarsus were a hub for the pagan religious life of the entire region.

By the first century AD, Tarsus had become a prominent center of learning as well, with a library purported to hold more than two hundred thousand texts. Tarsus also had its own philosophical academy that would produce a number of notable figures. Likely the most

---

3   While much could be said in a more detailed study, Resheph was an archer god of war and plague who was popular throughout the Levant and much of the Ancient Near East, even assimilated into Egypt. References to Resheph are found in various texts of the Hebrew Scriptures as a demonic power from which protection is sought. Several early depictions of Apollo as an archer with arrows of plague are considered to partake of the same well.

prominent was Athenodorus Cananites, a Stoic who would become the tutor of Caesar Augustus, the first Roman emperor. At this point in history, no separation was recognized between religion and philosophy, though members of philosophical schools embraced a somewhat stricter way of life than the general run of pagan peoples and held what they considered to be more sophisticated views of the divine.

Saint Paul's writings make clear that as a young man, he received some breadth of education within the philosophical circles of the city. He is later able to quote the comic playwright Menander (1 Cor. 15:33). He was able to carry on extended conversations in the philosophical hub of Athens (Acts 17:18–34). At a significant number of points, when speaking to Greeks in his epistles, St. Paul appears to use Stoic philosophy, especially as expressed by Seneca, as a touchpoint to explain important Christian ideas.[4] Nevertheless, it would be incorrect to assume that at any point Saul of Tarsus was a member of this or that philosophical school. While he possessed a knowledge of contemporary Roman thought and culture that he could later deploy in the service of the gospel, his way of life was always firmly Jewish.

Tent Making

Tarsus, situated near the place where the river Cydnus entered the Mediterranean, likewise stood as a central point in a number of trade routes. The city stood at the hub of the river, the sea, the Roman roads leading west, and the trade routes heading east, deeper into Asia, and south, to the Levant and eventually Egypt. In the first century AD, Tarsus and the surrounding countryside and farmland were home to some fifty thousand people, with seasonal swells likely more than double that number because of religious festivals and trade taking place at

---

4   Seneca was St. Paul's contemporary. The similarities between the language utilized by the Stoic philosopher and the apostle were well noted in the ancient Church. Saint Jerome reports that in his day, there were pseudepigraphic collections of correspondence between the two figures discussing philosophical matters.

the harvests. With its access to supply routes, Tarsus also became a hub of several industries, one of the most important being textiles.

Its location along trade routes and near a port made Tarsus an ideal setting for the textile industry. As a young man, Saul was apprenticed within that industry in tent-making (Acts 18:2–3). In the first century, temporary dwellings were made for all manner of purposes but were of particular importance to the traveling caravans who used the trade routes that ran through his home city. Tents were made from a variety of materials, notably woven goat hair and leather. Tarsus, however, was a major center of linen production in the Roman Empire. Saul would have been taught to use a loom to weave linen strips that would later be sewed together into a tent. The two key skills in such production were properly impregnating the linen canvas to prevent shrinking and correctly sewing waterproof seams between strips.

While the linen trade in Tarsus meant that this material would have been the primary mode of tent production in his apprenticeship, the fact that Paul was able in later life to ply his trade in Corinth means that he had also learned methods to work with leather. The Roman military favored leather tents, particularly for European campaigns. Working with leather required a Jewish person to regularly contract and be purified from ritual impurity, as leather is, after all, made from the skin of an animal carcass. Paul would have received the leather, likely also in strips, from a tanner after that skin had been soaked in sea salts and then a mixture of putrefying bark and berries. In this case also, young Saul would have learned the correct ways to form waterproof seams for the leather, which was prone to contracting, stiffening, and becoming brittle in ways that linen was not.

Tarsus and the Roman Empire

In the generations immediately preceding Saul's birth, Tarsus was a focal point in the geopolitical events surrounding the creation of the

Roman Empire. Despite having been annexed to Rome by Pompey, Tarsus had sided strongly with Julius Caesar in the Roman civil war. This allegiance was so strong that the city had been briefly renamed Juliopolis, though the change failed to stick. This allegiance continued in the subsequent civil war between Octavian and Mark Antony. It was in and around Tarsus that Antony and Cleopatra mustered their forces before the Battle of Actium in 31 BC.

By the mid to late first century BC, Tarsus and the surrounding region hosted a substantial Jewish population. The Jewish community in Tarsus chose not to segregate itself from the broader run of Greek and then Roman life in the city. Rather, they became intimately involved despite practicing a different way of life than either the rustic pagans of the countryside or the more urbane philosophers of the city. The Jewish people were a pillar of Julius Caesar's support in the region, so much so that he took note and granted them the right to freely practice their way of life, exempting them from Roman civic duties that would require them to compromise it. This edict of Caesar later became the basis for the broader toleration of Judaism practiced, albeit with some exceptions, throughout the empire.

In return for her support of Caesar, Tarsus was also made a free city and granted immunity. Status as a free city meant that Tarsus was able to largely govern her own affairs without significant interference from above. As the capital of Cilicia, this freedom allowed the entire province to flourish. Immunity not only granted the population an exemption from most imperial taxes but also gave the people of the city and region immunity from conscription for civic labor and military service. When this status was granted to the city, it came with a grant of Roman citizenship to the prominent members of the community, including the prominent members of the Jewish community. Saul's great-grandfather or grandfather would have been one of these recipients of citizenship, which he could pass on to his heirs, including Saul himself (Acts 22:25–28).

Jewish People in the Diaspora

The way of life of the Cilician Jewish community centered in Tarsus is described as Hellenistic Judaism. On one hand, the life of Saul's family in Tarsus was one deeply informed by the Torah, not only in the home but in public. They kept a Jewish home, and Saul would have been immediately identifiable as a member of the Jewish community by his dress and other practices. Rather than the temples and festivals surrounding the city, its god, and its heroic founder, the life of Saul and his family revolved around the local synagogue. Like most Jewish people in the Roman diaspora, Saul had a Jewish name and a Greek variant that he used in conversation with Gentiles. His parents named him Saul after the first king of Israel and the ancestral hero of their tribe, Benjamin. In the Hellenistic world he went by Pavlos, or Paul, which means "small man." The earliest physical descriptions of St. Paul describe him as being short, bald, and bow-legged, and suffering from persistent eye problems.[5]

The issue of food and eating represents a window into the tension faced by faithful Jewish families living in Roman cities. The Jewish diaspora was primarily an urban phenomenon within the Roman Empire, as the Jewish people were neither a people from outside the empire who were conquered and enslaved, nor were most Jewish people Roman citizens. This means that they were neither the object of rural land grants nor forced into labor on those estates. Within cities, the Roman diet, at all levels of society, consisted primarily of bread, cereal grains, and seasonably available vegetables and fruit subject to the region. Meat and fish were confined to the upper tiers of society.

A Jewish Roman citizen in Tarsus, even if possessing some wealth, faced an additional problem regarding the consumption of meat. Meat sold in Roman meat markets was, by and large, the product of the daily pagan sacrifices. These were, therefore, foods of which a faithful Jewish person could not partake. Most Jewish families in Tarsus likely

---

5   Though this description is repeated in many places, likely the earliest document in which it is recorded is the Acts of Paul.

baked their own bread from available grains to avoid the likewise common pagan grain offerings. In these cities, remaining faithful to the Torah's prescribed diet required, beyond vegetarianism, simplicity. Faithful Jewish people were satisfied with this quiet and simple way of life. Others sought after the good things of the world and in so doing abandoned or even repudiated Jewish practices as described in the Hebrew Scriptures.

At the same time, faithful Jewish people participated in many other aspects of civic life, albeit while maintaining their identity as Jewish participants. Saul became familiar, from the outside, with Greek and Roman ways of life, both philosophical and generally pagan. He was conversant in the ideas of the broader world beyond his own people. This way of being in the world as a Jewish person was a balance between the traditional and the cosmopolitan—a way of life fully embraced, but at peace with other, alternative ways of life being practiced within the larger community. Many elements of his Hellenistic upbringing would resurface in St. Paul's later works. Before this, however, Saul of Tarsus would forsake this balance in favor of an unencumbered zeal for the traditions of his people.

CHAPTER TWO

Era of Zealotry

As a young adult in his culture—considered an adolescent in ours—Saul of Tarsus was sent to Jerusalem for Torah study. He came of age as a member of the party of the Pharisees and, like many young men in strict religious environments, developed a great zeal for the traditions of his people. Jerusalem at this time was a hotbed of zealotry, resistance, and sporadic outright rebellion against the Roman imperial power. While St. Paul does not appear to have ever formally joined an organization dedicated to zealotry, he was, in our modern terms, radicalized from the perspective of the Pharisaic mainstream of the early first century AD. Great learning brought a love of tradition, and zeal for tradition led to an aggressive spirit in the young Saul. That aggression ultimately found targets at the fringes of the Judean community.

Jerusalem

The Jerusalem to which Saul came was in many ways the inverse of his home city of Tarsus. At that time the capital of the Roman province of Judea, the city was, more importantly to her Jewish inhabitants, the capital of Israel established by David the king. The united Israel David established there was short-lived—little more than a generation. The Davidic dynasty would continue to rule over the smaller nation of Judah for another three centuries at the beginning of the first millennium BC. Jerusalem and its temple were destroyed by the invading armies of the Neo-Babylonian Empire at the beginning of the sixth century BC.

This Jerusalem with its first Judean temple became more than a past historical reality. Through the Psalms, ubiquitous in Jewish worship, the post-Torah reality of David's united Israelite kingdom, his capital, and the temple built by his son became the paradigm of the blessed state. The heavenly city of God was the heavenly Jerusalem. The heavenly worship of the God of Israel took place in a heavenly temple after which the temple of Solomon had been patterned. One day, the son of David—the culmination of his eternal dynasty, the Messiah—would come to make these heavenly realities into earthly realities once again. Within sacred geography, the first Paradise in which humanity was created to live was relocated to the place of Jerusalem, and Jerusalem, as she existed in the hearts and minds of Judeans, was a lost Paradise to which they yearned to return.

The prominence of this ideal Jerusalem, her king, and her temple were not diminished, but rather enhanced by the subsequent return of the Jewish people to Judea, the rebuilding of the temple, and the rebuilding of Jerusalem. The Babylonian exile proper lasted only seventy years, but the Judea that was refounded was a Persian province, not an Israelite nation. The tribes that had formed the Northern Kingdom of Israel were lost to history, and despite promises from the prophets that God would restore all twelve tribes of Israel, this restoration becoming a reality seemed impossible. The temple was rebuilt and rededicated, but with none of the signs and wonders that accompanied the dedication of the tabernacle as described in the Torah or Solomon's temple in the books of the Kings. The reality of Jerusalem and Judea, with no king of her own, was a pale shadow of Judah, let alone David's Israel.

Revolt of the Maccabees

Following its conquest by Alexander the Great, Judea became a province of the Seleucid Empire ruled by the newly founded Antioch in Syria. While Judea had faced relatively little interference in her internal life from the Persians, the Greeks viewed the unwillingness of the Judean people to leave aside their tribal customs and be absorbed into the broader Hellenic culture as an affront. The refusal of the Judeans to observe and worship the gods of their conquerors was blamed for every form of misfortune that befell the regional empire, culminating in her being blamed for the loss of the armies of Antiochus IV Epiphanes to his Ptolemaic neighbors in Egypt. To right this perceived wrong, Antiochus sacrificed pigs on the altar of Yahweh, the God of Israel, in the Jerusalem temple. This act was held in Judean memory as "the abomination which causes desolation," the greatest possible affront to their God, their people, and their way of life. This pagan sacrificial act also began an era of direct persecution against those Judeans who sought to keep the Torah, to the point of children being tortured to death in front of their parents for refusing to eat pork.[6]

This persecution produced a violent revolt from the Maccabees, a group of brothers who spearheaded an ultimately successful revolution to establish an independent Judea. They set themselves up as a new dynasty of kings, the Hasmoneans, and rededicated the temple (1 Macc. 4:36–61). Again, however, even this independent Judea remained a weak impostor to the spiritual legacy of David's Jerusalem. Once again, the rededicated temple experienced no signs of God's favor. The Hasmonean kings were not descendants of David in genealogy or temperament. Judea maintained its independence for as long as it did through a series of foreign treaties including with Sparta and, fatefully, Rome. Beginning with John Hyrcanus, the Hasmonean

---

6   One example of these persecutions is recorded in 2 Maccabees. From these persecutions developed the idea of martyrdom, later to become of key importance in Christian communities. The person willing to die rather than forsake faithfulness to the commandments of God became a figure of primary importance in religious memory alongside the figures of prophets, righteous priests, and kings.

kings also took to themselves the high priesthood. Rather than a restoration of the twelve tribes, Hyrcanus in the mid-second century BC embarked on a brutal military attempt to reconquer former Israelite lands to enlarge Judea with no care for the actual people.

Roman Rule

The treaty between Rome and Judea facilitated the latter's annexation under Pompey in 63 BC. In the process, Pompey sacked Jerusalem and personally invaded the Most Holy Place within Jerusalem's temple with no immediate apparent consequence. From this point forward Judea and Jerusalem existed under Roman domination. The Romans, like the Seleucids before them, found the Judeans to be a particularly recalcitrant conquered people. Attempts to assimilate the Judeans into Roman culture produced rioting, localized revolt, and generalized hostility. For practical reasons and as a return favor for local support (as in the case of Tarsus), Rome adopted a general policy of toleration for the Judean people, provided that the general peace was kept.

Rome also gave the region a semblance of a king, making Herod the Great the ethnarch, or "ruler of the people." From Rome's perspective, the land, the natural resources, and the trade routes that ran through Judea were of great value—the people, as non-citizens, less so. Herod was able to live an opulent lifestyle beyond that of his fellow Semites (he was Idumean, not Jewish) but also was forced to maintain a careful balancing act in keeping the peace on behalf of Rome. The first Herod earned the title "the Great" primarily through his vast building programs across the region—most notably his massive, decades-long expansion of the temple complex in Jerusalem. While impressive to his Roman masters and many others, Herod's hands being involved in the second temple only served to further sully it in the hearts of religiously faithful Judeans.

Following Herod's death in 1 BC, even his nominal authority was diluted as his territory was split, with each of his four sons being named a tetrarch, or "ruler of a fourth." This was to emphasize the reality of the authority of Rome but also served to create four quasi-royal courts with petty bureaucrats, courtesans, and hangers-on attached. The members of these extended entourages, both real and aspirational, became known as Herodians and represented a faction within Judea with their own particular set of interests—chiefly further Roman collaboration for personal benefit.

The Sadducees

Similarly, the family that controlled the high priesthood and broader priesthood in the Jerusalem temple in the first century AD, along with their surrounding retinue of servants and those operating in their orbit, formed a party known in Scripture as the Sadducees. This title is a rendering into Greek of "Zadokites," as this party sought to portray themselves as the priesthood of the family of Zadok, whom the exilic prophets had prophesied would preside in rebuilding the temple. But they were in no way related to the historical family of Zadok. Their control of the temple, however, had given them unprecedented power within Judea under the Romans. Rome allowed them to levy the temple tax to maintain and support the temple. The high priestly family had used this power to gain ownership, by confiscation, of seventy percent of the land within Judea that was not directly owned and controlled by the Romans. Many tenant farmers were working what had been their families' own land for wages from the priestly families.

The Sadducean priesthood, then, was deeply invested in the on-the-ground status quo of the first century—so much so that when the temple was destroyed in AD 70, this party and family very quickly ceased to exist. The Sadducees' investment in Roman interests meant that the ideology of a heavenly Jerusalem greater than the corrupt, earthly one where they held power was a threat, with its heavenly temple and a coming king who would defeat the Romans in what seemed like treason to them. While it is anachronistic to discuss a "canon of Scripture" in the first half of the first century AD among Jewish groups, the Sadducees rejected the perspective of the post-Torah Hebrew Scriptures

19

that prophetically spoke of these ideas or made negative statements regarding the reality of the earthly Judea in contrast.

The Pharisees

Throughout the world, Jewish people practiced diverse Judaisms as they sought to live out their lives in the Roman world and, in some cases, beyond it. Various factions within Palestinian Judaism, however, were distinguished precisely on how they saw the earthly Jerusalem relating to the Jerusalem above and how the temple and Davidic monarchy would be restored. Often this meant defining themselves against the Herodians, the temple and its Sadducean priesthood, and the Roman governing power.

The most prominent party within Palestinian Judaism that would go on to form the core of later Rabbinic Judaism was the Pharisees. Their name refers to a separation they maintained between themselves and not only the Roman world but also the compromised elements of the Jewish world in Judea. The Pharisees fully embraced the overarching narrative of the entirety of the Hebrew Scriptures, seeing exile as the just and right result of the wickedness and disobedience to the Torah of the ancient Israelites and Judahites. The lack of signs, the incompleteness, and the incorrectness of the restored Judea, Jerusalem, and temple in all their postexilic forms were the result of the exile not truly being over. If exile was the result of disobedience and given by God with the purpose of bringing about repentance, then true restoration of the city, the temple, and the monarchy would come when Israel collectively repented.

This collective repentance had not yet happened. In fact, from the Pharisaic perspective, even within Jerusalem and Judea most people seemed content with the temple as it existed and life as it was. On the other side, the discontents expressed themselves in forms reminiscent of the Maccabees and Hasmoneans, seeking to bring about the Kingdom of God through force and violence. Neither of these, to the Pharisees, represented the way forward. The answer to all of Judea's suffering was for the Judean people to embrace the way of life pre-scribed by the Torah and to hold to it scrupulously, as the Pharisees did. The study and teaching of the Torah, then, were central acts of piety for the Pharisees, while their relationship with the existing Jerusalem temple was somewhat ambivalent until that temple might be cleansed.[7]

The Zealots

Also active within the first century AD in Judea were a number of zealot groups. Zeal was a phenomenon, not an organized movement, yet it gave birth to dozens of small radical groups. The phenomenon extended beyond these groups and influenced and radicalized mem-bers of other Jewish sects. Generally, what marked a zealot group was its willingness to use force and violence to push back against oppres-sion within Judea and/or to bring about the promised restoration of David's kingdom. For groups like the Sicarii, this went so far as to include the assassination of Roman imperial officials and Jewish col-laborators. In other cases, these groups were formed around would-be messiahs seeking to spark another Maccabean revolution. In all cases, their activities in the end served to increase the oppression of the Roman state as the Romans used violence to quell further rebellion.

There is no way to produce a comprehensive list of every Jewish fac-tion and subfaction even within the province of Judea in this period. Many small and short-lived movements left little or no historical or archaeological footprint. The community at Qumran, for example, which produced the Dead Sea Scrolls, retreated into the Judean des-ert to live a strict way of life founded around the Torah as interpreted through later Enochic texts. They created their own form of temple worship and followed their own calendar. Undoubtedly there were

---

7   It's worth noting that while the Pharisees are often portrayed as antagonists within the Gospels, the New Testament itself does not present the Pharisees as wrong in their religious teaching. Rather, they are criticized for not living up to their own teaching (see Matt. 23:2–3).

countless other separatist groups. Thus when Saul of Tarsus as a young man traveled to Jerusalem, he entered not into a united bastion of traditional Orthodox Judaism but into a complex religious, social, and political environment scarred by internecine violence.

Gamaliel

Young Saul was sent to Jerusalem to further his education in the Torah and the tradition of his people. While the term "school" is frequently used to describe various Rabbinic traditions within Palestine in the first century, this is not a reference to a school in the modern sense of an institution of learning. Rather, education was an interpersonal affair in which a learned teacher, scholar, and/or religious leader accepted students or disciples. These students quite literally followed their teacher, engaging with him whenever possible through asking questions but also hearing and observing his way of life, his interactions with others, and his means of addressing conflicts and disagreements.

Paul was accepted as a student by the rabbi Gamaliel (Acts 22:3). Our picture of Gamaliel is formed from references both within the Book of Acts and within various tractates of the Talmud. Gamaliel was the grandson of Hillel, one of the founding figures of Pharisaism, and a prominent leader within Jerusalem's Sanhedrin, the council of religious authorities that saw itself as the descendants of the elders appointed by Moses. Gamaliel likewise became a prominent member of the Sanhedrin in the middle part of the first century AD. One of the sayings preserved within the Talmudic tradition from Gamaliel describes different sorts of students whom he had encountered, giving evidence that he had accepted a significant number of disciples during his life.[8]

The disciples of Gamaliel shared a life in common. Unlike many philosophical schools within the Roman Empire, it was not generally

---

8   Ab. R. N. xl.

a part of Jewish tradition for a rabbi to charge disciples for instruction. Nonetheless, like any group of young male students, Gamaliel's students needed to feed and otherwise provide for themselves during their period of education. Their living was likely subsidized by prominent members of the Pharisees who had the means to do so, but like modern student life, it was hardly opulent. Many students participated in scribal activity as a means of further learning and supplementary income. Manuscripts of the Hebrew Scriptures were copied by hand, the typical method being a reader proclaiming those scriptures while a number of students each made a written copy of the text being read. The production of Torah scrolls aided in the memorization of the Torah, as well as generating many of the questions that would eventually be referred to Gamaliel as rabbi.

One part of Gamaliel's leadership position within Pharisaism and Palestinian Judaism as a whole was the answering of questions and the resolution of disputes for Jewish communities outside of Jerusalem. He did this through the composition of epistles, three of which have survived within the Talmudic tradition.[9] Two of these letters are answers to detailed questions concerning tithing—one sent to Galilee and the other sent to Jewish communities in the southern part of the Levant. The third letter was more broadly addressed to Jewish communities scattered throughout and even somewhat beyond the Roman Empire regarding the details of the calendar for the year of its writing. Gamaliel dictated these epistles to his scribe, Yohanan, and they were thereafter circulated and then later preserved when the Jewish traditions of the era were collected in writing.

Under Gamaliel's direction, Paul would have memorized the entire Torah in Hebrew and much of the rest of the Hebrew Scriptures. He learned to read the Hebrew Scriptures within the Pharisaic tradition, which understood that the exile of the people was still ongoing and looked forward to an eschatological divine intervention. The day would come when the Messiah, the son of David, would come

---

9   Sanhedrin 2:6, 11b, 18d.

to restore the kingdom to Israel. The temple would be purified and rededicated. The people would be judged and purified. The power relationship with the nations in general, and Rome in particular, would be reversed, and the messianic king would rule the world with the kings of the nations as vassals during a messianic age. During this age, justice would be established on the earth. Part of this justice would mean that the righteous dead would live again to receive the reward they were denied in life while the evil would suffer the penalty for their wickedness, likewise often evaded in this present age. The coming of the Messiah and this next age was to be hastened by the pursuit of righteousness—by faithfully following the Torah not only individually but collectively as a people.

Zeal

Zealotry was a phenomenon with its roots in the Hebrew Scriptures. The key figure for the zealot movements of the first century AD was Phinehas, who had begun the deliverance of Israel from a plague through violent action (Num. 25:10–13; see also Ps. 106/105:28–31). For those Judeans who saw the Roman domination of their land and the corruption of the temple and priesthood as a judgment from God, the obvious next question was what must be done to correct the situation and turn away God's wrath. The example of Phinehas offered one paradigm. This example was used to justify any level of force or violence necessary against both Roman oppressors and Jewish collaborators. For some zealot groups, those with charismatic leaders and would-be Messiahs, this took the form of seeking to touch off an organized revolt. For most zealot groups, however, Phinehas represented the example of a lone, righteous Israelite taking decisive action.

Through the early and middle parts of the first century AD, a constant flow of students and disciples from the Pharisaic tradition moved into various forms of zealotry. Young people becoming radicalized is a phenomenon that certainly did not end in that century. It is worth noting, however, that certain elements of Pharisaic thought do lend themselves to such radicalization. The beliefs that the current state of the people is a result of God's judgment against their wickedness and that a coming messianic intervention will restore the kingdom suggest the question of what form of activism might speed that result. Over against this tendency, Pharisaic leaders and, later, Pharisaism as a whole adopted a conservative position that the messianic age to come would be brought about by an unambiguous act of God, not by human efforts—especially martial.

For any given individual, zealotry existed on a spectrum. A limited number of self-described zealots personally carried out violence. Most merely served as apologists for and sympathized with various forms of revolt and violence when they took place. In between these two poles was a very common tactic of inciting and stoking mob violence. Those with sympathies running in the direction of zealotry—but who would shrink from carrying out violence themselves—might become a part of that violence when functioning as members of a mob. This mob violence was not an organized revolt by a given zealot faction, but an emergent collective action fostered by certain zealous persons in their midst.

We do not know where Paul was for the Passover in AD 30. Given that he would have been somewhere in Judea, it would seem likely that he was part of the huge influx of pilgrims in and around Jerusalem for the feast. This was the Passover during which Jesus of Nazareth entered the city with His own disciples. By the end of the week, He had been put to death by the Roman authorities at the urging of the mob and with the approval of a cross section of Jewish authorities. Nearly every competing faction in Jerusalem had a reason to want to be rid of Jesus. He actively spoke out against the wickedness and corruption of the Herodians and the Sadducees. He was increasingly embraced by His disciples and a faction of the people as the Messiah, suggesting the danger of some sort of revolt. The Romans responded to any whiff of burgeoning revolution with radically disproportional violence and terror, particularly during a period in which the population of Jerusalem had more than doubled for a feast. In the end, the counsel of the high priest Caiaphas, that it was better for Jesus to die at Roman hands than for the situation to play out and potentially doom the city and many more of the Jewish people, prevailed. Romans needed little excuse to execute a Jewish person (John 11:50).

Birth of the Christian Movement

Following the execution of Jesus by crucifixion, unlike most nascent messianic movements of the first century, His did not cease. His disciples, in fact, publicly proclaimed in and around Jerusalem that He had been raised from the dead to demonstrate His righteousness and had ascended to the heavens to rule as the Messiah at the right hand of God (Ps. 110/109). Further, they proclaimed that God would imminently intervene through Jesus the Messiah to restore the Kingdom in full. Though the disciples of Jesus were a mixed group and included only a handful of members of the Jewish leadership, the teaching of His disciples clearly reflects a modification of Pharisaic teaching. In a sense, their teaching is Pharisaism with the addition of Jesus of Nazareth as the Messiah.

During this period, from AD 30 to 35, Paul was radicalized, and his radicalization went hand in hand with the burgeoning of what would come to be called Christianity. This new sect of Judaism developing around Jesus as the Messiah was in the first place, from Paul's perspective, heresy. Wrong belief, however, was not enough to make one subject to violent retaliation in Pharisaic circles. Even zealot groups cared little about what someone thought. Rather, they retaliated against those who by their actions either grossly violated the Torah or collaborated with the Romans. Nascent Christianity, for the young Paul, was different from other forms of zealotry in that it represented a dangerous sectarian group.

The disciples of Jesus were not only continuing but recapitulating the situation that led to the death of Jesus Himself. Like St. John the Baptist before them, they were baptizing a separate group or sect, drawing off a following for themselves from among the people. Once baptized into the group, they were living separately and dropping out of the regular pattern of Jewish life in Judea and Jerusalem in favor of communal living. At the same time, their public rhetoric regarding Jesus as the Messiah was directly treasonous and punishable with death by the Romans. All of this occurred in the name of a condemned criminal. When the Romans decided some Judean faction was dangerous or treasonous, they were not careful in response—it had direct consequences for all of Judea. Messianic and zealot movements in the Jewish revolts would later draw just such cataclysmic responses.

Here, Paul split from his teacher Gamaliel, who counseled caution regarding the new movement: if it was from God, it would be unstoppable; if not, it would perish without the need for direct intervention (Acts 5:35–39). Paul believed that direct, even violent, action was necessary as the spread of what would become known as Christianity continued. In this earliest phase, a few significant members of the Jewish Sanhedrin even joined the new movement.[10] That said, it does not appear that Paul was ever in the business of direct assassination. Rather, he used the techniques of mob incitement and turning over Christians as dissidents to other authorities for punishment (Acts 9:1–2).

The most prominent such act by Saul of Tarsus recorded in Scripture surrounds the death of St. Stephen. Stephen had been a fellow disciple of Gamaliel, but one who had been baptized into the Christian movement. He had been given a position as one of the first deacons in the Jerusalem Christian community, overseeing ministry to Greek-speaking Jewish people (Acts 6:1–6). Within this ministry, certain Jewish people from the diaspora engaged in public debate with Stephen and lost. This led to their slander of him and ultimately

---

10 The most prominent of these is likely Menachem, a respected Pharisaic leader who helped found the Christian community at Antioch after his expulsion from the Sanhedrin. He is mentioned in Acts 13:1, and, according to Jewish tradition, after his expulsion he left with eighty of his disciples for the Syrian wilderness. Josephus, a contemporary source, describes Menachem's prominence and his joining of a sect without mentioning Christianity as such.

to him being called before the religious authorities to answer for himself and the movement he had joined. He made a full-throated defense for himself and an appeal for all those hearing to embrace Jesus of Nazareth as the Messiah. In response, Saul, along with others, helped incite the crowd until it erupted into violence and Stephen was stoned to death by the mob (Acts 7).

Paul had likely shared many a meal with St. Stephen. This event reveals that such was Paul's zeal—in his mind for the tradition and ways of his people and for the Torah—that he would even incite violence against someone close to him. Later in life, he would come to see that, in fact, it was he—not his opponents—who was twisting and perverting the Torah and the Pharisaic traditions in which he had been formed during this period. He would come to see this with no small shame. With the help of St. Nicodemus, a Christian and still a member of the Sanhedrin, Gamaliel buried the body of his disciple St. Stephen in his own family tomb.

CHAPTER THREE

Road to Damascus

At some point in AD 35, Paul continued his zealous crusade against those still committed to Jesus of Nazareth as the Jewish Messiah. By that point, this movement not only was not dying away; it was spreading. The fall of Jerusalem in the sixth century BC had created a broad Jewish diaspora. Groups of refugees, as described in the Book of Jeremiah, fled to Egypt while Jerusalem and wider Judah were falling to the Babylonians. The result of this migration was a large Jewish community in Alexandria centuries later engaged in scribal activity and theological writing. Philo of Alexandria, who wrote in the first century BC, is one representative of this community.

Jewish Diaspora

When the exiled Judahites were allowed to return to the Persian province of Judea, not all did so. A large Jewish community remained in Mesopotamia for many centuries. Following Alexander the Great's conquests, Judea ended up part of the Seleucid Empire, and trade and other commerce led to the spread of small Jewish communities throughout the region of greater Syria. When Antioch was founded on the Orontes River circa 300 BC, it was deliberately populated and subdivided into thirds. The original population was one-third Greek, one-third native Syrian, and one-third Jewish. Antioch's Jewish community thrived, and by the first century AD it was the second-largest center of Jewish life in the Roman Empire after Jerusalem. Additionally, imperial life, trade, and commerce led to Jewish people relocating throughout the Mediterranean basin in smaller settlements with their own synagogues for worship and Torah study.

The spread of Jewish people throughout the known world led to a diversity of practice. In an era in which travel was a long and expensive prospect, the synagogue eclipsed the Jerusalem temple in practical reality for most Jewish people. Relatedly, no central religious authority within Judaism was recognized across the diaspora. Certainly, diaspora communities corresponded with Jerusalem, and Jerusalem was seen as the mother of all the Jewish people. But this correspondence was just as likely to be addressed to a respected Pharisaic teacher like Gamaliel as it was to the currently serving high priest.

Pharisaic Judaism also had circulated throughout the diaspora. Thoroughgoing knowledge of the Torah and the ability to preach and apply it, answering questions of interpretation and application, carried with it its own authority. In short, the spread of the Jewish people created a broad diversity of opinions and religious experiences, and communities took on their own character. Some of these became organized local movements with names, such as the Theraputae in Egypt. In most cases, Jewish people felt no need to formally align with a group, movement, or faction. In the first century AD, with its variety of flourishing communities, *Judaism* became a catch-all term for the diverse religious experiences and practices of the Jewish people.

Following the death of St. Stephen, many members of the community dedicated to Jesus of Nazareth in Jerusalem now saw the city as a dangerous place to be. Those who had connections in other places returned to those places, taking their dedication to Jesus as the Messiah with them. Devotion to the Messiah Jesus began thereby to spread to a broader range of Jewish communities, at first as an internal faction. Very early, the movement took root in Antioch's large Jewish community and began to grow there. While followers originally referred to it as "The Way," at Antioch these Jewish people were the first to be labeled as Christians, or Messianists. In Antioch, followers of Jesus crossed their first major barrier—from the Aramaic-speaking Jewish people of Judea, Galilee, and Samaria to the broader group of Greek-speaking Jewish people in the diaspora.

The Threat of the Christian Movement

The more the movement spread, the harder it would be to uproot. There were any number of reasons why certain Judean factions saw the Christians as a threat: All the reasons for antipathy against Jesus of Nazareth Himself still applied. The occupying Romans viewed messianic claims as treasonous. And beyond the treason of a claim to kingship, Jewish messianic movements had in the past erupted into revolt against Rome and would do so in the future. Any resident of Judea who didn't believe that Jesus was the Messiah was loathe to suffer the wrath of the Romans over the claim that He was.

The party of the Sadducees in general and the high priestly family, in particular, felt this danger acutely, as their fortunes lay with their ongoing Roman collaboration. At the same time, few people were less popular in the eyes of an average Judean than a Roman collaborator. This reality required the high priestly family to maintain a constant balancing act of appeasing the Romans while not appearing to be Roman bootlickers. From a very early stage, the proclamation of Jesus as Messiah labeled the leadership class of Jerusalem, including the high priest, as complicit in Jesus' execution by the Romans. Handing over a Jewish teacher to the Romans for execution threatened this delicate balance of public perception regardless of whether one believed that teacher was the Messiah.

For these and other reasons, in the year 35, the high priest sent Saul of Tarsus with letters to Damascus. These letters lent the authority of the high priesthood to Saul's intent to detain Christian members of the Jewish community in Damascus and return them to Jerusalem for religious trial, likely before the Sanhedrin. In his mind, Paul was still a Pharisee. The leadership of the Pharisaic party in Jerusalem, however, was taking a very different, nonviolent approach to the Christian movement. Paul's continued zeal made for strange bedfellows. Central to the Christian proclamation was the Resurrection of Jesus from the dead. This Resurrection was claimed to be the beginning of the bodily resurrection, a doctrine central to Pharisaism over against other Jewish movements. Thus the Christian movement in its Judean expression was largely an intra-Pharisaic movement. For Paul, this was a dangerous heresy.

The high priest had no real civil governing authority in Judea, let alone Damascus. On the other hand, the Roman authorities cared very little about Jewish noncitizens. They were willing, at the whiff of public disruption, to execute them en masse. A Roman citizen with letters from any sort of official offering to take members of a dissident group off the Romans' hands would have been not only accepted but welcomed. Paul's endgame as he set out on his journey is unclear. Had he secured a number of Christians and returned with them to Jerusalem, it seems unlikely that he would have planned executions by mob violence as in the case of St. Stephen. Far more likely, he was confident that a hearing before the Sanhedrin, which included the greatest Torah scholars in Jerusalem at the time, could convince these errant sectarians that they were incorrect about Jesus' messianic identity. Such an approach could also produce a sort of countermovement, ready to refute those attempting to spread the proclamation of Jesus.

Paul's Journey Interrupted

The road from Jerusalem to Damascus was roughly two hundred miles. On horseback, this would have taken Paul about five days, traveling at roughly four miles per hour during daylight hours. Other men were traveling with him, likely sent by the high priest and likely members of the relatively small Jewish detachment that the Romans allowed to police the temple complex in Jerusalem. This group was part of a compromise between the high priestly faction and the

Romans. The peace had to be kept within the temple complex, especially when the population of Jerusalem swelled during festal periods. Jewish sensibilities, however, would not allow Roman troops in many areas of that complex. The Romans had, in the past, found that offending those sensibilities too overtly was a recipe for insurrection. When it came to the temple, the Jewish people were allowed to police themselves if they did so successfully. If they failed to maintain the peace, the Romans maintained other options at their disposal.

The long hours of travel left plenty of time for prayer for a Pharisee like Paul. Meditative prayer was an important part of Jewish religious life, particularly in the diaspora. This type of prayer in this period had an immediate object and then a larger goal. The immediate object was, in almost all cases, a portion of the Hebrew Scriptures, which could vary from Psalm verses to passages of the Torah. The most common focus for prayer, however, was the *shema*.[11] Prayer that concentrated centrally on God, particularly on His unity, focused and unified the mind. Extended periods of such prayer sometimes became the vehicle for visionary experiences for practitioners, and St. Paul reported having a significant number of these visions during his life.

The contents of such mystical experiences, when they could even be described, would vary. One mode of this spiritual experience was a variant of the visions of Isaiah and Ezekiel in which they beheld the God of Israel enthroned. The pursuit of such throne visions later developed into what would be called Merkavah mysticism within the Jewish tradition.[12] During his journey to Damascus, Paul experienced such a vision. In St. Paul's vision, however, the figure seated on a throne at the right hand of God was Jesus of Nazareth. Through questioning, Jesus made it clear that Paul was not attacking a human

---

11 Named for its first word in Hebrew, the *shema* is Deuteronomy 6:4, "Hear, O Israel, Yahweh our God, Yahweh is one."

12 *Merkavah* is the Hebrew word for "chariot." In Ezekiel's vision (Ezek. 1), he saw Yahweh enthroned on a chariot throne that could travel throughout the world.

movement within Judaism. Rather, Paul was attacking the Messiah Himself with all his vengeful ire.[13]

This was the first, but not the last time that Jesus would appear to St. Paul in person. Despite the vision happening at midday, it was accompanied by a light from the heavens stronger than the sun. Those with Paul on the road heard a voice but saw nothing. Jesus spoke to Saul in Hebrew, calling him by name and telling him to continue to Damascus, where he would be directed what to do. Though his companions did not see the light, it blinded Paul. They led him the rest of the way, taking three days to complete the journey. During those three days, Paul ate and drank nothing.

In popular description, this event has come to be referred to most commonly as the conversion of St. Paul. But this narrative presupposes something that is obviously not the case: that Judaism and Christianity were two separate religious traditions in AD 35. Paul's own understanding of this event and his subsequent life is not that this began an abandonment of Judaism, the traditions of his people more broadly, or even Pharisaism. Quite the opposite. He continued to see himself as Jewish and a Pharisee. What changed was his identification of Jesus as the Messiah. Pharisaic Judaism was already messianic. Paul came away from this event with the firm conviction that the messianic prophecies he had studied throughout his life had been fulfilled within his lifetime.

This is not to say that the revelation of Jesus as Messiah to Paul was not earth-shattering. Saint Stephen, a man dead, in part, at Paul's hands, was instantly proven to be right. As a zealot, Paul had placed great weight on the fact that his view was correct. He understood the traditions of his fathers. He knew the Torah. His cause was holy, pure, and just. He was not one of the sinners responsible for the ongoing exile and suffering of his people. He was someone who could teach them how to live righteously, as he did. This first vision immediately

---

13   This vision and the surrounding details are recounted four times in the New Testament in narrative form and in the reflection and preaching of St. Paul himself: Acts 9:1–19; Acts 22:6–21; Acts 26:12-18; Galatians 1:11–24.

told Paul that he was, in fact, a sinner—one of the worst of them in betraying innocent blood. He was blind, with nothing but his thoughts to occupy him for days.

Damascus the Roman City

Like Jerusalem, Damascus had been annexed in the first century BC by the Roman general Pompey. Damascus was already an ancient city, but it had been centuries since its prominence as an Aramean capital. The Romans almost immediately rebuilt the city according to the Roman pattern. The city as refounded by the Romans is what is known as the "old city" of Damascus to this day, with a roughly rectangular layout: three-fifths of a mile by nine-tenths of a mile, with the longer distance stretching from west to east. Damascus was walled, with massive gates at the points where the main thoroughfares, built on the north/south and west/east axes, left the city. The larger of the two roads that ran from west to east was known as the Via Recta, meaning "straight road" or "straight street." Damascus and its environs were home at that time to roughly one hundred and fifty thousand people.

When St. Paul arrived, the city was not yet prominent within the Roman system. It was nearly a century later that Damascus became a metropolis, the capital of the Roman province of Syria. Control of the city from the perspective of its people had been given to Herod the Great. After his death, it was his son Philip who gained Herod's domains in Syria. Philip became a major rival of Herod Antipas, his brother. Antipas had divorced his first wife to marry Herodias, who had been the wife of another brother. Saint John the Forerunner had been executed by Antipas in part for denouncing this illicit union (Mark 6:17–29). At the same time, Antipas's first wife had been the daughter of Aretas IV Philopatris, the king of the Nabateans, who ruled from Petra. Aretas launched an attack on Antipas with the assistance of Philip. Antipas appealed to the emperor for help, but a planned Roman invasion of Nabatea never happened. This chaos ultimately led to the dissolution of the Herodian experiment by Rome.

Philip attempted to reforge relations with his brother by marrying his niece, Salome. When Philip died in AD 34, through their military alliance, Aretas briefly gained control of Damascus and certain other holdings through his garrisoned troops.

Baptism

Paul, still blind, was taken by his companions to the home of a certain Judah on the Via Recta. Over the next several days, still eating and drinking nothing, he processed his recent experience. Then he had another vision—this one of a Jewish man coming to him and miraculously restoring his sight. Elsewhere in the city, St. Ananias also had a vision. Ananias was a Torah scholar who had previously made his home in Jerusalem. While there, he had become committed to Jesus as the Messiah. In the wake of St. Stephen's death, he had fled to Damascus and, because of his reputation and learning, had become a leader in both the Jewish community more broadly and the Christian movement within it.

In Ananias's vision, Jesus appeared to him and instructed him where to find Saul of Tarsus to heal him. Ananias was fully aware of Saul's activities but was told the purpose for which Jesus had called him into service. He was faithful to his vision and found Saul as directed. When Saul's vision was restored, physical blockages fell away from his eyes. Ananias baptized Paul and then laid hands on him to receive the Holy Spirit, as was the pattern for receiving members of the Christian movement.

Baptism was an inherited rite. Jewish practice included any number of ritual washings for various situations. One set of them formed a part of the rites for proselytes, non-Jewish people who wanted to fully embrace the Jewish people and way of life. Saint John the Forerunner had, beginning roughly a decade earlier, begun baptizing people in the Jordan River. Calling people out of the cities, villages, and settlements of Judea to the wilderness, specifically the Jordan, carried significant historical resonance. Joshua had crossed the Jordan with the people on the way into the land of Canaan when it was first conquered and settled by the Israelites. The language of the Hebrew Scriptures cited around the ministry of the Baptist is the language of return from the Babylonian exile.[14] This prophetic action combined with the setting presented as imminent a time of reckoning for Israel, her restoration, and the end of the exile.

The baptism practiced by St. John was for the forgiveness of sins. The connection between washing and the removal of sin and its effects may seem obvious. It required, however, participants to confess their sins. Identification as a sinner was something that the Pharisees and the Sadducees of Judea found disagreeable for different reasons, leading them, for the most part, not to participate. From the perspective of a Pharisee like St. Paul, their identity was forged as those who observed the Torah fully and correctly, in contrast to sinners.[15] After the death of St. John, it is clear that the disciples of Jesus continued to baptize new followers during His lifetime (John 3:22; 4:1–2). Before His Ascension into heaven, Jesus made baptism and instruction in His commandments the mission of His disciples as He sent them out as apostles (Matt. 28:19–20).

Following the celebration of Pentecost in AD 30 when the Holy Spirit descended upon the apostles, baptism came to include a second element: the laying on of hands to receive the Holy Spirit. The indwelling of the Spirit of God was a phenomenon in the Hebrew Scriptures. However, it had been largely confined to certain individuals—primarily prophets but also kings and sometimes priests. In some cases, as in the Books of Joshua and Judges, the Holy Spirit would come upon someone abruptly and then depart. That Pentecost, however, was seen as the day on which this changed to a

---

14   Most prominently Isaiah 40:3f.

15   Certainly, Pharisees accepted that they committed sins and needed repentance. The Torah includes provisions for repentance and restoration after sin, and following these was part of keeping Torah. The Pharisees worked to keep these provisions as well. The sinner, then, was the notorious sinner—the unrepentant sinner. These sinners flocked to St. John for baptism, putting off the observant Pharisees.

continuous indwelling of the Holy Spirit in every faithful follower of Jesus following their baptism and the rite of laying on of hands. This indwelling was itself a prophetic sign within the Hebrew Scriptures that the messianic age had begun (see Joel 2).

Paul's acceptance of baptism and the laying on of hands after his Damascus experience was therefore an act of repentance. He had reached the point of understanding himself as a sinner in need of purification. After the baptism, Paul broke his fast and ate. He then spent some amount of time in Damascus both learning from St. Ananias and proclaiming Jesus as the Messiah within the Jewish community. His reputation had preceded him, so this was confounding. Those Christians who had come from Jerusalem or heard from believers there were both astonished and suspicious that their enemy had suddenly joined their movement. The members of the Jewish community who had likely originally expected to host and collaborate with Paul now found him arguing with them that Jesus of Nazareth was, in fact, the Messiah. This disruption began to escalate and came to the attention of Aretas's garrison in the city, leading to St. Paul needing to make an escape by night. The gates closed; he was lowered down outside the city wall in a basket.

Arabia and Paul's Sense of Calling

After this flight from Damascus, St. Paul journeyed to Arabia. While modern readers may assume this refers to the Arabian Peninsula proper, in the first century AD it indicates Arabia Nabatea, the kingdom of the Nabateans that was then ruled by the same Aretas. When St. Paul mentions this journey, he doesn't refer to any cities (Gal. 1:17). He writes about this journey in the context of a discussion of receiving his teaching directly from Jesus the Messiah rather than from the apostles. Significantly, the only other place in which Paul mentions Arabia in his writings is in the same Letter to the Galatians, referring to it as the location of Mt. Sinai (Gal. 4:25). While this verse has been grist for a certain brand of modern Christian archaeologist, there is no reasonable reading of Exodus that allows the historical Mt. Sinai to be located in a region called Arabia. Paul's references may be deliberately evocative.

Paul spent roughly three years in the Nabatean desert, not staying in any particular city or settlement. He emerged from this sojourn in the desert with a fully formed, coherent understanding of Jesus as the Messiah and what this means on a range of theological and practical subjects. Certainly, St. Paul's education in the Hebrew Scriptures gave him plenty of raw material from which to craft doctrine after the missing piece of the Messiah's coming was added. This is not, however, how Paul himself speaks. Rather, Paul attributes the details of his proclamation about the Messiah to Jesus Himself. The clearest explanation is that this period was a period not only of Paul coming to terms with his past life and newfound calling, but it was also a period of visionary revelation from Jesus Himself. In other words, Arabia became Mt. Sinai for Paul.

The Torah was the revelation that Moses received at Mt. Sinai. Moses was, therefore, the paradigm of what it means to be a prophet of God. While not paralleling himself with Moses, Paul came to see himself as standing within Israel's prophetic tradition. His prophetic calling was not only, or even primarily, based on his visionary experiences. Rather, the core of prophethood in the Hebrew Scriptures and in the life of St. Paul is an encounter with God enthroned, followed by a calling and the sending out of the prophet on a mission. Paul describes his initial vision of Jesus the Messiah enthroned at the right hand of God as an encounter with God Himself. Because this vision was bestowed upon him, he takes it to be a calling to be a prophet. The vision was not a result of some technique employed by Saul or of some other kind of attainment. It was given as a gift to him and not to others, thus designating him. In describing the vision on the road to Damascus, he deliberately uses the language of Jeremiah to parallel himself with the prophet (Gal. 1:15–16; see also Jer. 1:5).

Central to St. Paul's identity for the rest of his life was his role as an apostle. The Greek word *apostolos* refers to "one who is sent." Paul was on a mission from God. He was sent for a task, to proclaim Jesus as the Messiah. He was sent to an audience, to the people of the nations throughout the world. Paul's view of the life of Christians in the world came to center on this understanding of calling. His calling was particular, but every person has one. For Paul, the standard by which God will someday judge people's lives is one's faithfulness to the unique call that God has given them.

A Calling to the Nations

Saint Paul came to see his particular calling as bringing the proclamation of Jesus the Messiah to the nations. In many English translations, the understanding of the nations in the Jewish world of the first century AD is obscured by the translation "Gentiles." *Gentiles* is the Latin word for "nations." In popular modern usage, however, the word tends to connote simply "non-Jewish people." This presupposes our modern understanding of ethnicities and is not germane to the theological understanding of early Judaism.

The origin of the nations is found in Genesis 10 and 11. The scattering of people across the earth that happened following the Tower of Babel produced seventy nations spread throughout the world with their languages and cultures. At this point, no entity related to Israel yet existed. Israel would be founded as a nation only at the Exodus. Abraham, the forefather of the Israelite people, was called out of one of the seventy nations to live separately from it. Once Israel came into existence, the relationship between Israel and the seventy nations became an important emphasis in the Hebrew Scriptures and Jewish thought.

This scattering was seen as the source of the idolatry into which the seventy nations fell.[16] The gods of the nations were not seen as concocted fiction or primitive science. Jewish authors of the first centuries BC and AD were unanimous in affirming that demonic powers lay behind pagan worship. The precise relationship between demonic powers and pagan religious practice varies, but their worship was held

---

16 See Deuteronomy 32.

to be the worship of demons rather than God. It placed those who participated in it under demonic control. This spiritual reality would manifest itself, in Jewish thought, as the violent bloodshed and sexual immorality that were all too common in the ancient world. Because the demonic powers were hostile to God, they were also seen as the source of the hostility that other nations often had toward Israel, Judah, and later Judea.

Nevertheless, the Hebrew Scriptures did not view the seventy nations entirely as enemies. Israel was called to exercise a priestly role toward them, interceding for them and offering sacrifices. A clear example of such a sacrifice is the offering of the seventy bulls for the seventy nations at the Feast of Tabernacles. The nations were deluded, participated in shameful and vile behavior, and were on their way to destruction, but this was not the cause of rejoicing. An undercurrent running through the Hebrew Scriptures is God's desire that all people would repent and live.

From the earliest portions of the Hebrew Scriptures onward, a prophetic thread proclaims that just as the nations were scattered, they will one day be drawn back together. Shem, the father of the Semitic peoples, is told that he will one day open his tents in hospitality to the descendants of Japheth (Gen. 9:27). Abraham, the forefather of the Jewish people, is told that all the nations would be blessed through him (Gen. 12:3; 17:4). One element of the prophecies aimed at the messianic age is that the seventy nations and their kings would come and worship the God of Israel, having destroyed their idols and repented. Saint Paul, over his years in Arabia, came to understand his calling to be the enactment of this regathering of the nations. Since Jesus the Messiah had come, as a Pharisee Paul now understood that a number of things would take place. The gathering of the nations to worship the God of Israel was the element that had been placed under his authority by the Messiah Himself.

This calling came with a profound sense of urgency. God had dealt with the nations to date in a particular way. In their ignorance and separation from Him, He dealt mercifully with them in patience and

41

long-suffering. Individual nations, tribes, clans, and people groups could descend to a level of evil and depravity at which point God would intervene. He would act dramatically, in judgment, to put an end to that evil and prevent the further victimization of the weak and innocent. Now, however, the people of the nations were being given another chance to draw near to God through the Messiah. This meant that God would soon judge the whole world through the Messiah Himself. Now was the time to be saved from wrath and judgment.

CHAPTER FOUR

Jerusalem

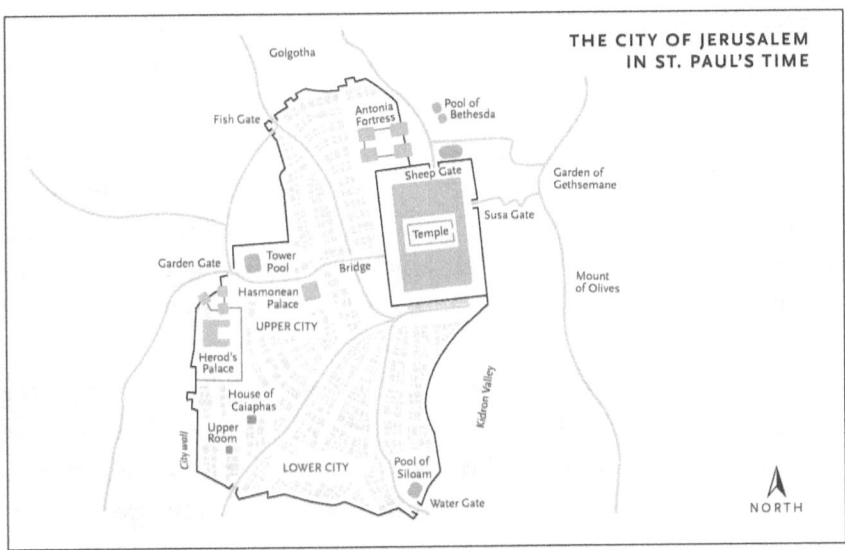

THE CITY OF JERUSALEM
IN ST. PAUL'S TIME

Golgotha

Fish Gate

Antonia
Fortress

Pool of
Bethesda

Sheep Gate

Garden of
Gethsemane

Susa Gate

Temple

Garden Gate

Tower
Pool

Bridge

Hasmonean
Palace

Mount
of Olives

UPPER CITY

Herod's
Palace

House of
Caiaphas

Kidron Valley

Upper
Room

City wall

LOWER CITY

Pool of
Siloam

Water Gate

NORTH

Following his sojourn in Arabia, St. Paul made a brief return to Damascus then set out to return to Jerusalem more than three years after he had left it. By this time he had arrived at a firm sense of his purpose in serving Jesus the Messiah and the Christian movement. Even though three years had passed, however, and despite rumors of his repentance having reached Jerusalem, Saul of Tarsus was still to the Jerusalem community's mind a violent enemy of the Christians. Paul's purpose was not to try to assume a leadership role in the Christian community in Jerusalem, or even to join it. Neither was his purpose to attempt to bring his Pharisaic compatriots to recognize Jesus as Messiah. Rather, his purpose was to meet with the leaders of the Christian movement as a whole—those who had known in person the Jesus who only recently began to reveal Himself to Paul. To gain an audience with this leadership, he needed a certain Barnabas, a member of the local community, to vouch for him.

Peter and James

Paul spent just over two weeks—fifteen days—meeting with two leaders in particular: St. Peter and St. James the brother of the Lord. Peter is the Greek name used by Simon Bar-Jonah, a Galilean fisherman who was the foremost of Jesus' inner circle of disciples. *Petros* likely began as a nickname given by Greek-speaking Galileans meaning, roughly, "Rocky." Peter lacked Paul's extensive Torah knowledge and Pharisaic connections. He had, however, been one of Jesus' closest and most intimate friends. He knew better than anyone who Jesus was, the validity of His claims to be the Messiah, and the reality of His Resurrection.

Peter's older brother Andrew had been a disciple of St. John the Baptist. Following the Baptism of Jesus by St. John, Andrew became convinced that Jesus was the Messiah and brought his brother Peter to become a follower as well. Jesus had an inner group of twelve disciples and within that group an inner circle consisting of Peter and the sons of Zebedee, James and John. With these other two, Peter was privy to Jesus' most intimate moments, His greatest miracles, and His clearest and plainest teaching. Peter had also had a major moral failure at the time of Jesus' arrest and trial: he ultimately failed not only to protect or defend his master; he actively denied even knowing Him out of fear, a betrayal that Jesus made clear He knew happened (Matt. 26:69–75; Mark 14:66–72; Luke 22:55–62; John 18:16–18; 25–27).

But this was not the end of Peter's story. After Jesus rose from the dead on the third day, He appeared to Peter and restored him. As the disciples were preparing to be sent out as apostles, Peter was particularly chosen not only for this restoration but for commissioning to be a leader among the group of disciples as a whole. Saint Peter answered this call and became a significant leader in the Jerusalem community. His ministry was not based on public debate or reasoning from the Scriptures. Rather, like much of Jesus' ministry, it appears to have centered on miraculous manifestations of power, primarily in the form of various healings that demonstrated a continuity of his ministry with the Messiah's. Peter and the other apostles had actually taken a step back from the day-to-day matters of community life, appointing the first deacons, including St. Stephen, to administer food distribution and other practical tasks.

Saint James had not been one of Jesus' disciples or even followers during His earthly life. Rather, he had been a part of Jesus' family. James, the anglicized form of the name Jacob, was the oldest son of Jesus' adoptive father, Joseph. Like the other children from St. Joseph's previous marriage, James had not accepted the claims made about and by his stepbrother and, for the most part, found His preaching and movement embarrassing to the family (Mark 3:31–32; John 7:3–5). James had then become the leader of that family following the death of his father.

James had a profound reputation in Jerusalem that stretched well beyond those who held that his brother was the Messiah. Although he was a Galilean without a great deal of formal Torah education, James was a profoundly devout and pious man. He kept the commandments of the Torah consistently and with zeal. It is said that his knees became like those of a camel due to the callouses he developed praying on his knees in the temple.[17] His reputation was so great that his later death during an outbreak of mob violence was considered by Josephus, the

17 Eusebius, *Ecclesiastical History*, 2.23, citing Hegesippus.

Jewish historian, to form part of the reason God allowed the destruction of the temple and the city.

Neither James's reputation as a righteous man nor his familial connection led to his leadership role over the Jerusalem community, however. Following His Resurrection from the dead, Jesus had made several appearances over a period of forty days, including an appearance to His brother James (1 Cor. 15:7). During this appearance, Jesus appointed St. James as the overseer, or shepherd, of the community of His disciples in Jerusalem. While Jesus' apostles exercised a particular role within the Christian movement throughout the world, St. James was the leader of a particular community in a particular place. This distinction lies behind the later identification of James as the first Christian bishop.

The Community in Jerusalem

Jerusalem did not host a Jewish community; it *was* a Jewish community. As already discussed, there were different schools and factions within that community, and by the time St. Paul returned there, the community of Christians in Jerusalem had swelled in its numbers despite the scattering of so many of its members after St. Stephen's death. Before that fateful Pentecost in AD 30, the disciples of Jesus had numbered roughly 120. After that day, it quickly swelled into the thousands and remained significant until the destruction wrought in the city by the Romans in AD 70.

Within the larger Jewish community of Jerusalem in the first century, the Christians do not seem to have been treated significantly differently from other groups and movements. Zealots like St. Paul would occasionally attack the Christian community, but many other groups within Jerusalem and its environs came under zealot attack for perceived collaboration with the Romans, heresy, and other issues. Members of other Jewish groups were able, in this period, to speak of members and even leaders of the Christian community in Jerusalem as their fellow pious Jews. When tensions arose, it usually surrounded attempts by certain Jewish Christians to convince members of other Jewish groups to join their movement.

Like other Jewish groups in Jerusalem, Jewish Christians in the first century made use of the temple, convening there daily at the hours of prayer. They participated in elements of the sacrificial life of the temple while it still stood. They took Nazirite vows. They continued to observe the Sabbath. They gathered in Jerusalem for important feasts, though many of these feasts began to take on a transformed meaning: They celebrated Passover, marking the death and Resurrection of the Messiah at that time. They celebrated Pentecost, but now as the anniversary of the New Covenant and the coming of the Holy Spirit. And they began to celebrate new days of commemoration, such as the day of the martyrdom of St. Stephen.

The primary practical distinction between the Christian community and Pharisaic Judaism was the Christians' communal way of life. They lived together in common, sold most of their possessions, and shared the proceeds to support the community as a whole. The apostles appointed deacons to oversee the practical elements of this communal life, such as food distribution. This way of life was, for obvious reasons, more attractive to the poor, widows, and slaves than to the wealthy and self-interested. During Jesus' life on earth, His followers had had a similar demographic makeup.

This communal life centered not on the temple nor on the Sabbath but on the Lord's Day. This term refers to the first day of the week, the day after the Sabbath, and emerged very early in communities dedicated to Jesus as the Messiah. In addition to their observation of the Sabbath, members of the Christian community gathered together exclusively on that day, the day of the week on which Jesus had risen from the dead. These gatherings, like synagogue gatherings, included the singing of Psalms, the reading of the Scriptures, and the preaching of the apostles.

The Eucharistic Gathering

The center of the Christian gathering was the Eucharist, Greek for "thanksgiving." The Eucharist was a sacrificial meal following the general pattern of a thank offering, as the name implies.[18] Like other sacrificial meals, it took place within the context of a broader meal. In addition to the bread and wine that were offered sacrificially, all manner of other foods could be found on the shared table. The thank offering, in certain forms, is the one offering that was always technically allowed to be celebrated outside the temple, making its celebration more intuitive to Jewish Christians.

Beyond the offering of bread and wine to God and its consumption, the meal functioned as a remembrance. The eucharistic celebration was not the sacrifice itself but was a means of connection to another sacrifice, that of Jesus the Messiah. Fundamental to the early Christian understanding of the death of Jesus was that He offered Himself as a sacrifice to God on behalf of the people.

Jesus' offering of Himself aligned with a theological understanding of martyrdom that had developed in Jewish circles during the period of Seleucid domination. The Jewish person who was willing to die rather than betray his God, his people, or the Torah was seen to offer himself as a sacrifice pleasing to God through his faithfulness even to the point of death. That the sinless Messiah would do this would be the sine qua non of such sacrifice. Eating and drinking the Eucharist, identified by Jesus before His death as His broken Body and shed Blood, was not to receive the benefits of His sacrifice but rather to participate in it. The one who participated worthily offered his whole self to God and was thereby united to the Messiah, becoming bone of His bone and flesh of His flesh.

In Jerusalem St. Paul received the story of the institution of the Eucharist as a sacrificial meal by Jesus, recounted during its administration on the Lord's Day. Already at this point, as seen in Damascus

---

18   Stephen De Young, *The Religion of the Apostles* (Chesterton, IN: Ancient Faith Publishing, 2021), 260–262.

and elsewhere, Christian communities were taking root in other major cities of the empire. These communities existed, however, in largely non-Jewish environments. Understanding and navigating the construction of Christian communities in relationship to Jewish minorities in non-Jewish cities would become St. Paul's life's work. Much of that work would surround the Eucharist.

The Gospel

Over the period of time that St. Paul met with Peter and James, he laid out the understanding of Jesus from his visions and his time spent in Arabia. The core of this understanding was Jesus' identity as the Messiah, but this then radiated out into other areas of teaching. Jesus being the Messiah led to a particular way of seeing the relationship between Jesus and the God of Israel, Jesus and the people of Israel, and Jesus and the Torah. The proclamation of Jesus the Messiah did not take the form of logical or philosophical arguments to establish these particular points of interpretation. Rather, this proclamation took the form of a narrative that saw the life, death, and Resurrection of Jesus in a cosmic frame. This mode of viewing events in the life of Israel from the perspective of the spiritual world forms the genre of Jewish apocalyptic literature.[19]

Paul had come to see Jesus as embodying the Torah—a goal that Paul would have sought as a Pharisee. In the first place, this meant that Jesus led His life in a way that was in harmony with the commandments of the Torah without exerting a great effort or becoming involved in legalistic disputes. The Torah was written in His person and actions. Further, Jesus knew how to teach and apply the Torah to the daily lives of peasants. He was also able to publicly correct well-educated Pharisees and Torah teachers. All of this is summed up

---

19 Apocalyptic literature as such is typically written from the perspective of a figure who takes a spiritual journey through the cosmos and sees the spiritual realities underlying events in the visible world. Prominent examples include 1 Enoch and the Apocalypse of St. John in the New Testament.

in the statement that Jesus as the Messiah "fulfilled the Torah." Fulfillment is not a matter of perfect rule keeping or checking off a long list of boxes. It means to fill the Torah until it overflows into life. For St. Paul, the way of life Jesus exemplified is centered on perfect love that fully lives out the Torah while surpassing what Paul thought possible during his Pharisaic education. As the Messiah, Jesus delivers on the promise of Pharisaism.

As the Messiah, Jesus also embodied Israel as a people. In His life, he experienced their journey, their suffering, and their sorrow. The Hebrew Scriptures were clear that the suffering—and ultimately the exile of the people—was the result of their sin and rebellion. Jesus endured these same things despite being without sin. The northern tribes of Israel had been utterly destroyed by the Assyrians. Judah in the South had ended up in ongoing exile and servitude to foreign powers. Ezekiel summarizes the state of Israel as being dead, dry bones, bleached by the sun. With this characterization came the promise of a resurrection to new life (Ezek. 37:1–14). As a Pharisee, St. Paul saw the resurrection of Israel as the precursor of the bodily resurrection of the dead. The Resurrection of the Messiah, embodying Israel, was the first fruit of Israel's resurrection.

As the Messiah, Jesus also uniquely embodied the God of Israel. Part and parcel of the Davidic line that would produce the Messiah was the Son of David's identity as the Son of God (Ps. 2:7). A son is, by nature, the image of his father. The function of Israel's king was to embody the rule of God over the creation in his establishment of justice within the kingdom. He and his court were an icon of God and the divine assembly. As the Messiah, the Davidic king, Jesus fulfilled this role by being the perfect image of the Father. Within the life of Jesus, He experienced the rejection by the people that God had experienced throughout the Hebrew Scriptures. He fed the people, healed the people, taught the people the Torah, loved the people, and in return received rejection and ignorance. As the Messiah Jesus continued to love and to return love for hate, the reconciling love of God for His people was revealed.

These emphases, with much more nuance, were arranged as a story of the life of Jesus the Messiah, beginning with Jesus' Birth and submission to the Torah and moving through His Crucifixion, Resurrection from the dead, Ascension, and sitting at the right hand of God. The story culminated in an impending future appearance of Jesus that would signal the resurrection of all the dead and their judgment according to their works. This Day of the Lord would inaugurate the age to come, an age that would have no end. Saint Paul and other apostles referred to this narrative proclamation about the Messiah Jesus as "the gospel."

The Greek word *evangelion*, commonly translated as "gospel," is a word that had broader use within the Roman Empire. The word was generally used extrabiblically in the plural: "gospels." These gospels were lists of the credentials and accomplishments, particularly focused on military victories, that were read before the arrival of a Roman official to a city. The entire narrative of Jesus represented a great victory over all the spiritual powers arrayed against humanity, including the demonic powers, sin itself, and death. It could be referred to variously as the gospel of Jesus the Messiah or the gospel of God.

Saint Paul could also refer to Jesus' victory as "my gospel" because he had formulated these thoughts and interpretations on his own, with the witness of Jesus Himself and in the midst of prayer. He carefully laid out his understanding of the gospel before Peter and James, and they gave agreement to all that he said. This confirmation, following his own independent efforts, emboldened Paul, and he began to engage more directly with the Jerusalem community, particularly with the Greek-speaking Jewish members, to argue the truth of the gospel narrative. This began to create instability within and around the community, and Paul was dispatched back to his native Tarsus (Acts 9:28–30).

CHAPTER FIVE

Tarsus and Antioch

Saint Paul returned to Tarsus and remained there for the better part of a decade. During this period, he produced no writings that have survived to this day. This period of his life is also not recounted by St. Luke in the Book of Acts. In his later letters, Paul writes that his sense of mission and purpose as one sent by the Messiah had already crystallized before this point. Nevertheless, there is no mention of Paul beginning that mission or even beginning to make preparations for a lengthy period of years in which he seems to have remained in his home city.

Was St. Paul Married?

While this silent period is difficult to explain, it likely gives a window into answering another persistent question regarding St. Paul. It would be exceedingly strange for the young Saul of Tarsus not to have been betrothed by his family to a Jewish woman. In Jewish communities, a man was expected to be married. This was not an option. A man remaining unmarried well into adulthood was refusing to be married—tantamount to refusing to be an adult, refusing to be a man. For someone like Paul, who was pursuing Torah study at the highest level as a Pharisee, such a refusal simply would have disqualified him.

On the other hand, it is very clear in both St. Paul's epistles and St. Luke's narrative of his subsequent life that he does not have a wife. He asserts his right to take a wife but labels it as a right unused (1 Cor. 9:5). Likewise, he never mentions having any biological children. He frequently used familial terms of father and child to describe his relationships with people with whom he is not biologically related. He says that he thinks that it is good for people who are unmarried to remain unmarried like him.

The answer to all these mysteries may be found in the precise wording of one of the places in which Paul addresses the subject. Specifically, he writes, "To those who are not married and to widows, it is good for them to remain as they are, the way I do" (1 Cor. 7:8). Paul's statement is not only addressed to the question of someone choosing to live a celibate life but also to the question of remarriage after widowhood. Everything Paul says about his not marrying in order to devote himself to his mission for the Kingdom of God can be read just as easily as his decision not to remarry after being widowed.

Certainly, there is no mention of Paul's wife in the New Testament, despite a few strained modern arguments. On the other hand, there is likewise no mention of the wives of any of the apostles, nor those of St. James or St. Jude the brothers of the Lord, other than St. Paul's passing reference in 1 Corinthians 9:5. Aside from the reference there, the only place the New Testament speaks to St. Peter being married is oblique, when Jesus heals his mother-in-law (Luke 4:38–39). That no details are given about Paul's marriage reveals very little about whether it existed.

Our earliest extant witness to extrabiblical traditions regarding the apostles is St. Ignatius of Antioch, writing at the end of the first century AD and the dawn of the second. In the fourth chapter of his Epistle to the Philippians, St. Ignatius refers to St. Paul as one of the apostles who was a "married man." In his surviving letters that are uncontested in their authenticity, Ignatius shows familiarity with the contents of St. Paul's writings. It seems unlikely that this is just a mistake or bit of ignorance on his part. Rather, it would seem to reflect his personal knowledge of St. Paul's history that did not necessarily make it into the text of the New Testament.

Based on all the available information, the most reasonable conclusion seems to be that Saul of Tarsus was indeed a married man and that he returned to his wife and his extended family when he returned to Tarsus. He would much later write to St. Timothy regarding the necessity of a man having set his house in good order before assuming a position of leadership in a Christian community. At some point in this period of years, possibly closer to its end than its beginning, Paul was widowed. To pursue his calling from Jesus the Messiah, he made the decision not to marry again but to devote himself to this calling fully.[20]

In addition to a wife, St. Paul was part of an extended family in Tarsus. He had at least one sister, and that sister had at least one son (Acts 23:16), neither of whom are named. He also had two relatives, unidentified in their exact relationship to him, named Andronicus and Junia (Rom. 16:7). He refers to them as having joined the Christian movement before he did. Based on what he would later say in his letters, St. Paul believed firmly in the importance of family authority structures. He would have considered his responsibility to operate within these structures, even in relation to his calling from God, as critically important. He would have navigated these familial responsibilities as a precursor to the full beginning of his mission in the same way that he would later navigate Roman civil authority structures during his missionary journeys.

This was clearly a complicated matter for Paul. The fact that it took him some years to pursue his calling attests to this. We also hear little to nothing of his preaching activities in Tarsus, in the synagogue, or

---

20 Clement of Alexandria and Origen make a different argument: that Paul and his wife agreed to end their marriage so that Paul could leave her and travel freely. This is an argument they make based on a certain reading of certain texts; they do not claim it to be a historical tradition they received. This idea would also contradict much of St. Paul's teaching about marriage in his epistles. While making St. Paul a hypocrite, this idea would fit nicely with the views of human sexuality espoused by Clement and Origen. All these factors mean that this idea is easily disregarded.

in Christian communities. We hear of him working no miracles there. He will not write or refer to the Christian community of Tarsus in the future, though one very likely existed. Paul seems to have been a prophet without honor in his own country. Whatever the critical matters were in Tarsus from which Paul sought to extricate himself, he was finally able to move on following the arrival of Barnabas.

Barnabas

The Barnabas who arrived in Tarsus seeking Saul was the same Barnabas who had previously vouched for him in Jerusalem with the apostles (Acts 9:27). His given name was Aramaic: Joseph Bar-Nechma. The name Barnabas, which he used in Greek-speaking circles, is a Greek version of his surname. Though that surname is likely simply a result of his father being named Nechma, the meaning of that name is "encouragement," "comfort," or "consolation." He was Jewish and from the tribe of Levi.

Saint Barnabas was born in the city of Salamis on the island of Cyprus, and the beginning and end of his life show a great devotion to his homeland. Salamis and the other major Cypriot cities had thriving Jewish communities. Many cities in Cyprus, including Salamis, were already ancient, having stood for a millennium by the time of the rise of the Roman Empire. Even in the Roman era, Cyprus had a great sense of itself and its own traditions independent of the empire. The last king of Cyprus killed himself in 58 BC rather than allow himself to be captured by the Romans.

The Jewish communities of Cyprus were eradicated in AD 117 after a general uprising by zealot groups in various parts of the empire. The urban Jewish communities in Cyprus joined this revolt in 116 and, according to Roman records, two hundred and fifty thousand Greeks in Cyprus were killed in the attacks on Roman officials, government representatives, and imperial infrastructure. Rome responded by massacring the Jews, expelling those who survived, and passing laws that prohibited any Jewish person from setting foot in Cyprus. These revolts set the stage for the Bar Kochba rebellion which, over a decade later, brought about the destruction of most of the Jewish communities in Judea.

Barnabas had left Cyprus to become a student of Gamaliel before the arrival of Saul of Tarsus. Rather than leaving Gamaliel to pursue zealotry, Barnabas had left the great rabbi to follow Jesus of Nazareth after His arrival and public preaching in Judea. In addition to Jesus' circle of twelve disciples, He had had another concentric circle of seventy, and Barnabas was among them. These were not incidental numbers. Jesus had deliberately paralleled the structures of the twelve tribes of Israel and the seventy elders of Israel in His ministry.[21] Barnabas had become a leader within this group of seventy and maintained that position through and after the Crucifixion and Resurrection of Jesus.

Barnabas's leadership position was within the growing Christian community in Jerusalem. He had become one of its benefactors by selling a significant piece of property and giving the proceeds to the community (Acts 4:36–37). When Saul of Tarsus arrived after meeting Jesus and joined the Christian movement, St. Barnabas became the one who vouched for him and connected him with Ss. Peter and James. Likely, Barnabas's shared connection with Gamaliel and his students gave him some familiarity with Paul and allowed him to recognize the transformation that had taken place.

Peter and Cornelius

During Paul's years in Tarsus, a massive expansion of the Christian movement had begun in Antioch where, early on, the community had reached into the Greek-speaking Jewish population. Now, however, it had begun even to reach non-Jewish people. During these years, St. Peter crossed a Rubicon when he preached the gospel to a Roman

---

21 Many of Jesus' followers who had considered Him the Messiah likely thought that this group was intended to replace a Sanhedrin that, despite a few genuine luminaries at the time, had become corrupt.

centurion who was a God-fearer. God-fearers stood at the edge of Jewish communities as non-Jewish people who nonetheless revered the God of Israel. They frequently endowed synagogues, contributed to Jewish communities charitably, and participated—as they could—in prayers to Israel's God. They were not motivated to become Jewish through the process of circumcision and incorporation into the Jewish community for a variety of reasons, primarily because the Jewish communities themselves did not encourage such conversions.

That St. Peter went into the home of a centurion named Cornelius and ate with him would have offended the sensibilities of the strictest members of the Pharisaic movement, who advocated for a high degree of separation from Romans like Cornelius. Such Romans' bodies and food maintained the vestiges of idolatrous worship and pagan immorality regardless of how much they might have recently come to fear the true God. Because of a revelatory vision that Peter had received, however, he had gone further. Though not Jewish, Cornelius had been baptized into the Christian community and received the Holy Spirit through the laying on of hands along with his whole household. They then existed as Christians while still being outside the Jewish community. A new space had opened up.

Antioch

As already mentioned, Antioch on the Orontes River—to distinguish it from several other cities with the same name—was founded in 300 BC to serve as the capital of the newly created Seleucid Empire. Its first ruler, Seleucus the First, the Victorious, had been one of Alexander the Great's chief generals. In the wake of Alexander's death, he carved out an eastern empire for himself from conquered territories. At its founding, the city's history was tied up with the worship of Zeus, and Alexander was believed to have built an altar to Zeus there. The official story of its founding, however, stated that an eagle was given a piece of meat from a ritual offering on that altar to Zeus and flew with the meat to the later site of the city. Beyond the official founding myth, Antioch stood at the intersection of two water routes to the Mediterranean and three major trade roads to the west, east, and south.

A few early village settlements in the area were incorporated into the city, which, at the time of its founding, was one-third Greek, one-third native Syrian, and one-third Jewish. This made the Jewish community a significant part of the city's history. It also meant that when the Seleucid persecutions of the Jewish people began, the Antiochene capital was ground zero. Second Maccabees relates the story of seven brothers, their mother, and their elderly teacher of the Torah who were tortured to death rather than violate the commandments of the Torah at Antioch. The remains of these Jewish martyrs were the center of a shrine in Antioch in the first century AD that had become a pilgrimage site for Jewish people in the region.

Under Rome, Antioch had become the eastern capital of the Roman Empire. While Alexandria was larger and more culturally influential, it lacked access to the empire's eastern frontier. Like Tarsus, Antioch had been made a free city by Julius Caesar. Augustus had expanded the temple to Zeus on the central high place of the city into a massive temple to Jupiter Capitolinus. This localization of Jupiter honored the Jupiter of the Capitoline Hill in Rome, where the empire's central temple to its chief god was located. Rome thereby assimilated the local religious traditions into its own. The expanded temple was to be a direct spiritual connector to the capital, making Antioch an extension of the city of Rome in the East. Throughout the first century, Roman emperors and other leaders like Herod and his successors continued building projects in the city, adding a forum, a circus, an expanded theater, and eventually even a hippodrome.

In the first century, the population of the city of Antioch was roughly two hundred and fifty thousand. If those living in the surrounding country are also counted, the total population was closer to half a million. The Jewish community had continued to thrive there despite persecution and had come to be the second-largest Jewish population in the world after Jerusalem. The Christian community in

Antioch had come to take on a somewhat different character than that in Jerusalem, and the shape of the relationship between the Christian and larger Jewish communities in Antioch became the paradigm for the relationship between such communities as the Christian movement spread through the Roman Empire.

The Christian community in Antioch began as a subset of her large Jewish community, which was a subset of the larger community of Antioch. Jewish life there surrounded the life of the synagogue for most purposes and most of the year, although proximity to Jerusalem certainly made pilgrimages for feast days possible. The life of the synagogue and sabbath gatherings for the reading of the Torah and other Scriptures, community prayer, and teaching formed the Jewish community. In its earliest phase, the Christian community was simply composed of those members of the Jewish community who continued to embrace Jesus of Nazareth as the Messiah.

The identification of Jesus as the Messiah made a substantive difference in the interpretation and preaching of the Hebrew Scriptures. These differences were not necessarily the subject of division in Jewish communities in the first century, though in particular times and places they could be. Christians, very early on, created communal links with each other without withdrawing from the Jewish community. This took the form, primarily, of a second gathering of only the Christian members of the larger Jewish synagogue community. Like the Christian community in Jerusalem, the Antiochian Christians gathered on the day after the Sabbath, the first day of the week, the day on which Jesus had risen from the dead. It was referred to as the Lord's Day.

The core purpose of the Lord's Day gathering was Christians' celebration of the Eucharist. As at Jerusalem, this sacrificial act of worship took place within the context of a broader meal. The Eucharist was led by the leaders of the Christian community, and only baptized Christians participated in it. As non-Jewish Antiochenes were baptized, functionally this meant that they were brought into this community to celebrate the Eucharist on the Lord's Day with their fellow

Christians. They were not, however, incorporated into the city's Jewish community. Many early non-Jewish Christians had likely lived for some time on the fringes of the synagogue community, and joining the Christian community left them in that same peripheral position.

The term that was used to describe these Christian communities was the Greek *ekklesia*.[22] This term had been used in Greek translations of the Hebrew Scriptures for the Hebrew *qahal*. The *qahal* was the gathering, throughout Israelite and later Jewish history, of the people of God, generally to hear from God's prophet. It became a natural term to use to describe the gathering together of Christians while also expressing continuity with the Judaism that Christians still professed.

The Christian community in Antioch began to experience great growth, particularly among non-Jewish members. As a new development, this raised concerns, particularly among those who took a very strict interpretation of the commandments regarding purity in the Torah. They maintained that these commandments required a radical separation from non-Jews. Even for those without such scrupulosity, this view presented all manner of new challenges for communal life that needed to be managed through reliable leadership. The apostles in Jerusalem chose to send St. Barnabas to Antioch.

Barnabas saw in St. Paul a potential partner in this leadership and in Antioch an opportunity for Paul to focus on answering his calling. Barnabas traveled to Tarsus, sought out Paul, then returned with him to Antioch. There the two of them helped establish the order of the community. A major part of that work was the integration of the Christian community into a single whole. Jewish Christians in Antioch had one pattern of life, still centered around the synagogue, with the addition of their Christian gatherings. For the non-Jewish Christians, the eucharistic gatherings were central to their life while they maintained, at best, a partial relationship with the synagogue.

---

22 *Ekklesia* is most commonly translated into English in the New Testament with the word "church." In the Old Testament, it is most often translated as "assembly" or "congregation."

That distinction or separation naturally tended to carry over into the eucharistic gathering itself, particularly the meals, which ended up being segregated on Jewish/non-Jewish lines. While Paul and Barnabas were working to integrate these factions, St. Peter visited Antioch. While he had actively engaged in eating with the non-Jewish Christians for some time, when certain other members of the community in Jerusalem came to visit, he instead ate solely with the Jewish Christians for the sake of their sensibilities. Many other community leaders, including Barnabas, did likewise. Paul rebuked Peter publicly, aiding in the reintegration of the two portions of the community (Gal. 2:11–14).[23]

Each Christian community across the empire was forming independently at this time, taking on its shape in part based on the shape of the Jewish community with which it overlapped. As more non-Jewish people were baptized as Christians, their influence was also felt. Nonetheless, despite certain levels of diversity, these communities were not completely independent. They saw themselves as connected with the church in Jerusalem, which served as their mother. This understanding parallels the way in which most Jewish people at the time understood the relationship between their scattered synagogue communities and Jerusalem. The term *ekklesia*, then, could be used to describe any given Christian community in a particular place or to describe the entire gathering of Christians throughout the world.

Part of the leadership role received by Ss. Paul and Barnabas in Antioch entailed serving as the representatives of the Jerusalem ekklesia. The first major example of this was their response to a famine in Judea. The Christian community of Antioch sent relief aid to the mother community in Jerusalem, and Paul and Barnabas served

---

23 Saint John Chrysostom, among other Fathers, suggests that this public incident was primarily theater. Saints Peter and Paul planned the confrontation as a ruse to help accomplish the reintegration of the community by having a figure well respected by the more scrupulous Jewish parties publicly repent. While this may, at first, just seem an attempt to prevent there being any real disagreement between the apostles, such a portrayal would find precedent in certain actions taken by the Hebrew prophets.

as representatives to deliver this aid (Acts 11:27–30). While in Jerusalem, Paul witnessed further persecution of the Christian community at the instigation of Herod and his party, resulting in the death of James the Son of Zebedee—one of the Twelve. When Saul and Barnabas returned to Antioch, they brought with them Yochanan, or John, who went by the Roman name Marcus or Mark.

CHAPTER SIX

First Missionary Journey

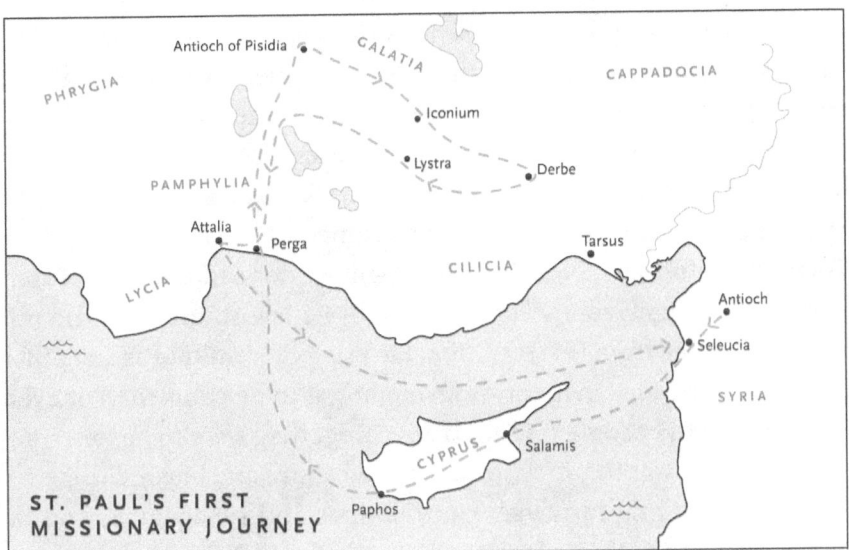

ST. PAUL'S FIRST
MISSIONARY JOURNEY

Working in Antioch with those from the nations who had come to view Jesus as the Messiah represented the beginning of Paul answering Jesus' call. The time came for Paul to continue to follow that calling in its fullness. Scattered throughout Jewish communities in the Roman Empire were Jewish people who followed Jesus as the

Messiah. In many, if not most, cases, they had not been organized into formal communities, though some may have had eucharistic gatherings. Sometimes non-Jewish people were being baptized and received somewhat haphazardly as Christians. These communities needed to be more fully formed, stabilized, and integrated in terms of Jewish and non-Jewish Christians.

Beyond this, however, Paul felt called to something further. Not only was he called at the community level to integrate non-Jewish followers of the Messiah into Christian communities; he was called to proclaim the gospel in its narrative form to all the nations. With the coming of the Messiah, an epochal shift had taken place. The time had come when people of all nations were called to leave behind their idolatry and wickedness and return to the worship of the true and living God. Saint Paul had been sent as the agent of this calling of the nations. The Day of the Lord and God's judgment were coming, and the time was now for repentance and the forgiveness of sin.

Judaism had never substantively proselytized. Various groups were more or less willing to receive converts, but there was no call to attempt to persuade outsiders to be circumcised and begin to keep the Torah in its fullness. Non-Jews were simply not called by the Torah or the rest of the Hebrew Scriptures to live a Jewish life. Paul did not actually diverge from this tradition. He was as committed as any other Pharisee to the idea that non-Jews ought not to be compelled or even incentivized to become Jewish. If anything, they were to be deterred. Paul's mission was to proclaim something above and beyond this.

Saint Paul came to Jewish communities and synagogues, and he taught from the Hebrew Scriptures that Jesus is the Messiah. He also proclaimed Jesus as the Messiah to non-Jewish people. What this meant for them was that the God who had created the world and all its people wanted them to return to Him in worship and faithfulness. This meant leaving behind idolatry, fornication, and other sinful desires. It also meant being set free from the power of the evil spiritual forces whom they had worshiped in the past and who had dominated their lives. Paul wanted Jews to continue in their way of life, knowing that the Messiah had come and that these were the last days. He also wanted non-Jews to know that these were the last days and that their way of life must fundamentally change—not to the Jewish way of life, but to one now emerging for faithful followers of the Messiah from the nations.

This full-orbed mission of St. Paul to spread the gospel as he had formulated it from his encounters with Jesus began in earnest with a move of the Holy Spirit in the leadership of the Christian community in Antioch. Paul and Barnabas had already represented them to the mother church in Jerusalem. Now they would represent the Antiochian Christians to other Christian and Jewish communities. This mission would begin for them in Barnabas's native Cyprus.

The Journey

SALAMIS, CYPRUS

Barnabas and Paul sailed to Salamis, Barnabas's home city, taking John Mark with them. There they began by preaching Jesus as the Messiah in the local synagogue. This was not to the exclusion of non-Jewish audiences; the first people from the nations who would hear the teaching of the gospel would be those God-fearers at the edges of the Jewish community. The preaching in Salamis went well, and a regularly functioning Christian community began meeting on the Lord's Day. Saul and Barnabas then traveled from city to city through much of the island, meeting with similar success.

The Roman provinces in this period were overseen either directly by the emperor or by the Roman Senate. The emperor oversaw the frontier and border provinces of the empire where the military, which he commanded, was stationed. Interior, established, stable provinces were left to the oversight of the Senate. Each was ruled by an appointed governor called a proconsul because he governed as a representative of one of the Senate's consuls. In the city of Paphos in Cyprus, St. Paul made his first high-profile convert to the Christian community: Sergius Paulus, who was serving there as proconsul on behalf of the consul Claudius, who would later become emperor.

Paul and Barnabas's activities came to the attention of Sergius Paulus, and what he heard interested him. One of his advisors was a certain Jewish man who had nonetheless become involved in Roman religion and sorcery. This man, named in the Book of Acts as Bar-Jesus, or the son of Joshua, was likely serving as an augur or an astrologer for the proconsul. Proconsuls were barred from making use of the Roman military's haruspices,[24] but this did nothing to deter their reliance on signs and omens. Paul publicly rebuked Bar-Jesus for his opposition to the gospel, and the latter was struck blind. This miraculous sign convinced Sergius Paulus to join the Christian movement.

PERGE AND ANTIOCH IN PISIDIA

Barnabas and Paul sailed from Paphos in Cyprus to Perge, a city in the Roman province of Pamphylia Secunda. This port city was on the coast at the western end of Asia Minor, now modern Turkey. Perge had been left to Rome at the death of her final king and was another city that was already ancient by the first century AD. The Romans subsequently connected this port with roads to other major imperial cities. Upon their arrival at Perge, John Mark left Paul and Barnabas and returned to Jerusalem. Paul and Barnabas, meanwhile, set out for the city of Antioch in Pisidia on the Via Sebaste. This road was built by the Romans from 26–5 BC. The road ran for 120 miles, traversing the Taurus Mountains. Over the course of its length, its width varied between 20 and 26 feet.

After several days' journey, Paul and Barnabas arrived at Antioch in Pisidia. This Antioch had been founded by the same Seleucid monarch who founded Antioch on the Orontes. The region around the city was the settlement site of a large group of Europeans known as the

---

24 A *haruspex* was a diviner who based his predictions on inspection of the entrails of sacrificial animals.

Galatians. The Galatians became a persistent problem for the Greek kings, and Antioch in Pisidia became a military encampment under Seleucus's son Antiochus. When the Romans took possession of the area, they named it Galatia and began the process of building Roman settlements throughout the area. These new settlements were founded by veterans who had completed periods of service in the Roman legions and were rewarded with land grants, primarily in border regions of the empire or other areas where the Roman way of life had not taken firm root. In the case of Galatia, Rome did not want to experience the same difficulties with the local Galatians that their Greek predecessors had. The region had the status of a *colonia*, meaning that it was considered to be an outpost in conquered territory.

At first, St. Paul and Barnabas's interactions in the city were not with any of the major imperial centers or figures but directly with the local synagogue and Jewish community. They were invited to preach following the readings from the Torah and Prophets at the synagogue, as was common at the time for visitors. The account of Paul's preaching in the Book of Acts gives a window into the content of his proclamation (Acts 13:16–41). From this summarized sermon, a number of themes emerge regarding the gospel as Paul proclaimed it.

Paul addresses himself to both the members of the Jewish community and to the God-fearers who may be in attendance. He begins by surveying the history of Israel from the perspective of the rise of David as king. He then addresses the promises made to and about David to show that at least some of those promises can be fulfilled only by David's descendant, the Messiah, rather than David himself. Key to this argument is the promise that David would not see decay and that his reign would have no end. Paul sees the narrative of the death and Resurrection of Jesus as the way in which this prophecy was ultimately fulfilled.

Jesus, the Messiah who had come, presented to the Jewish community in Antioch an offer and a demand. The offer was the forgiveness of sins beyond what was possible in the Torah. For St. Paul, the sacrificial system within the Torah served to manage the sin of the people of

Israel through repeated sacrifice and atonement. This allowed them, as long as their repentance was real, to continue to have the holy God live in their presence. Paul saw the Messiah as having dealt with sin once and for all, freeing from sin entirely the person who is faithful to Him and who follows the Spirit of God. The demand was faithfulness to Jesus as Messiah.

The message delivered by Paul was well received by the Jewish community and God-fearers, and word of it tantalized the curiosity even of the general Roman citizenry. But the majority of the Jewish community, unsurprisingly, was not convinced by one Sabbath's preaching to join the Christian movement. The following Sabbath brought a crowd from outside the community to the synagogue to hear more, raising further suspicions from the unconvinced members of the Jewish community. The Jewish leaders began to speak against Paul, and though a Christian community began forming in Antioch in Pisidia, it was primarily made up of non-Jewish converts. Paul saw this too as a prophetic fulfillment and hoped that non-Jews finding salvation would make the non-Christian Jews jealous, leading them to embrace their Messiah.

ICONIUM

The Jewish leaders went on to communicate to the important Roman members of the community that Paul and Barnabas were troublemakers bound to cause problems in the city. This made them decidedly unwelcome, and the apostles moved on to Iconium, a journey of roughly ninety-seven miles. Iconium was another ancient city with a history stretching back to 3000 BC. The city that became Iconium passed through a number of empires from the Hittites to the Cimmerians, and by the first century AD it had been bequeathed to Rome by her last king. In her founding myth as understood by the Romans, Perseus had founded the city after defeating Medusa and using her head as a weapon.

Paul and Barnabas spent productive time in Iconium, adding baptized members to the Christian congregation both from the local

Jewish community and from outside it. In addition to their preaching, they worked a number of miraculous signs in the city that testified to the truth of their proclamation. The ongoing success of Paul's mission work in the city left it divided: both the Jewish community and the broader community had members joining the Christians. While the Jewish Christians did not necessarily leave the Jewish community, the non-Jewish converts removed themselves from much of civic life, which revolved around pagan rites. Jewish leaders who did not accept Jesus as the Messiah increasingly saw the Christian community as a dangerous and divisive cult. Learning of the growing hostility toward them in the city, Paul and Barnabas departed and headed toward nearby Lystra. At Iconium, Paul also met his later companion St. Thekla.[25]

LYSTRA

Saul and Barnabas then traveled to Lystra, only about twenty miles from Iconium. Lystra was a small village—a Roman colony established in 6 BC. Upon their arrival, a strange scene unfolded. Paul spotted a beggar attentively listening to his preaching. The man had been unable to walk since his birth, and Paul healed him, making him able to walk. The crowds, made up primarily of local Galatians, identified Barnabas and Paul as Zeus and Hermes respectively and made desperate attempts to offer sacrifices to them. Through Ovid's *Metamorphoses* we know the ancestral myth in Lystra that likely occasioned this response.[26]

In the ancient myth, Zeus and Hermes in human guise arrived in the region around Lystra and sought shelter for the night. They were refused hospitality by every home until they came to that of an elderly couple, Baucis and Philemon, who welcomed the gods with hospitality. When Zeus and Hermes, in their wrath, wiped out the population

---

25 See the appendix.
26 Ovid, *Metamorphoses*, book 8.

of the region that had spurned them, they preserved Baucis and Philemon, transforming the elderly couple into a tree—really two trees of different species forever connected. This tree was identified as a pair of intertwined ancient trees that were still extant in the area in the first century AD.

The display of miraculous power by Paul likely made the Lystrans think that history was repeating itself. The people were, for obvious reasons, disinclined to repeat their ancestors' mistakes. Sacrifice, as hospitality offered to gods, seemed the correct response to Ss. Paul and Barnabas. Paul attempted to explain the real nature and source of the miracle as the true and living God, but he failed to win over many of the people. People from the Jewish communities of Antioch and Iconium, however, soon arrived in Lystra and began to incite the crowds against Paul and Barnabas. Paul then found himself on the receiving end of the same mob violence that he had previously wielded against Christians during his period of zealotry. He was stoned and physically thrown from the city, though he did not die.

DERBE

Barnabas and a recovering Paul went on to the city of Derbe and organized a Christian community there. The journey of seventy-five miles likely took several days, especially given Paul's condition. The small town proved a fertile field, and a dynamic Christian community was established without major opposition or incident. In Derbe, Paul met a young man named Timothy and his mother, Eunice, a devout Jewish woman who became part of the Christian community. Timothy's grandmother Lois likewise became an important Jewish Christian. Saint Timothy would later become not only a traveling companion of St. Paul but his most trusted successor and the coauthor of several of his letters.

The Return Trip

The apostles then passed back through the cities they had previously visited to make sure the Christian communities there were secure. Important to the stability of these communities was the appointment of elders. The local Jewish pattern of leadership relied on the elder men in the community, and Paul followed this pattern. These elders, *presbyters* in Greek, were responsible for adjudicating disagreements and teaching within the communities. Most critically, however, they presided at the eucharistic meetings on the Lord's Day when the apostles were not present. They were the offerers of the eucharistic sacrifice.

Having checked on their newly organized communities, Paul and Barnabas sailed back to Antioch in Syria. There they reported everything that had happened to the Christian community and gave thanks to God. For Paul, this first missionary journey not only was a successful initial foray but gave him a pattern for future travel and community organizing. The pattern included not just a knowledge of what had brought them success but also an awareness of sources of opposition, as well as the delicate balance he would have to maintain both within Jewish communities and concerning the Roman governing authorities. Before he could embark on a second such journey, Paul would have to return to Jerusalem to resolve a controversy with the other apostles.

CHAPTER SEVEN

Council of Jerusalem and Epistle to the Galatians

In Syrian Antioch, the nascent Christian community faced its most serious crisis to date. The ekklesia was made up of members of the Jewish community of Antioch who remained members of that community and also of non-Jewish converts to Christianity. Previous tensions regarding eating together had been resolved. Only the most scrupulous of Pharisees refused to have any contact with non-Jews whatsoever. The nature of the Christian gathering on the Lord's Day, however, was the central act of the offering of the Eucharist.

The Fellowship of the Eucharist

The Eucharist was a thank offering that was offered by the presbyters—the elders of the people who presided at the celebration when an apostle wasn't present. The Jewish Christians understood that the sacrificial system of the Torah demanded that sacrifices be offered in purity. While the level of purity required by those making and partaking of the offering was not as high as that required for those who presided, these purity demands were not negligible. The Jewish Christians continued to keep the Torah's commandments, which allowed them to maintain the purity necessary to approach and come into the presence of God.[27]

Baptized non-Jews did not keep the commandments of the Torah that were addressed specifically to the Jewish people. They weren't supposed to. But non-Jews also weren't supposed to participate in sacrificial worship at the same level as the Jewish people. The Torah was given in part to allow the Jewish people to be the ones to offer sacrifices and offerings on behalf of the nations and the world.

Further, the Eucharist was associated not only with a general sacrifice or a thank offering but was closely tied to the Passover because Jesus had implemented the Eucharist as an offering at the Passover. The Eucharist served as a participation in His death and Resurrection, which occurred at the Passover. The Passover not only was the central and most sacred feast of the year, but its celebration is central to Jewish identity. To be Jewish, at its most minimal definition, was to be circumcised and to eat the Passover. No one uncircumcised could eat it (Ex. 12:48). The analogy to the Eucharist, to many Jewish Christians, seemed obvious.

This issue opened up a world of questions and decisions that St. Paul had to address if he was going to fulfill his calling to bring the people of the nations to God through Jesus the Messiah. He was not dealing with the modern idea of ethnicities; rather, what it meant to be a Greek, a Phrygian, a Roman, or a Laodicean was to worship certain gods and observe certain festivals that bound the people to these gods and to each other. Sexual immorality was a primary feature of many of these festivals. To join the Christian community and come to worship the God of Israel meant, largely, to these converts that they had to cease being Greeks, Phrygians, Romans, or Laodiceans—at least as those identities had previously been understood.

How should they live? What could and couldn't they eat? How should they dress? How should their households be restructured?

---

27   In the commandments of the Torah directed to the people of Israel, their central purpose was to allow the Israelites to maintain the purity necessary to dwell safely with God in their midst.

How should they relate to their former kin and countrymen? All these questions and many more needed answers in the Christian communities that Paul was founding and building. The easy answer to many was that they should just become Jewish. After all, the Torah and its way of life are from God. How could following it go wrong?

Saint Paul, however, understood the Hebrew Scriptures differently as he had reflected on them with his visions of Jesus. The prophets did not say that the nations would all become part of Judah. They did not prophesy that the distinctions between peoples and nations would be eradicated. Instead, they prophesied that the nations, with their identities intact, would come to worship the God of Israel. Paul's mission was not to make the Greeks, Galatians, and Romans in the Galatian communities that he founded into Jewish Christians. He wanted them to be Greek Christians, Galatian Christians, and Roman Christians. He also wanted Jewish Christians to remain Jewish Christians and continue to follow the Torah. For the others, the practical outworking of Paul's mission was that what it meant to be Greek, Galatian, or Roman would become something very different, transformed by the Messiah.

The Council of Jerusalem

In Antioch, Jewish members of the Christian community pressured non-Jewish members to be circumcised and take up a Jewish way of life. Given that this was not a concern confined to Antioch but would ultimately involve newly founded Christian communities all over the known world, the matter was to be submitted to the apostles and presbyters of the mother community in Jerusalem. Paul and Barnabas, along with a few others, were sent there from Antioch to represent the case. As they traveled, they visited Jewish and Christian communities and related what was happening with people from the nations coming to worship the God of Israel through Jesus the Messiah. This news was well received everywhere, but Jerusalem's Christian community included a number of Christian Pharisees who presented arguments in favor of these non-Jewish Christians being circumcised and keeping Torah if they wanted to be fully included in the eucharistic gathering.

After a great deal of debate, St. Peter presented his experience with Cornelius. He pointed out that the Spirit of God came to dwell in Cornelius, a Roman, without him needing to be circumcised. It was not the place of the apostles to yoke these new Christians to the Torah when God had not—especially as they themselves had often failed to keep Torah as they should have. Paul and Barnabas then described the miraculous signs and wonders that had accompanied their preaching to both Jewish and non-Jewish audiences. They agreed with Peter that God was moving with miraculous power not only within the Jewish people but through them in every nation of the world.

As the one appointed by the risen Jesus, His stepbrother St. James issued the final decision of the Jerusalem mother community on this issue. James took a strict reading of the Torah as the basis for this decision. Within the Torah, particularly in the Levitical legislation, most commandments are directed to the people of Israel. Only four are directed to both Israel and the foreigners who may dwell within the land. They are found in Leviticus 17, which describes a series of regulations for Israelite sacrifices. Within this discussion, both the house of Israel and the stranger or foreigner in their midst are forbidden from eating blood (vv. 10–14). Clean and unclean animals are described in Leviticus 11, but all the commandments regarding them are directed solely to the people of Israel. Only the commandment against eating blood is extended also to foreigners. Leviticus 18 is made up of commandments for all people regarding sexual morality: sexual immorality is forbidden to the Israelites and to the stranger, or else the land will vomit them out (vv. 26–28). Leviticus 20 forbids idolatry—and particularly sacrifice to Molech—to the sons of Israel and the foreigner (vv. 2–5).

James agrees with the perspective of Peter and Paul that the inclusion of non-Jews among the Christians is the fulfillment of prophecy. Now that the Messiah had come, it was time for the nations to abandon idolatry and immorality and come to worship Israel's God.

The place for them to do that was the Christian community, with the offering of the Eucharist as its central act of worship. For non-Jewish Christians to live in a community with Jewish Christians, they needed only to keep the commandments directed to them in the Torah. Saint James outlined these four commandments in a letter that was sent to Antioch with Paul and Barnabas, along with their companions Silas and a certain Judah from the Jerusalem community.

The Epistle to the Galatians

Though the apostolic decision served to settle this issue for the Jerusalem community, the integration of Jewish and non-Jewish Christians into single communities remained an issue throughout the world. Working through the challenges in various communities would become much of the work of the rest of St. Paul's life. During his absence, Paul learned that this integration had become an issue in the communities he had helped found and organize in the province of Galatia. Certain Jewish Christian parties were applying pressure to non-Jewish Christians to be circumcised and live as Jews. This led to St. Paul writing the first of his extant letters to those communities.

Paul writes to the Galatians and describes as a different gospel the message being preached to them by those asking them to be circumcised. Their message is a different narrative of the Messiah and a different view of who He is. Paul emphasizes that the gospel he had preached to them was given to him directly by Jesus Himself, and he tells of his experience of his calling on the road to Damascus. In describing his call from the Messiah, he utilizes language from the prophet Jeremiah about that prophet's own call (Jer. 1:5).

Paul recounts his subsequent history in Arabia with Barnabas, interacting with the Jerusalem apostles. In explaining his calling, he parallels his ministry to people coming to Jesus the Messiah from the nations with the ministries of Peter and James to Jewish people who embrace Jesus as the Messiah. He describes those seeking to require that non-Jewish Christians be circumcised and take up the Jewish way of life as a continuous, bedeviling problem. He then relates the episode with Peter at Antioch. Whether or not one accepts the idea that the event was staged, St. Paul certainly uses the retelling of that confrontation to demonstrate that even the most prominent Jewish Christian leaders were not on the side of compelling circumcision.

In his Epistle to the Galatians, Paul makes a distinction that will be important throughout his written work. To distinguish between the commandments of the Torah directed only to Israel and those directed more broadly to all people, Paul referred to the former as "works of Torah" or, in most English translations, "works of the law." These were commandments given specifically to the people of Israel that defined Israelite and later Jewish identity. They were required of the Jewish people at Mt. Sinai to preserve the people's holiness. A holy God dwelling amid a sinful people represented danger. God had not similarly come to dwell in any other nation, and so those nations did not need to maintain the same level of holiness.

Paul is keen to point out that standing before God, or the ability to please God, was never restricted to only the Jewish people, nor did it require the keeping of the commandments that defined the Jewish people as such. Paul points out to the Galatians, as Peter had at the Jerusalem Council, that the non-Jewish members of their community had received the Spirit of God despite not having kept to the particularities of the Jewish way of life. It therefore made no sense that in order to bring their salvation to completion and live a life pleasing to God, they now would need to become Jewish.

How, then, does one please God? By being faithful to Him. Paul returns to Abraham, the first father of the Hebrew people, to point out that he was found to be pleasing to God—even before he was given the sign of circumcision—because he was faithful. Abraham was faithful to the calling he received from God, to leave Ur and travel to the other side of the known world on the promise that he would have many descendants who would inherit that land. God promised that all the nations would be blessed in Abraham, not only the people of Israel. Thus the real son of Abraham is the one who mirrors his faithfulness.

For Jewish people, Paul has no problem in saying that faithfulness takes the form of following the Torah. But faithfulness will have a different shape for someone to whom the Torah was not given, just as it did for Abraham before the Torah was given. Further, the Torah describes problems that beset humanity. Every human dies. Every human struggles against the power of sin. Every human lives in a world dominated by evil spiritual powers, though these powers have especially ensnared the nations. The Torah points to these problems and their origins in human sin, and it presents a way of managing that sin for the Israelites and later Jewish people to live lives pleasing to God. But the demonic powers, sin, and death remain active in the world until, for Paul, the Messiah deals with them.

Paul points out that the promises to Abraham use the Hebrew word *zera*. This word, like the typical English translation "seed," is a collective noun. It can be either singular or plural, given a particular context. In Hebrew, wordplay is common. Using a grammatically inconclusive word to imply more than one of its possible meanings is a regular feature of interpretation. In one reading, all the promises to Abraham are to his seed plural. As they are reiterated in the Book of Genesis, the large number of Abraham's descendants constitutes one of the promises. On the other hand, there was a singular element to the promises from the beginning. The promises were inherited by Isaac, not Ishmael, and by Jacob, not Esau.

This singular line, for Paul, led ultimately to Jesus as the Messiah, the recipient and bringer of the promises. Jewish Christians had finally and fully received these promises in their Messiah. People from the nations could gain a share in these promises through that same Messiah and live lives of faithfulness. Before the Messiah came, the Jewish people were guarded, shepherded, and taught by the Torah. Before the Messiah came, the nations were enslaved to the demonic forces whom they worshiped in the form of idols. The coming of Jesus as the Messiah brought those under the Torah to fullness and maturity as sons and heirs of God, recipients of their inheritance. The coming of Jesus as the Messiah also set the nations free from idolatry and the demonic powers that enslaved them, leaving them free to come to know and serve the living God.

For Paul, a Jewish person continuing to keep Torah was good and right. But for a non-Jewish Christian to be circumcised and attempt to keep the whole Torah was fundamentally a mistake. The non-Jewish Christian had already received adoption, freedom, the Spirit of God, and the blessing of Abraham through the Messiah. To try to gain these things through becoming Jewish would be to deny already having them in the Messiah. For that person, Torah-keeping represented a rejection of the Messiah.

While Paul does not seek to subject non-Jewish Christians to Jewish identity markers, he does not see the Torah as irrelevant to them for the shape of a life pleasing to God. As he points out to the Galatians, the whole Torah is summed up by the commandment to love one's neighbor as oneself. Non-Jewish Christians were to follow the Spirit of God, who was given to them not instead of the Torah, but because the Spirit of God would never lead them to violate the Torah. A life filled with love, joy, peace, patience, kindness, goodness, faithfulness, gentleness, and self-control is pleasing to God and violates none of the commandments. Non-Jewish Christians have been set free not *to* sin, but *from* sin, to please God.

In addressing the Christian way of life for both Jew and non-Jew, St. Paul reorients this discussion. Jewish identity is not, for Paul, what allows a person to live a life pleasing to God. Either a Jewish or a non-Jewish person can live a life pleasing to God. Paul describes two ways of walking. His consistent use of the verb "walk" in his epistles is not a coincidence. Within the rabbinic circles from which Paul came, the discussion and application of the commandments of the Torah to daily life were referred to as *halakha*, derived from the Hebrew verb "to walk." For Paul, the commandments of the Torah do apply to non-Jewish Christians, but they must be applied by qualified leaders through a process of discernment.

Paul explains that the two ways in which one can walk are the way of the Spirit and the way of the flesh. The way of the flesh consists of following sinful desires to attempt to satiate and please them. This way leads to all the sin that has plagued the nations in the past, from idolatry to anger to drunkenness, violence, and sexual immorality. The other way of walking is to follow the leading of the Spirit of God. Walking in this way pleases God and produces the fruit of love, joy, and peace. When someone in the community is walking in the wrong way, Paul reminds the Galatian communities that their task is to attempt to restore him to the right path.

In this first epistle, as will become common in many of his later letters, St. Paul adds a line written with his own hand—often simply signing his name. Many ancient descriptions of Paul describe ongoing problems with his eyes beyond the blindness and scales that were cured in Damascus. When he makes his mark on a letter, he often comments on how large and unwieldy his handwriting is, likely a by-product of bad vision. The task of writing the kind of epistles that Paul would send to various Christian communities did not involve him writing longhand. Instead, the process by which Paul composed his letters was dictation to an *amanuensis,* or secretary. After the dictation was complete, Paul would review the letter and make any corrections. The secretary would then be sent to the recipients to read the letter aloud and answer any questions. The Epistle to the Galatians does not give the name of its secretary, but this person would have been dispatched to Galatia to travel between the communities that Paul and Barnabas had established.

CHAPTER EIGHT

Second Missionary Journey

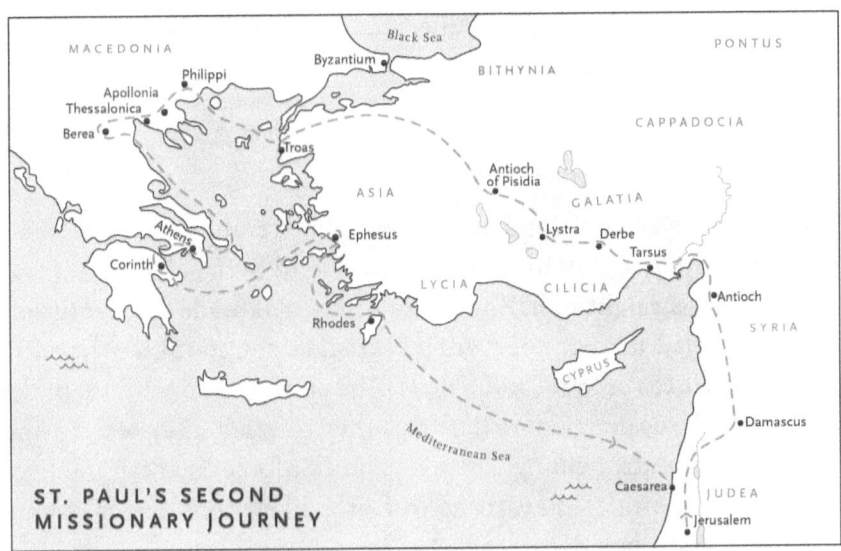

ST. PAUL'S SECOND
MISSIONARY JOURNEY

In Antioch, Paul began to plan a second, more ambitious mission-ary journey that would take him into Greece. He would begin by traveling back through and revisiting the communities organized on the previous journey before embarking on new territory. Barnabas wanted once again to bring John, also known as Mark, with them. But Paul remembered how John had left them early on and did not trust that he would endure any better in this case. This disagreement led to a falling out between Paul and Barnabas, which led to their parting ways. Barnabas and Mark sailed for Barnabas's native Cyprus. Paul then formed a new partnership with Silas, who had accompanied them back to Antioch from Jerusalem after the council.

The name *Silas* in Greek is slightly mysterious. Saint Silas had the Latin name *Silvanus*, which is normally transliterated into Greek as Silouan(os). Some have suggested that Silas is a shortening of this longer name. If so, it is not significantly shorter. There is also some evidence that it may be a Greek version of the Aramaic way of writing the name Saul. The use of the form *Silas* makes this option convincing biblically, primarily when he is discussed alongside Saul of Tarsus. Using a unique form of his name, rather than referring to two Sauls, makes a great deal of sense. When he is referred to elsewhere, his Latin name is used (e.g., 2 Cor. 1:19).

The Journey

Paul and Silas set out for Derbe, this time traveling via land. This meant a journey of 240 miles from Antioch in Syria, although it was not made in a straight shot. Rather, Paul and Silas made frequent stops as they traveled to visit flourishing Christian communities throughout the provinces of Syria and Cilicia. The apostles had with them the letter of the Jerusalem Council, and as they traveled, they relayed and taught its contents, helping organize and reinforce the ongoing lives of these communities. Returning to Derbe likely took several weeks with these visits included.

Upon his return to Derbe, Paul found St. Timothy now of age and ready to accompany him as both an assistant and a disciple. He would serve as Timothy's mentor, and ultimately Timothy would be Paul's primary successor in leadership in the Christian communities. Before Timothy left with Paul and Silas, Paul arranged for him to be circumcised within the local Jewish community. Timothy's mother and grandmother were devout Jewish women, but his mother was married to a Greek man who had not had him circumcised (Acts 16:3; 1 Tim. 3:14–15). From Paul's perspective, Timothy was a recipient of generations of Jewish tradition through his mother and was therefore a Jewish Christian. It was right, then, that he be circumcised and live as a Jewish Christian.

Paul, Silas, and Timothy revisited the Christian communities in Lystra, Iconium, and Antioch in Pisidia. After some years, Paul found these communities thriving. He shared with them the results of the council held in Jerusalem and gave them additional guidance and teaching. When they moved on into new territory, they traveled through the provinces of Phrygia and Galatia. Eventually they reached the province of Mysia, which made up the entire northwest section of Asia Minor. This journey along Roman trade roads covered roughly two hundred miles.

Paul began to experience significant visionary activity during this journey, including what he interpreted as encounters with the Spirit of God and with Jesus once again. These visions steered him away from the province of Bithynia. Reaching the Roman trading post at Dorylaion, an important crossroads, he and his companions turned directly west and traveled the road to Troas, a major port on the northwestern Aegean coast of Asia Minor. This represented another journey of 200 miles.

Alexandria Troas and Luke

Troas is an abbreviation of the full name of the site, Alexandria Troas, which differentiates it from the existence of several other Alexandrias. Within the walled city lived roughly one hundred thousand people. It had been made a free city shortly after becoming Roman territory and served as the major port between Europe and Asia, granting easy access to trade routes running both east and southward through the Levant toward Egypt. Across the Aegean lay the great Greek city-states and trade routes westward toward Rome. Troas was so strategically located that Julius Caesar had considered making it his capital had he managed to fully ascend the imperial throne. Constantine also later considered it before ultimately settling on the village of Byzantium and rebuilding it as Constantinople.

Paul wanted to continue his mission, but because of recent visions and experiences, he was unsure of where to go next. Troas made sense as a centrally located base camp from which to plan future travel. There, St. Paul had another vision in which a Macedonian man pleaded with him to come next to the province of Macedonia. In Troas, Paul was joined by another trusted and important companion, a certain Lucas, a physician. Lucas, a Roman name, is the only name ever used for this figure in the New Testament or in subsequent tradition. He was a native of Antioch in Syria and was likely a native Syrian—a non-Jewish person of Semitic background.

Lucas, or Luke, had been at the edge of the disciples of Jesus of Nazareth during His life. It is not known for how long he followed Jesus in His itinerant preaching ministry, but Luke was present for its end in Jerusalem. Following His Resurrection, Jesus appeared to Luke and another disciple named Cleopas on the road and even ate with them at the village of Emmaus (Luke 24:13–35). This would make Luke one of the earliest non-Jewish members of the Christian community when he returned to Antioch. It is not entirely clear whether he traveled from Antioch to Troas to find St. Paul specifically or if other business took him there when he encountered and joined St. Paul. In either case, Luke knew Paul from Antioch.

As a physician, Luke was part of the most educated class in the Roman Empire. Education in the Greek style was practiced by a consistent method throughout the entirety of the Greek-speaking world at this time, giving Luke a broad familiarity with Greek literature and a special familiarity with the Hippocratic corpus, a working collection of Greek medical texts and commentaries by other physicians and philosophers. This placed Luke in a unique position among Paul's followers. He would go on to write a two-volume historical work that narrated the life of Jesus, followed by the early life of the Church. Much of the latter volume, the Acts of the Apostles, focused on his mentor, Paul. He recorded and summarized several of Paul's sermons within this narrative. The first volume, known to us as the Gospel according to St. Luke, shows clear signs of being structured around the gospel as Paul received and preached it. In addition to his understanding of history and his writing ability, Luke was also accomplished as an artist, particularly in the field of portraiture.

Philippi

Paul, Silas, Timothy, and Luke sailed from Troas to Samothrace, entering the province of Macedonia. They immediately traveled from there to Neapolis, a small city ten miles from the major city of Philippi that served as its port. Philippi possibly had been the most important city of the Macedonian kingdom when it had an independent existence. Shortly after its founding, it had been renamed for Philip of Macedon, the father of Alexander the Great. A nearby gold mine had brought it wealth and made it the site of the kingdom's mint. It lay along the major trade road running through Macedonia, which had long since been incorporated into the Roman Via Egnatia. This Roman road ran nearly 700 miles, from the city of Dyrrachium on the Adriatic Sea to the village of Byzantium, the later site of Constantinople.

When the independent Macedonian kingdom fell into decline, Philippi and its significance greatly dwindled until the first century BC, when a major battle in the Roman civil war following the death of Caesar was fought nearby. Augustus then made Philippi into a Roman colony, meaning that he began to resettle Roman veterans there on a series of land grants. The city was administered, like most Roman colonies, directly from Rome. Her civic life was overseen by two Roman military officers charged with enforcing Roman law and keeping the peace.

While Paul and his companions had passed through several other cities, Philippi was the first one in which they stopped to preach. Even as he entered Europe, St. Paul still began his ministry by connecting with the local Jewish community. Philippi at this point did not have a structured synagogue; rather, the Jewish community, which consisted primarily of women, gathered on the Sabbath near a river for prayer. One of the women in this group was a certain Lydia, a non-Jewish woman who was a God-fearer. She was originally from the city of Thyatira and was a dealer in purple-dyed cloth, making her a woman of some means. Upon hearing the gospel from Paul, she was baptized along with her entire household. She went on to host and fund the efforts of Paul and his companions. Lydia's household—and likely her physical home—became the foundation of the Christian community in Philippi.

SPIRITUAL WARFARE

In the various kinds of oracular activity that had been common in Greece from well before the Roman period, certain individuals would be possessed by spirits, either permanently or temporarily, during rituals. People could then consult these spirits regarding esoteric knowledge or predictions of the future and request favors. The most well-known example of this activity is likely the oracle at Delphi, who was believed to be possessed by Apollo. Similar mediums and spiritists were common throughout the Roman Empire, doing business on a smaller scale.

Paul and his companions remained in Philippi for some time, building and organizing the community until a series of incidents caused them to move on. On the way to the place where Sabbath prayer gatherings happened, Paul and Silas passed through the agora, the large open-air market in the city. An enslaved young woman who was possessed called out after them, identifying them as servants of the Most High God and their message as the way of salvation. Paul responded by casting the demon out of the woman.

Among the Judeans, demonic spirits were identified as unclean, and possession was seen as an affliction. But the Greek and Roman perceptions were quite different. Those who claimed to own the young woman cared little for the fact that she was enslaved or in what ways the spirit possessing her might afflict her. She was a persistent source of revenue for them.

These owners dragged Paul and Silas back to the market to the Roman overseers of the city. Rather than describing the financial difficulty that had resulted from their activities, the accusers merely identified Paul and Silas as Jews and advocates of unlawful practices. Roman officials did not need much more than this to respond. The vast majority of Jewish people were not Roman citizens and, therefore, had no substantive legal rights. Because they opted out of everyday Roman life and religion, they were frequently the target of blame for everything from natural disasters to military losses. Additionally, many Romans saw certain Jewish practices such as circumcision as barbaric and backward.

PAUL AND SILAS IMPRISONED

The governors of the city of Philippi therefore treated Paul and Silas as they would any Jews accused of making trouble in the city. They let the mob have them, then had them beaten with rods and thrown into prison. Their imprisonment was not the first step in some form of due process. Rather, they would remain in prison until the officers who sent them there changed their minds. If they were simply forgotten, as happened often, they would stay there until they died. For Paul and Silas, that death was likely not far off. After they were beaten, their ankles were chained to the floor. Imprisoned people were left to lie in their own filth as well as the filth and potentially the decaying remains of the previous occupants. Rats were common in Roman prisons, as were disease and infection. Enslavement was widely considered the better option to imprisonment.

The officer in charge of the jail had a simple job: keep everyone in the prison. There was no duty of care; he was not responsible for keeping his charges healthy or even alive. As in any Roman military context, dereliction of this duty was punishable by death. The public shame would extend to his family, leading to the potential confiscation of property and the enslavement of wives and children. Therefore a prisoner making any small move toward escape would be summarily executed.

Paul and Silas occupied themselves in this dank prison by continuing to pray and sing hymns to God together. In the middle of the night, a massive earthquake in the prison opened the gates and broke the chains of the prisoners. Seeing the potential for mass escape and the dire consequences for himself and his family, the officer in charge of the jail prepared to kill himself.

Paul and Silas not only declined to escape, but they ensured that no one else did either. The officer of the jail, dumbfounded, invited them to his home, cleaned their wounds, and listened to what they had to say about Jesus the Messiah. He and his household were baptized before the night was over, and they ate together. In the morning, the officers in charge of the city sent word to authorize the men's release. Paul pointed out, however, that he and Silas were Roman citizens, and their imprisonment instantly became a grave matter for the city officers. Not only were they not allowed to publicly beat and imprison Roman citizens without charges and a hearing, but they also had a duty to protect Roman citizens from mob violence. Now they were the ones in danger of being found derelict in their duties. Issuing profuse public apologies, the officers encouraged Paul and Silas to move on. After meeting with the Christian community again, they did indeed depart.

Thessalonica, Berea, and Athens

Paul and his companions traveled the Via Egnatia deeper into the province of Macedonia. The next major city with an established Jewish community was Thessalonica, the capital of the province. Over the course of the 105-mile journey, they stopped in the cities of Amphipolis and Apollonia. These mid-sized cities were important to Roman economic life in the region but had no substantive Jewish presence. For Paul, proclaiming Jesus as the Messiah to the Jewish people and then inviting those of the nations to come to worship Israel's God in the Christian community was not just a habit or matter of course. Paul believed that Jesus, as the Messiah, represented the resurrection and restoration of Israel. It was this renewed and empowered Israel into which those of the nations were invited to come, sojourn, and worship Israel's God. The ongoing resistance and rejection that Paul experienced from his fellow Jewish people was therefore not just an annoyance to him or a problem in pursuit of some goal. It represented a theological problem that Paul would later work through in writing.

OPPOSITION IN THESSALONICA

Thessalonica had a population of two hundred thousand people. Not only was it a provincial capital on the Via Egnatia, but the city also lay at the intersection of that most important road and the one that ran from the Balkans through the Axios and Morava valleys. When Paul and his companions arrived, they immediately connected with the local Jewish community, where Paul was given the opportunity to speak on three consecutive Sabbath days at the synagogue. Luke summarizes this teaching as arguing from the Hebrew Scriptures that the Messiah would suffer and die and then rise from the dead, followed by the identification of Jesus as the Messiah (Acts 17:3).

Based on this public teaching, several members of the Jewish community, as well as God-fearers and leading women of the city, were baptized and brought together to constitute a Christian community. These believers met at the home of one of the baptized, Jason, on the Lord's Day to celebrate the Eucharist. Other members of the Jewish community who rejected Paul's teaching viewed this development as dangerous. The growth of this Christian group jeopardized the position of the broader Jewish community in the city in significant ways. These opponents instigated a number of non-Jewish people of the city who in turn incited a mob that attacked the house of Jason, where Paul and his companions were staying. Paul and company were, however, not there at the time, so Jason and other members of the Christian community were dragged before the city officials and accused of treason.

The element of Paul's preaching on which the accusation hinged was the proclamation of Jesus as the Messiah, who was identified as a king. The idea of a king was abominable to the Romans, who associated it with the tyrants who had ruled Rome before the founding of the Republic. *King* was the one title that Caesar never took for himself, because of these sensibilities. Proclaiming someone as the true king—over against Caesar—and forming groups of followers was the worst form of sedition in the view of Roman officials. Jason and the others managed to defend themselves but were released only after posting considerable bond. The Christian community smuggled Paul and Silas out of the city so they would not be caught up in the unrest.

THE GOSPEL IN BEREA

Paul and his companions then traveled fifty miles roughly west to Berea. Berea was another city that had been of some great importance in the Macedonian kingdom but had not maintained its prestige once it surrendered to Rome. Roman Berea was primarily a cultic center with significant temples to a number of the Greek gods. While its permanent population was relatively small, the city's numbers frequently swelled at times of pilgrimage. In Berea, Paul and his companions found another Jewish community centered on an established synagogue. The Jewish people there greeted Paul's preaching warmly and actively read and discussed the Hebrew Scriptures to which he pointed in arguing for Jesus as the Messiah. Here again, in addition to Jewish Christians, non-Jewish parties were being baptized, including many leading women of the city.

In Roman culture, Paul's gospel appeared radically egalitarian. The word *physis* in Greek, generally translated as "nature," was used to describe the generally inherited properties of a particular living thing. The social stratification of Roman society was therefore considered natural; it conformed to the nature of the humans being governed.

Roman citizens were of a better stock and type of human than the run of the mill, which was why they ruled and held special prerogatives. The emperor was so far beyond other humans as to be divine. Slaves were slaves because they had an inferior nature, and slavery was the proper place for them. Women, though generally viewed as human by the first century AD, were considered to be defective humans, incapable of higher reason.

As a Jewish scholar of the Torah, St. Paul taught that male and female persons were equally human, and both were created by God in His image. He understood that every human on earth was descended from one human; thus all heritable qualities were an equal possession of humanity. Paul did not believe that there was no difference between a man and a woman, or between a Jewish person and a non-Jewish person, or between an enslaved person and a freeman. Rather, he taught that they all shared the same human nature and that they shared that human nature with the Messiah Jesus. Jesus, through His life, death, and Resurrection, had elevated and transformed that nature. Every human person was able to live a life pleasing to God, though the way they did that would be different, based on all these factors.

This radical teaching on the shared nature of humanity made Paul's preaching, and the Christian movement, incredibly popular with women and slaves within Roman society. His was the first rational, religious voice that recognized their humanity and invited them to find salvation. The growth of Christianity among women and slaves, in turn, made it look all the more repugnant to cultured Romans. A religion of Jews, women, and slaves was clearly degenerate and to be rejected on its face.

While the earliest stage of organizing a Christian community in Berea went well, that first phase was not destined to last. Before long, opposition parties from the Jewish community in Thessalonica learned that Paul and his companions were in Berea. Some of them traveled to Berea and began to instigate trouble there as well. The Berean Christians then sent Paul twenty miles away to the nearest coastal port, from which he sailed around the coast to Athens. Silas and Timothy remained in Berea until Paul arrived in Athens and sent word to them to join him.

THE PHILOSOPHERS OF ATHENS

To describe the history and significance of Athens, even only up to the first century AD, goes well beyond the scope of this book. Athens is one of the most ancient human settlements in the world, going back at least five thousand years. The city was central to the Mycenean civilization of the Bronze Age. It collapsed with nearly everything else at the end of the Bronze Age but went on to have perhaps even more significant influence in the Iron Age, particularly by the middle portion of the first millennium BC.

Athens produced the first experimentation with something resembling a democratic system, and she produced the greatest rhetoricians of the ancient world. Tragedy and comedy both emerged from sacrificial rituals in Athens. Philosophy and the first philosophical schools were born and took root there, existing for centuries. The writing of history as such first emerged in Athens. Hippocrates, the founder of medicine, was born there. Athens was filled with ancient temples. After its conquest, Rome immediately made Athens a free city with respect to her cultural achievements.

While all this is true, there is another side to Athens that must not be forgotten. The Athenians believed that they were created as a special race, from the soil around Athens, by the gods Athena and Hephaestus. Even at the height of Athenian democracy, only male Athenian citizens of a certain social status had the vote. Athenians owned many slaves. Pericles, one of her greatest orators, was also ambitious and attempted to organize the free cities of the Delian League into an Athenian empire that would subjugate her neighbors, especially Sparta. It was Athens's defeat by the Spartans in the Peloponnesian War that stifled these ambitions. Greek tragedy portrayed a world in which violence and horror were always just below the surface of culture, waiting to break out. Her philosophers embraced, rather than rejected, the ancestral pagan religion of the city, albeit with nuance that set them above the common folk.

The Athens at which St. Paul arrived was an aging city in need of renewal. That renewal would eventually come at the hands of the emperor Hadrian in the second century. When the apostle arrived, major building projects had been left incomplete for lack of funding, and buildings and infrastructure were showing their great age. The intellectual life of the city continued but against a backdrop slowly falling into disrepair. The great philosophical schools continued to accept disciples within the city, and the temples continued in their function. Athens's population was around one hundred and fifty thousand, considerably smaller than it had been five hundred years before.

Paul was deeply disturbed by the paganism of the city. He also, however, was much better able to get a hearing in Athens than in some other cities. The intellectual life of the city was such that philosophical debate was the major pastime. Athenians wanted to hear any new idea they could find, at least for the purpose of martialing arguments against it and rejecting it. Thus Paul was able to take a two-pronged approach. On Sabbath days, he received a hearing in the established Athenian synagogue. There he could speak to the Jewish community and to the God-fearers of Athens. On other days, Paul stood speaking in the marketplace to anyone wishing to engage in discussion or debate.

Some of Paul's hearers believed that he was preaching about two new gods from some foreign place, named Jesus and Anastasia, the latter being the Greek word for "resurrection." He was invited to present his teaching at the Areopagus to the leading men of the city. The Areopagus is a rocky outcropping at the edge of the Acropolis in Athens, the high part of the city that held the most sacred temples and government buildings. It was believed to be the place where Ares, the god of war, had once stood trial for murder. Murder trials seem to have been the cause for the earliest gatherings of the city leaders at the spot, but this group of elders eventually became a governing council. Owing to the antiquity of Athens, the Romans allowed the city to continue to be governed in most matters by this council.

Invited to speak before this gathering, Paul proclaimed the same gospel, but he told the story from a different perspective. He was now speaking not to members of the Jewish community or to God-fearers at its edges. He used the Hebrew Scriptures, but not the same passages he used in the synagogue. Instead, he took as the occasion for his remarks an altar to an unknown god in Athens. While Athens may have erected such an altar as a means of being cosmopolitan, either as an inclusive gesture to visitors who worshiped foreign gods or as a catch-all to cover all the bases, Paul made another identification. For Paul, this "unknown god" could refer only to the God who, long ago in their ancient past, the Athenians—and the Greeks in general— abandoned in favor of idolatry.

He spoke to them of this singular God who created everything, does not live in buildings of human manufacture, and doesn't need to be fed and dressed and cared for by humans. God gives every human everything, so how could He have needs? He speaks of God creating all humans, over against the popular pagan models, and scattering the nations across the earth, assigning them their territory. Within Athenian paganism, echoes of this event could be found in the ancient past, performed by a god no longer worshiped.[28] Paul, rather boldly, then gives two quotations from pagan poets: the first from Epimenides of Crete and the second from Aratus's poem "Phainomena" (Acts 17:28). Both these quotations are addressed to *Theos*, the Greek word for "God," but it is rather clear that this word in the context of these writings refers to Zeus. In his speech, Paul follows a long pattern of the Hebrew Scriptures in taking praises and titles lavished on the pagan gods by their worshippers and applying them, correctly, to the true and living God.

It was at this point that Paul segued to the Christian gospel. Everything that he had just said, with which he expected his highly educated pagan audience to agree, contained within it an implied critique of idolatry. After making that latent critique direct in pointing to the

---

28 E.g., Plato, *Critias* 109b–c; *Laws* 713c–e.

98

pagan gods' supposed need to be served by humans, Paul pointed to the wickedness of this idolatry. In the past, God had shown great patience with the nations, but now He was calling them to repent and return to worshiping Him. A day of reckoning was coming when God would judge the world through Jesus the Messiah, whom He raised from the dead.

The idea of the bodily resurrection, though one of the critical doctrines of Pharisaism, was doubted by most other Jewish groups and schools of thought. Further, to Greek philosophy, which by and large agreed with Plato that the body was the prison house of the soul, it seemed absurd. Paul's proclamation of it therefore led to derision from a significant portion of the council. A number of its members, however, took Paul's message seriously, and they joined the ranks of the Christians. Saint Luke names two of them: Dionysius, a member of the Areopagus council, and Damaris, a prominent woman of the city. Both would later hold important leadership positions in the Athenian Christian community.

Now that he had begun the work of establishing a Christian community in Athens and forming the beginnings of its leadership, Paul was able to leave the city peaceably. He traveled west from Athens to Corinth, a journey of roughly forty-eight miles. One can argue that Paul's missionary journey ended only when he returned to Antioch, but at the very least, when he arrived in Corinth, his travels were put on a lengthy pause. Paul's relationship with the community in Corinth would open a new chapter in his mission and sense of his calling.

CHAPTER NINE

Epistles to the Thessalonians

During his time in Corinth, word reached St. Paul of certain confusions and difficulties in the community he had helped establish in Thessalonica. Backtracking the many miles to return to the city
in person was not a possibility. Additionally, Thessalonica had been a
hub of resistance to Paul's mission and message. So, over the course of
the time he spent in Corinth, the apostle wrote two letters addressed
to the Thessalonian community from himself, Silas, and Timothy. In
these letters he attempts to resolve certain confusions that remained
following his first visit and his initial preaching.

First Thessalonians

Paul begins his first letter by letting the faithful in Thessalonica
know the good reputation that they have everywhere he has traveled in Greece. While there were Jewish Christians in Thessalonica,
non-Jewish Christians seem to have predominated. Paul frames the
coming of the gospel to them as their turning away from the worship
of idols to the living and true God. This would have been the case for
either God-fearers or outright pagans who had been baptized into the
Christian community.

101

The community in Thessalonica not only received Paul's teaching, but they saw his way of life while he was there with them. Paul viewed the way he carried out his life publicly as part and parcel of his teaching and preaching. One of his foremost principles was that he and his companions would support themselves by working in any city they visited. In the first century AD, it was commonplace for disciples of a philosophical teacher and even some rabbis to pay their instructors. Paul always affirms that there is nothing innately wrong with this arrangement but that he chose otherwise. He always wanted to remain free from accusations of greed or preaching for money. This practice also allowed Paul to point to himself and his own way of life as a guide for other people's decision making in his absence.

Paul believes that the Thessalonians have two great confirmations of the truth of his preaching in their community. The first demonstration was the miraculous power of God that manifested itself in healings and other signs while he was there. The second is the resistance that they face from outsiders. Paul points out that the prophets were persecuted, the Messiah was persecuted, the Christian community in Jerusalem has been persecuted, and now so have they.

Though he was not able to go himself, Paul earlier had sent Timothy to visit Thessalonica and report back to him about the situation and the difficulties there. He was happy with Timothy's report, despite the difficulties they faced, and assured the community of his continued prayers on their behalf. Paul reiterates the need for them to walk now in holiness. When teaching non-Jewish Christians, one of the most radical disjunctions with their former way of life was sexual morality. Sexual continence had simply not been a concern for most of them before, so it became Paul's focus. Paul's frequent emphasis on this area was not based on prurient interest but on the continuing education and reorientation of former pagans.

But the primary area of confusion regarding Paul's teaching in Thessalonica surrounded the resurrection of the dead. In particular, it seems to have been unclear in the community how the bodily resurrection related to the coming of the Messiah to judge the world. The

Thessalonian Christians understood that Jesus would appear to establish justice in the world permanently and eternally. They understood that at that time they would enter into the Kingdom in its fullness. But the fate of those members of their community who had died before Christ's appearance was unclear to them.

As Paul had experienced in Athens firsthand, the idea of the bodily resurrection was ridiculous and undesirable to pagans. Even within Jewish communities, a strong belief in the necessity of the bodily resurrection was a distinguishing feature of Pharisaism, but it was not accepted across the board. Paul had spoken to the Thessalonians of the imminence of the Day of the Lord—that it can come at any time. In his letter, he does not back off from that teaching. As he clarifies the teaching of the resurrection, in fact, he reiterates all that he had already taught them about the coming of the Messiah in the fullness of His Kingdom.

He also explains, however, that one of the signs of the coming of the Day of the Lord will be the resurrection of all the dead. The first of those to rise, Paul says, will be the dead in the Messiah—those who died in the hope of His coming, either before or after the Birth of Jesus. Then he says that the living followers of the Messiah will be transformed and enter the Kingdom. The Messiah's judgment of the earth will be a judgment not only of those alive on the earth at that time but of all those who have ever lived. Both positive and negative judgment come on that day. The Christians in Thessalonica should grieve their departed loved ones in a way that also reflects the hope they have in the Resurrection of the Messiah. Paul then ends his first letter with general encouragement and reminders to the community.

Second Thessalonians

Paul's second letter, again from himself, Silas, and Timothy, followed not too long after. This letter was considerably shorter and more focused on a single issue of clarification. Some people in the community were teaching that the Day of the Lord had already happened.

Whether this was an additional issue beyond what was discussed in the first letter, or a more detailed address of the difficulty is not entirely clear. In the teachers' scenario, not only would the departed miss out on entering the Kingdom, but potentially the entire community would as well.

Paul refocuses his response on the signs that will come before the Day of the Lord arrives. Here he deals with two traditions in particular: The first is that before the Messiah comes, there will be a great falling away into faithlessness, leaving only a small remnant. This idea is found frequently in the Hebrew prophets. At least at this point in his life, Paul does not identify this falling away with the rejection of Jesus as the Messiah by the Jewish people. He sees this, rather, as a future falling away into sin and faithfulness by those who had previously been followers of the Messiah.

For Paul, this falling away is tied up with a second tradition that was then current in much of the Judaism of the period: The coming Messiah would overcome an adversary. The conception of this adversary was both spiritual and material, embodying both the spiritual forces allied against God's people and their human oppressors from the nations. The most common label given to this figure is Belial. The name Belial is derived from the Aramaic term *Beli ol,* meaning "the yokeless one" or "the lawless one." He is the one who revolts against all the commandments of the Torah. The Book of Proverbs refers to the "man of Belial" in this context (6:12–15). Paul uses the Greek words that mean "man of lawlessness" in place of these Hebrew and Aramaic terms.

This figure will be unveiled before the Messiah appears, at which point the Messiah will defeat and utterly destroy him. The man of lawlessness is a figure with political power and authority to attack and persecute God's people. He is also a figure who declares himself to be divine. In the Roman Empire, the culmination of the kingdoms of the ancient world, Caesar likewise declared himself to be divine. Not too long before the composition of the letter, Caligula as emperor had tried to have a statue of himself placed in the temple in Jerusalem.

So had countless generations of kings, rulers, chieftains, and strong-men before him. The number of these so-called god-kings who had attacked and even attempted to exterminate Israel was nearly endless. From pharaohs to kings to emperors, those grasping to set themselves up as gods opposed the true God. Unable to strike at Him, they struck at His people.

Paul, like many other Jewish people of this period, believes that an ultimate man of Belial will appear—a lawless one who, along with his treacherous followers, will be defeated once and for all by the Messiah. Already, however, as everyone who knew the history of God's people was aware, the mystery of lawlessness—the power and influence of Belial—was at work in the world. It was a spirit that manifested itself in all those who came to oppose and oppress them.

In light of this persecution that the Thessalonian community already faced and would continue to face until the end, Paul exhorts them to stand firm. He encourages them to hold tightly to everything he has taught them in person and also everything that he has told them in his two letters. He urges them to follow his example in the way of life that he led in their midst and to fight back against the mystery of lawlessness through love of their brothers and sisters, by doing good, and even by being kind to the enemies who attack them.

CHAPTER TEN

Two Years in Corinth

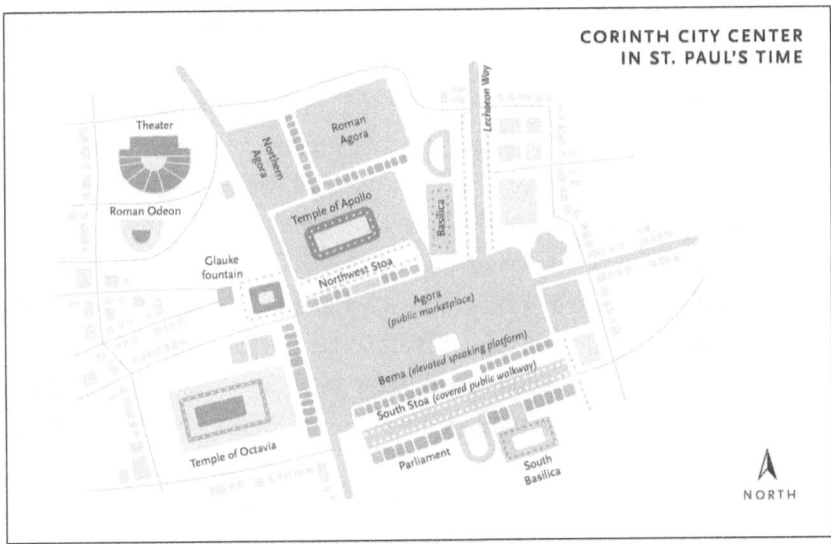

CORINTH CITY CENTER
IN ST. PAUL'S TIME

Paul arrived in the city of Corinth, but rather than visiting for a few weeks and then continuing his journey, he spent two years living, working, and leading the Christian community that he helped to found. Following these two years, Paul would eventually send at least four—and perhaps as many as six—letters to the Christian community there, seeking to give them further guidance and support. The only other local community with which Paul would develop something approaching this kind of bond would be Ephesus.

Corinth was another city that was already ancient when St. Paul came to it. By that point, it had been the site of a human settlement for at least three thousand years. Its geographical location in the Peloponnese made it of great strategic importance in wars fought over several centuries before the Birth of Jesus. A small, four-mile-wide isthmus connects the Greek mainland to the Peloponnese, and Corinth stands in that isthmus. Corinth also stood at the center of the league of cities that resisted the Persians, the Spartan alliance against Athens in the Peloponnesian War, and the Greek alliance against Macedonia. In this last case, Corinth had allied itself with Rome, only to attempt later to play both sides during the Roman invasion of Greece. This potential betrayal of Rome led to Corinth being leveled to the ground in 146 BC by the Roman legions.

One hundred years later, the Romans rebuilt Corinth in a display of power no less amazing than the city's previous destruction. The recolonized Corinth that St. Paul first visited was less than a hundred years old but was the capital of the Roman province of Achaia and heir to the history of her predecessor. Not all of that history was as shining as her history of bringing together her brother cities for the common defense. Ancient Corinth also had a reputation for debauchery, drunkenness, and sexual profligacy. Its vices were known among other Greek city-states as well as in Jewish and Christian circles. "To Corinthianize" became a slang term among Achaeans for pursuing indulgence.

Paul arrived in this new city with its ancient heritage at the peak of its renewed glory. Two hundred thousand free people lived in the city as well as five hundred thousand slaves. This imbalance was not uncommon in the Roman world. The Greek residents were ruled primarily by the Roman military veterans who had been sent to recolonize her. Every aspect of Corinth's civic life, from temples to theaters to its massive agora, had been reinvigorated quite deliberately by Rome to solidify the Roman adoption and adaptation of Greek culture.

Time in Corinth

Immediately upon his arrival, as usual, Paul connected with the local Jewish community at the synagogue. Claudius, who had succeeded Caligula as emperor, had expelled all the Jewish people from Rome, and Jewish refugees had dispersed to various cities all over the Roman world, including Corinth. Two of these refugees, Aquila and his wife, Priscilla, recently had arrived in the city following the expulsion. They worked in the tent-making trade and allowed St. Paul to live and work with them while he stayed in the city. He preached every Sabbath in the synagogue to both the local Jewish community and Corinth's God-fearers.

Paul's extended stay introduced a new dynamic into his relationship with the Jewish community. Typically, his preaching that Jesus is the Messiah was accepted by some Jewish people and rejected by others. Paul's continual preaching, week after week, began to grate on those who disagreed. This ultimately led to a confrontation in which Paul stated that he would cease preaching in the synagogue and instead take the gospel message to the non-Jewish citizens of the city to bring them into the Christian community. A non-Jewish Christian named Titius Justus lived in a house next to the synagogue. In addition to organizing Lord's Day meetings of the Christian community in Titius Justus's home, Paul began preaching there as well. But he did not refuse Jewish converts. In fact, Crispus, one of the synagogue leaders, subsequently embraced Jesus as the Messiah. The Jewish community was not, however, Paul's focus.

Paul stayed in Corinth for a long time. He was partly motivated by another vision in which Jesus appeared to him and told him to remain and that He would protect him. With this long sojourn, Paul's ministry took on a new character. While it seems that Silas and Timothy did most of the baptisms, along with the presbyters appointed for the community, Paul was there as the leader. He presided at her eucharistic gatherings and was present for baptisms, weddings, and to bury the dead. Though the period of his stay would ultimately be only somewhat over two years, he experienced a familiarity and a bond with this group of people that he would later compare to fatherhood (1 Cor. 4:15).

During the latter part of his stay, a major faction within the local Jewish community, led by a certain Sosthenes, attempted to get the Roman proconsul Gallio to eject Paul from the city. Sosthenes likely intended to frame his argument in a way that portrayed Paul as a disturber of the Roman peace. Instead, Gallio concluded that whatever God this was and whatever Torah was, this was an intra-Jewish matter that he didn't care to be involved in. In typically imperious Roman fashion, he dismissed the complainants, who ended up being subjected to mob violence themselves.

Return to Antioch

Eventually, the time came for Paul to return to Antioch. Taking Aquila and Priscilla with him, he traveled eight miles to Cenchrea, the nearest port, to sail across the Aegean to Ephesus. At Cenchrea, Paul chose to take a temporary Nazirite vow. It is not clear whether this vow was related to prayer for the community he was now leaving, the long sea journey that lay ahead of him, both, or other factors. He shaved his head and planned a return trip that would take him through Jerusalem so that he could make the required sacrificial offerings at the temple at the conclusion of the vow.

Paul did not stay for long in Ephesus, though Aquila and Priscilla remained there. He did, however, pray that he might return. This proved fateful, as Ephesus would soon become the center of his ministry and activities. At this point, however, he sailed down the coast to Caesarea, then traveled to Jerusalem. There, he visited the mother Christian community there, fulfilled his vows, and then journeyed onward to Antioch in Syria, with his second missionary journey completed.

CHAPTER ELEVEN

Third Missionary Journey

ST. PAUL'S THIRD
MISSIONARY JOURNEY

By this period, the mid-50s AD, other apostles had embarked on their own missions to spread the gospel of Jesus the Messiah. Some, like St. Thomas, had set off for the Far East, forming Christian communities primarily from non-Jewish converts. Some worked in Judea, Samaria, and Galilee. Some traveled to Alexandria and other parts of Egypt to the Jewish communities there. Others, like St. Paul, made their way into Europe. One such apostle who moved in St. Paul's European circles was Apollos. Despite the Greek name, Apollos was a member of the Jewish community in Alexandria who had been baptized by St. John the Forerunner and who had embraced Jesus as the Messiah. He had not, however, been in any regular contact with the Christian community in Jerusalem.

While Paul was making his way back to Antioch, Apollos arrived in Ephesus. Apollos had a thorough working knowledge of the Hebrew Scriptures. He spoke in the synagogue at Ephesus and argued from the Scriptures for the identity of Jesus as the Messiah. Priscilla and Aquila regularly attended this synagogue, and they encountered Apollos there. Speaking with him, they discovered that he did not have the full picture of the Christian movement, and they gave him further instruction. After preaching in Ephesus, he traveled to the province of Achaia in Greece and visited many of the Christian communities that Paul had helped organize.

Ephesus

Paul, meanwhile, had a third journey in mind, particularly to the city of Ephesus, which was one of the most important cities of the Roman Empire. The region in which the city lies was the site of some of the earliest known human settlements at the end of the Neolithic period. Ephesus had been a Hittite, Cimmerian, and Greek city in its history. The mythic founder of the city was Androklos, an Athenian prince who fled that city and came to Asia Minor. The oracle at Delphi guided him to found Ephesus by a series of signs given to him. A major shrine to this founder adjoined the major central temple. This was held to be the site of his grave, and the blood of sacrifices was poured into it to satiate and preserve his shade in Hades.

The primary deity of Ephesus, without doubt, was a particular form of the goddess Artemis. The temple of Artemis at Ephesus, though long since destroyed, was reported in the Roman world to be the largest temple—possibly the largest building—on earth and was listed as one of the seven wonders of the ancient world. The central statue within the temple was made, at least in part, from a piece of ancient meteorite that was considered to be a miraculous sign. The temple was a site of pilgrimage from across the Roman world and points east that associated the goddess with their own Kybele. These pilgrimages were not about tourism or seeing the building as an archaeological marvel; initiation into the mysteries of Artemis was a spiritual status symbol and an honor within Roman paganism. The political, economic, and spiritual significance of the site led to its domination over the life of the city, setting its rhythms and calendars.

Despite its importance, Ephesus did not have a massive population in the first century AD. It likely had considerably fewer than one hundred thousand inhabitants, due primarily to its geography. Ephesus, as a port, did not have room to sprawl out as a city or to overflow into farmland. But in recent history, Ephesus had seen a vast promotion in status after Augustus moved the capital of western Asia Minor from Pergamon to Ephesus. Between the pilgrimage site, the Aegean port, the access to trade roads east, and the Roman governing power, Ephesus was booming when St. Paul arrived.

Paul was not the only apostle who would spend time in Ephesus. Although he was instrumental in the growth and organization of its Christian community, St. John the son of Zebedee would later settle there, bringing with him Jesus' mother, the Theotokos. Saint Mary Magdalene would also ultimately settle in Ephesus and become an important part of its Christian community. In earlier decades the city of Jerusalem was clearly the center of the Christian movement, but as the Jewish revolts approached, and certainly thereafter, the center of gravity for the movement shifted to Ephesus.

Paul traveled overland to Ephesus, revisiting the communities he had helped establish in Galatia and Phrygia on the way to Antioch in Pisidia. By this point, he had covered hundreds of miles on foot—thousands of miles if sea travel is included. Days spent walking Roman roads were long, punctuated by brief stops at the side of the road to eat and relieve oneself. The road from Antioch in Pisidia to Ephesus, a road Paul was walking for the first time, was itself roughly 225 miles long.

A TWO-YEAR STAY

Upon his arrival, Paul found that some in the Jewish community inhabited a sort of liminal space at the edge of the Christian community, much as Apollos had. They had been baptized by St. John the Forerunner and were aware of Jesus, identifying Him as the Messiah, but they were not fully aware of and on board with the movement proper as it had spread from Jerusalem. This lack of connection likely happened as a result of Jewish pilgrims from Ephesus to Judea encountering St. John and Jesus during His public ministry. Not everyone who had such encounters, even those who believed Jesus was the Messiah, dropped everything to remain in Judea and become His followers. Instead, they returned to Ephesus before truly becoming a part of the Christian movement. Paul gave them the laying on of hands for them to receive the Holy Spirit, establishing the standard procedure for dealing with such cases.

Paul ended up taking up residence in Ephesus for two years. As in Corinth, this meant that he became a part of the day-to-day life of the local community as one of its leaders. His stay in Ephesus, however, seems to have been considerably more eventful than his time in Corinth. Paul began by preaching in the synagogue, where he had some success in growing the Christian community with newly baptized Jewish Christians. He had, however, learned from past experiences. After three months of preaching there, he began to receive pushback from those in the Jewish community who did not accept his message. Once this began, he stepped back from the synagogue and instead taught in the home of one of the non-Jewish Christians in the city, as he had done in Corinth.

During this period, yet again miracles and wonders surrounded Paul's ministry as signs related to his preaching. Chief among these were the healing of the sick and the casting out of demons. At a certain point, a group of Jewish exorcists attempted to use the names of Jesus and Paul in a talismanic way to cast out demons—to disastrous results. The exorcisms appear to have carried a great weight with the non-Jewish residents of Ephesus, and many who were baptized publicly burned magic and ritual texts from their pagan pasts.

Some of St. Paul's time in Ephesus appears to have been spent in prison, although St. Luke makes no mention of this in the Acts of the Apostles. He gives only a rough summary of this period. But the majority of Paul's letters were written during his time in Ephesus, and a number of them refer to being written from prison or to Paul having been imprisoned. There are even indications that he may have been sentenced to face wild beasts while in Ephesus (1 Cor. 15:32; 2 Cor. 1:9).[29] Given some of the trouble Paul faced in Ephesus and other places, the idea of several short stays or even a moderately lengthy stay in custody in the house reserved for Roman citizens seems to be the best way to explain Paul's words.

RIOT

After two years, Paul began to make plans to move on. He intended to return to Macedonia and Achaia to revisit the communities he had helped organize, then return to Jerusalem. He sent Timothy and a certain Erastus ahead of him to prepare for the trip. At this point, the success of St. Paul's mission in Ephesus began to rub up against the basis of the broader community's life. A certain Demetrius, a silversmith who made idols and other sacred objects for the worship of Artemis, had begun to see a decline in business. Part and parcel of Paul's proclamation of the gospel of the Messiah was that idolatry must be shunned and abandoned. This cost the Ephesian economy customers and pilgrims and also shifted the balance of power and control in the city away from the local and imperial religion.

---

29   The Acts of Paul and Thekla preserves the tradition that Paul faced a lion in the arena.

Demetrius incited a riot. The mob grabbed known associates of Paul and dragged them to the theater. A member of the local Jewish community, Alexander, attempted to address the situation but was shouted down once it was known that he was Jewish. Paul himself wanted to address the crowd, but the danger prevented him from doing so. Ultimately, one of the town officials dispersed the crowd, referring Demetrius to the courts. The official reminded the crowd that if they were declared to be rioting, the Roman military authorities would be quick and violent in restoring order. While the Christian community continued to thrive in Ephesus, Paul moved on from the city after this incident.

Achaia and Troas

After passing through the communities in Macedonia, Paul spent three months in Achaia visiting the communities there. By this point, he was traveling with a small retinue of disciples that he had gathered in Derbe, Thessalonica, Berea, and elsewhere. After finding out that strong opposition awaited him deeper into Greece, Paul turned back and returned through Macedonia, revisiting those communities. He then sailed back from Philippi to Troas, where he had agreed to gather with his companions and disciples shortly after the Passover.

While in Troas, at the eucharistic gathering on the Lord's Day after the Sabbath meeting in the synagogue, St. Paul preached late into the night. A young man named Eutyches fell asleep and then fell out of a window to his death. Paul raised the young man from the dead and brought him back to the meeting for the eucharistic meal. This major sign would serve as confirmation not so much of Paul's words to the Christian community in Troas but to Paul himself. His life and ministry were about to enter their final phase. This began with Paul's decision to return to Jerusalem, hoping to arrive there by Pentecost, several weeks later.

CHAPTER TWELVE

Epistle to the Romans

The longest of St. Paul's letters is his Epistle to the Romans. Paul composed this letter with the assistance of a secretary named Tertius during his time in Ephesus. This letter is different from others written by Paul in that it was sent to a Christian community that he had no hand in organizing. At the time of its writing, he had not yet been to Rome. The letter therefore has a somewhat different tone than the others. It lacks the fatherly quality with which Paul addresses those whom he has baptized, taught, and lived with in community. Paul writes to the Christians in Rome not because he has direct pastoral feelings of responsibility or concern, but because they face difficulties that he can help them navigate with his expertise.

Claudius had expelled all the Jewish people from Rome. Two years later, he rescinded his imperial edict, and they were allowed to return. Some Roman Jews remained resettled in other areas. Others returned to Rome to attempt to rebuild their previous lives. This had a profound effect on the Christian community in Rome, which overlapped the Jewish community in a way similar to the communities in the Greek cities where Paul had labored.

The foundational group of Christians were members of the Jewish community who embraced Jesus as the Messiah. They remained members of the Jewish community and the synagogue but also began gathering as Christians on the Lord's Day. They were then joined by non-Jewish people, at first primarily God-fearers, who likewise embraced Jesus and the Messiah and were baptized.

When the Jewish people were expelled from Rome, the Roman authorities took no notice of whether or not they happened to be members of the Christian movement. Nor did membership in the Christian movement make a non-Jewish person a Jew in the eyes of Roman law. After the edict, Jewish Christians disappeared from the city and from community life, but non-Jewish Christians remained and continued to meet. Those members of the Christian community who had been God-fearers no longer had a synagogue to attend or a Jewish community to join, even at its fringes. Thus over the course of two years, the Christian community in Rome began to take on its own character.

One Community, Not Two

With the removal of the edict, Jewish people, including Jewish Christians, returned to the city. With the return of the Jewish community, its life, centered on the synagogue, began again. The Christian community, however, faced new challenges. Should non-Jewish members of the Christian community attempt to reintegrate with the non-Christian Jewish community at any level? How would Jewish Christians who had held longtime leadership roles in the Christian gatherings be reintegrated with those who had stepped into those leadership roles in their absence? How much of the structure of Jew and non-Jew in Christian communities was good and necessary, and how much was just a matter of historical accident related to the proportion of Jewish Christians in a particular place at a particular time?

What Paul feared was the existence of two separate communities. There easily could have been a Jewish Christian community, perhaps existing solely as a subset of the Jewish community in the synagogue, and a non-Jewish Christian community that continued just as it had over the previous two years. From Paul's perspective, this would be a disaster in both directions.

For Jewish Christians not part of a Christian community, separation would serve to relativize the meaning of their commitment to Jesus as the Messiah. Over generations, these Jewish Christians would likely just be reabsorbed into Judaism as a whole without distinction. On the other side, without Jewish Christians, the Christian community in Rome would lack its root and its ballast. For Paul, these Christians were being brought into the house of Israel to worship Israel's God through Israel's Messiah. Their connection to Judaism and to the Jewish people was not just theoretical or a theological principle; it was real and needed to remain a reality in the Christian community.

To help the community in Rome navigate these difficulties and succeed in reintegrating, Paul wrote his letter. A decade later, when Peter and Paul both arrived in Rome to organize and build, they found a healthy community there despite persecution. This was likely in part a result of the success of Paul's letter. Paul did not write to them about abstract theology. Philosophical and theological treatises existed in the first century AD, and Paul was certainly educated enough to write one. If he did write any, none are still extant. But the Christians in Rome were a real community facing real difficulties, and Paul's Letter to the Romans, like all his other epistles, is a pastoral letter directed at assisting with the pastoral problems of real people.

Paul begins his letter by acknowledging that his relationship with the community in Rome has taken place over a distance. He has heard many reports about them and their faithfulness. He has the desire to go there and visit them in person, but it simply hasn't happened yet. He goes on to frame what he is doing in his answer to their current difficulties as the application of the gospel that he preaches. Understanding who Jesus the Messiah is and what He has done has implications for what a Christian community looks like, how it is organized, and even how Jewish and non-Jewish Christians relate to each other. Jesus is, after all, the Jewish Messiah prophesied in the Hebrew Scriptures.

The Faithlessness of the Nations and the Jewish People

In his letter, Paul speaks to each group, non-Jewish and Jewish Christians in turn, rhetorically drawing them together and uniting them in a way that he hopes will be persuasive and draw them together in fact. He begins speaking to the non-Jewish Christians in a way that is familiar from his preaching to non-Jewish audiences in the Acts of the Apostles. For countless generations, God has exercised patience with the people of the nations, but now the Day of the Lord and the time of judgment approach.

At one point all the peoples of the world knew God. God is still knowable in and through His creation. But the people of the nations wanted to indulge their sinful desires, they wanted power, and so they rejected and suppressed the truth of God to chase after these vain things. They used idols to worship demons. They became sexually immoral, violent, and cruel. They were filled with greed and hubris. They didn't want to know God, and so God gave them what they thought they wanted, and it was a disaster.

Addressing Jewish Christians, Paul points out that yes, they had received the Torah, but had they kept it? This is not primarily an individual question. The arc of the Hebrew Scriptures describes the failure of Israel and Judah to keep Torah and the consequences of that rebellion. They may be tempted to judge the non-Jewish members of the community for their past, but that judgment based on the Torah applies to them as well. Paul points out that people among the nations chose to follow God as best they knew how and kept the requirements of the Torah without having received it. Certainly, they were in a better position before God than a Jewish person who violates Torah.

Paul is not, however, saying that being Jewish has no value. Jewish people have the Scriptures, they have the covenants, they have the traditions handed down from their fathers. Yes, the Hebrew Scriptures showed that most of the Jewish people were not faithful to the Torah God has given them. But God's faithfulness to His covenant is much greater than human faithlessness. Of course, the fact that God always brings greater good out of human evil does not mean that people should go ahead and sin, knowing that God will be faithful and bring about good anyway. This, for St. Paul, is a ridiculous suggestion. He wants to be clear, however, that just being Jewish doesn't make one pleasing to God. The Torah brings knowledge of God but also knowledge of our sinfulness.

Faithfulness to God

At the time when Jesus the Messiah came, the nations were utterly lost in wickedness, and the Jewish people were suffering in exile for their sins, having rejected God's Torah. None of them could claim to have a right standing before God. For Paul, the mission of Jesus corrects this. Both Jewish and non-Jewish people can receive a new beginning through His death and Resurrection. Israel has been brought back to life and given a new start with a renewed covenant. The Jewish people can begin again to keep Torah but will be empowered to do so by the Spirit of God dwelling within them. Those of the nations have the opportunity, in Jesus the Messiah, to be set free from idolatry and sin to worship the true and living God.

The Greek word *dikaiosyne* is an important one in the Epistle to the Romans. It has become commonplace to interpret this and related words, especially in this epistle, in terms of their broader Greek usage.[30] This is a misinterpretation. In Jewish circles, *dikaiosyne* was used to translate Aramaic terms dealing with purification and things being put back in order (see Dan. 8:14). Paul's use of this term in Romans comes repeatedly in the context of discussions of sacrifice in general and the offerings of the Day of Atonement in particular. He makes reference to cleansing with the Messiah's blood. When using this terminology, Paul has in mind purification and a life that is pure and therefore pleasing to God as a sacrifice.

---

30   In their extrabiblical usage, these terms are often used in judicial or forensic contexts.

Paul explains that in His death, Jesus the Messiah offered Himself as a pleasing sacrifice to God. The Jewish people already held a concept of martyrdom by which a person who was suffering and dying for their faithfulness to the God of Israel would offer his life to God as a sacrifice. The Messiah is then the perfect example in doing this for all people. God received this ultimate sacrifice by Jesus, so Jesus' blood purifies the faithful from sin. The Messiah's Resurrection, then, begins a new life, and that new life is granted to the faithful. Baptism, for Paul, is the way in which a person participates in the death of the old self and the sin that enslaved them, followed by participation in the Resurrection and the beginning of a new life.

For Paul, the key issue facing all Christians is faithfulness—specifically, faithfulness to the call that any given person has received from God. The shape of this faithfulness differs for different people, as they have different callings. For Jewish people, faithfulness includes keeping Torah. For non-Jewish people, that includes keeping the commandments of the Torah that apply to them, but without becoming Jewish.

Abraham is the ultimate example of this faithfulness. He left Ur and traveled to the other side of the known world after receiving a promise from God, who found his faithfulness pleasing. This was before he was circumcised, with circumcision then serving as a sign of his faithfulness. One part of the promises to Abraham was that he would be the father of many nations. This promise is fulfilled in him being the father of those who are circumcised and keep Torah and also of those who are not circumcised but live a life that is faithful to God.

A Holy Tree with Abraham as Its Root

A central concern of Paul's in this epistle is understanding why so many of the Jewish people have rejected Jesus if He is, indeed, the Jewish Messiah. His answer to this question also reveals his understanding of the role of non-Jewish Christians in the salvation of Israel. In the first place, Paul points out that this is an area of intense sorrow for him. He would be willing to be cut off from the Messiah and cursed if it could reconcile the rest of his people to God in Jesus. He still holds hope that their rejection of Jesus might change someday soon.

But in explaining how it has happened, Paul begins by pointing out that being an Israelite was never just a matter of birth. Abraham had other biological children in addition to Isaac. Isaac had Jacob and Esau. This second example is revelatory in another way. Jacob had the status of firstborn, and so it was he who inherited the promises of Abraham. Esau was counted a coheir of these promises for as long as he remained in covenant with his brother. When his Edomite descendants turned on Judah, they were cut off.

The Hebrew Scriptures describe how the much larger Northern Kingdom of Israel—most of the Israelites—was disobedient to God and wiped from the face of the earth. Paul wants to be clear: this is not a failure of the Torah or of God. One could ask, if God knew they were going to end in destruction, why did He bring them out of Egypt? Why give them inheritance in the land? Why bless them? Why send them prophets? Why blame them for not answering a call that He knew they wouldn't answer? Paul's answer to these questions is that God is kind to the sinful and wicked and gives them the good things of this world. In the case of Israel, though, a faithful remnant has always existed within the larger body of Jewish people.

Paul envisions Israel as a holy tree with Abraham at its root. Many branches bud and grow and are born in the tree. Those who are faithful remain connected to the root and are supported and nourished by it. Those who are faithless are pruned away. God has cultivated this holy tree through the centuries. The nations, then, are other trees also all planted by God, but He has allowed them to grow wild for a time. Branches grow on those trees that are good and sound and faithful to Him, nonetheless. God is now retrieving those branches from the wild trees and is grafting them into the holy tree so that they can be nourished by the holy root. If branches that were cut off become faithful again, they can be grafted back in and begin to grow again.

Paul hopes that seeing people from the nations come to worship the God of Israel through Jesus the Messiah will make Jewish people jealous, and the transformation of non-Jewish people will persuade the Jews also to accept Jesus as the Messiah. Further, he sees these non-Jews being grafted in as the fulfillment of prophecy in the Torah. When Israel blessed Joseph's son Ephraim, he said that he would become the fulness of the nations. Ephraim, with the rest of the Northern Kingdom, was scattered into the nations like seed. Paul sees the non-Jewish Christians as the harvest. This is how, for Paul, Ephraim will be restored and all Israel will be saved.

For Paul, a person can choose to walk in two ways. One of these is to follow the desires of our sinful flesh. That way leads to death and destruction. The other is to follow the Spirit of God. That way leads to the life of the age to come. If someone is living indulgently according to their flesh, then all the Torah does for them is reveal their sinfulness and their need to repent. If someone is walking according to the Spirit, then the Torah brings life because the Spirit empowers them to keep it. The real keeping of Torah in the Spirit for Paul is not just a matter of keeping commandments externally. Rather, through the Spirit, a person begins to truly love his neighbor—even his enemies. Someone who truly loves keeps the whole Torah.

By this point, Paul was planning an ambitious missionary journey that would take him to the most far-flung Jewish community in the Roman Empire. He hoped to eventually sail for Spain, specifically the Roman province of Baetica in the south. This province was essentially at the western end of the earth from the perspective of people at the time. It represented, then, the ultimate conclusion of Paul's westward journey with the gospel. With this mission in mind, it seemed sensible to Paul that he would get a chance to stop in Rome on the way. This would not just be a visit to the community to which he was now writing. He also hoped it might provide an opportunity for another part of Paul's endgame: to one day preach the gospel to the emperor himself.

CHAPTER THIRTEEN

First Epistle to the Corinthians

From Ephesus, Paul wrote a number of letters back to the Christian community in Corinth. It is not totally clear how many there were and how many of them survived. What we now call the First Epistle to the Corinthians as found in the New Testament is actually his second letter, the first now being lost. What we call 2 Corinthians appears to have been written after another missing letter, though there are signs that the letter as it now exists may incorporate material from multiple letters. Some scholars hypothesize as many as six letters to the Corinthians with at least parts of five of them being incorporated into the two canonical letters. All this, however, ultimately amounts to conjecture.

Paul had a special relationship with the Christian community in Corinth, having spent more than two years sharing his life with the people there. He clearly kept in close contact with them and made multiple return visits to help with the resolution of problems and the building up of the community. His canonical letters to them are eminently practical, dealing with solving real issues within the community. They also focus heavily on helping non-Jewish Christians adopt a distinctively Christian way of life within their own cultures and traditions, rather than by becoming Jewish.

Non-Jewish Christians in a pagan city like Corinth faced difficult choices. All civic and community life included elements of pagan worship and practice: The trade guilds offered sacrifices to the gods. Families sacrificed to gods at family gatherings. The meat in the meat market came from the temple sacrifices. Civic festivals involved the gods. For non-Jewish Christians to reject and abstain from idolatry meant breaking ties with their families, their trades, their friends, their city, and the shared history that gave them identity. Rejecting idolatry was even seen as a rebellion against Roman authorities in some cases. Jewish people had an exemption to follow their own way of life that was often, though not always, honored by Roman authorities. Non-Jewish Christians had no such exemption.

In contrast to the pagan way of life, Paul frequently refers to those in the Christian community as holy ones. Sometimes he will further disambiguate and refer to those who have been made holy, are being made holy, or who are called to be holy ones. He will use any and all of these phrases to refer to the same people. The Greek term Paul uses, *agios*, is used in the Greek translation of the Hebrew Scriptures to refer to angelic beings who serve God. This should be understood in the context of how Paul typically refers to the life of the age to come. He refers to it as the "glory." Paul thereby refers to the glory of God that is shared with humanity. This glory is deeply connected with the presence of the Holy Spirit, whom St. Paul sees as the down payment or deposit on that inheritance to come.

The Danger of Factions

At the beginning of Paul's first extant letter to Corinth, he deals with the issue of factions. Some in the community had formed an allegiance to a particular apostle, leader, or worker among them. This was, of course, common in the Greek world from which many of the Corinthian Christians came. Philosophical schools bore the names of their founders, and within those broader schools of thought, people became disciples or proponents of individual teachers. So, in Corinth some claimed St. Peter, some Paul, some Apollos, and they sought to make whatever distinction they detected in their respective preaching into badges of some sort of superiority.

Against this, Paul's response is two-pronged. First, all those philosophical schools considered the gospel to be foolishness. There was more than a whiff of hubris in this attitude that certain members of the community were taking toward others. They held an idea of intellectual superiority that was unwarranted. Paul hadn't come there making philosophical arguments or trying to impress them with his rhetorical style. This is because, in the second place, the gospel isn't about Paul, or Peter, or Apollos. None of them were crucified for the people of Corinth. The faithful weren't baptized into the name of any apostle. They all belong to Jesus the Messiah, and He is not divided.

Paul asks them to realign their view both of the leaders of their community and of themselves. Their leaders, Paul and the other apostles included, are servants of the Messiah working for their good. They, as members of the community, are not there to pick a team but to work as they have been called by God. He compares the gospel of the Messiah that they have heard and embraced to a foundation that has been laid and on which every member of the community builds. When the Day of the Lord comes, everything they have built will be subjected to fire. The dross, the garbage will be burned away. But what is good and true, done in service of God, will be purified and will stand for eternity.

The Effect of Sexual Immorality on the Community

The sexual morality that non-Jewish Christians needed to practice was a radical departure from anything in their pagan culture. Roman culture viewed male sexuality as a biological function, like using the restroom. When the time came, one found a receptacle. For Romans, this very often wasn't one's wife but a male or female slave of any age, a friend or compatriot, or a prostitute. Women, on the other hand, were expected to be faithful and chaste. In essence, the Christian movement began to demand this same continence from men.

The community in Corinth was a place where many non-Jewish Christians struggled to make a clean break with their past way of living. Paul was not overly concerned with momentary failings. Sins could be dealt with in the community. What did bring Paul great concern was unrepentant, public sexual sin. In Corinth at this time a man was sleeping with either his mother-in-law or his stepmother. This was an ongoing matter that was publicly known. The man was unrepentant. Paul's concern is not to lambast the man in question. Rather, he is concerned that the community has tolerated this and has done nothing to correct him. It seems that some members of the community were even taking a form of pride in how nonjudgmental they were.

Paul explains that this cannot happen. This man's wickedness, when allowed among them, affects the whole community. It stains everything they do together. Ultimately, it shows a lack of concern for this man who is on his way to destruction. Paul here articulates an understanding of what would come to be called excommunication. As in the Torah, certain sins, especially when not repented, require that a person be cut off from among the people. This man's behavior was such a sin. But being cut off, being removed from the Christian community, was not a final punishment. Rather, it was a last-ditch effort to bring the offending party to repentance and restoration.

Paul reinforces what it means to escape the sexual immorality that had enslaved Christians in their former lives. Most people in the community should be married, and the only person with whom they should be having sexual relations is their spouse. A small minority of people in the community, like St. Paul, may have a special calling from God where it is better for them not to be married. If that is the case, God will also give them the continence and self-control to make that possible. If that self-control is not there, the person should be married or, if widowed, remarried. Divorce should not happen unless a wife is abandoned; then she is free to remarry.

Sacrificial Meals

The other major concern of Paul for the Corinthian Christians is that they make a clean break with all practices of idolatry. The primary issue at hand was the eating of food that had been offered to idols. This was a challenge because the vast majority of the meat in Corinth's food markets came from her temples. Traditionally, Jewish people in this situation had essentially become vegetarians apart from animals they raised themselves. Non-Jewish Christians were not called to keep kosher by following the diet outlined in the Torah. At the same time, they could not continue to participate in the feasts of idol's temples as they had in the past.

Some in Corinth appear, from Paul's response, to have made particular arguments about why it was still all right for them to eat this food. They argued that idols are just wood and stone, and the gods being worshiped aren't the true God. They argued that they were free from the food regulations of the Torah. They argued that the Messiah had come to set them free, not to further restrict them. All these arguments contain elements that are true, and so Paul does not dispute the truth of those premises. Rather, he gives a series of reasons throughout the letter why the Corinthian Christians should, nonetheless, not eat meat offered to idols.

One of these reasons is simply love. Regardless of whether someone thought it was all right for them to eat in an idol's temple, what message did this send to the one who saw it? Might that lead them into sin? Love means being willing to sacrifice some of your freedom for the good of another. Paul points out all the things that he is free to do but that he didn't do while living among them, or doesn't do in general, because his abstention benefits the people to whom he ministers.

Paul refers them back to their spiritual if not genealogical forebears, the Israelites who were led out of Egypt under Moses. They passed through the Red Sea in the way the Corinthian Christians were baptized. They passed through the cloud of glory just as the Corinthian Christians received the Spirit of God. They ate the manna from heaven and drank the water from the rock just as the Corinthian Christians receive the Eucharist. But when the Israelites turned to idolatry and sexual immorality with the golden calf, that whole generation ended up dead in the desert. Eating food offered to idols is playing a dangerous game.

The Eucharist Is a Sacrifice

Paul presents the Eucharist explicitly as a sacrifice in explaining its role in the community. He compares the communion in the Body and Blood of the Messiah in the Eucharist to the communion in the altar for those who worship at the temple in Jerusalem, and also to the communion with demons of those who sacrifice to the pagan gods. After establishing these parallels, he points out the basic logical problem with thinking that someone can be in a community with demons and in a community with God at the same time. There is no fellowship between the two. While the Eucharist is the very center of their life, like the temple and the holy sacrifices, there is an element of danger. For someone to come into the presence of God unworthily is as much of a threat of illness and even death as to come into the sanctuary in an unworthy way.

While he constantly insists that the gospel he preaches came from Jesus Himself, Paul presents the celebration of the Eucharist as something that he received. After his baptism, he participated in the eucharistic gathering long before he presided at one. When he relates what he passed on to them, Paul speaks of the Eucharist being celebrated through the retelling of the story of Jesus, on the night He was betrayed, first initiating it with His disciples (1 Cor. 11:23–26). This mode of celebrating the Eucharist identifies it as a particular kind of sacrifice.

Typical sacrifices in the Book of Leviticus, including thank offerings, are described in terms of the butchering and apportionment of the offering. There is no wider ritual or storytelling element to the typical daily offerings. Certain offerings, however, like Passover, involve ritual storytelling. The story of the first Passover is told in such a way that those participating in the present, as they eat the offering, are made a part of the event in the past. On that night, they, not their ancestors, are brought out of slavery in Egypt. For Paul, the Eucharist likewise has this memorial quality. Not a memorial in the simple sense of remembering, but by making the past event present again so that every generation at every time in every place can participate.

Gifts and Roles in the Community

Paul describes the Christian community as the body of the Messiah in order to explain the different gifts and callings of the various members. Just as each body part has its own purpose, and the body is healthy when they all function together harmoniously, so also for the wider community. He points to love as the greatest of all gifts because, as he said to the Romans, through love one fulfills the whole Torah.

He pays special attention to people who have the gift of languages. Corinth was a cosmopolitan city whose residents spoke many different languages. Apparently, people wanting to preach and pray out loud in different languages was contributing to confusion in their gatherings. Paul says in response that they ought to use only two or three languages in a given gathering, and only if there is someone there who can translate for the other people in attendance so that everyone can benefit.[31]

---

31 Certain modern interpreters have taken to reading St. Paul's use of the common term for languages, *glossai*, literally "tongues," as a reference to ecstatic utterances rather than spoken languages. This interpretation ignores the context of the cosmopolitan city of Corinth and multilingualism within the Eastern Roman Empire. This interpretation is also unaware of the issues surrounding the use of languages in synagogues during this period, a subject of hot debate within Judaism. There is no clear reason in the text to resort to esoteric interpretations when the plain meaning, in context, addresses a contemporary issue in the community to which St. Paul is writing.

Women, Hair Coverings, and Sexuality

Paul makes comments regarding women in the community in Corinth that are often misinterpreted through a modern lens. Specifically, he speaks about women remaining silent during the gatherings and later addressing any questions to their husbands. It must be remembered that in the broader pagan context, women were not taken as disciples by any of the philosophical schools or by major Jewish teachers. They were considered to be unable to learn beyond a rudimentary level. Husbands and fathers made decisions for the family without consultation. Paul is arguing that women need to practice silence and listen. They too need to come to understand the gospel and live faithfully to the Messiah. If they have questions, they need to have them answered. Paul is continuing what Jesus began when He took women as disciples.

Saint Paul's comments on head coverings and women's hair have long caused confusion and, in recent years, debate (1 Cor. 11:2–16). Within this section, St. Paul moves back and forth between discussing the Eucharist, as opposed to pagan sacrifice, and the dangers of sexual immorality. These two ideas were intimately intertwined for Corinthian pagans. Sexuality in Greek and Roman pagan circles was a means of worship—in particular, of enacting fertility rites. In contrast, Paul wants to distinguish between these two things clearly. No form of sexual display is appropriate for Christian worship.

The direct connection between a woman's hair and overt sexuality is less obvious to us in the modern world. For Paul and the Corinthians, however, it was clear. He gives a series of reasons why this is inappropriate. The first of these is that any display of a woman's sexuality should be directed toward her husband within her marriage—not publicly and not in the context of the worship of God. Paul points to the pagan sexual ritual activity that produced the Nephilim, the giants of Genesis 6:1–4, in alluding to the presence of the angels. Finally, he points to the Greek medical science of that time.

Within the Hippocratic corpus, the standard medical texts of the time, hair was seen as serving a function in fertility and procreation, in tandem with male gonads. The latter emits seminal fluid, and a woman's hair was believed to draw that fluid up into the body to allow for conception. Women who cut their hair short or men who grew theirs long generally did so, in line with this thinking, to present themselves as prostitutes. Paul therefore says that a woman's hair was given to her in place of a testicle. Just as genitals must be covered in worship, so also must a woman's hair. Paul is not here endorsing this now quite strange anatomical understanding as correct. He merely uses the Corinthians' knowledge of it as one more argument to explain his case for Christian worship to be and to remain desexualized.

Bodily Resurrection

As when he wrote to Thessalonica (see chapter nine), Paul expended some effort explaining the importance of the resurrection of the dead. As already noted there, belief in the resurrection was not universal in Jewish circles and was virtually nonexistent in non-Jewish circles. Paul explains that the Pharisaic view of bodily resurrection is a basic presupposition of the gospel of the Messiah that he preaches. This begins, of course, with the fact that Jesus rose from the dead, and Paul lists off those who saw Him after the Resurrection, many of whom, he points out, are still alive.

Paul then argues that the Resurrection of Jesus is not a one-off miraculous event but the beginning and guarantee of the resurrection of every human person who will stand before God's judgment. He further points to the already extant practice of taking the name of a departed holy man or woman at baptism.[32] What would be the point

---

32 For a more complete breakdown of St. Paul's reference to baptism for the dead, see Stephen De Young, *Religion of the Apostles* (Chesterton, IN: Ancient Faith Publishing, 2021), 141–46.

of this, of creating a relationship with a heavenly patron, if that person were simply dead and gone? And what sense would martyrdom make? Why would anyone sacrifice the good things in life if this life is all there is?

In terms of what the resurrection means and what our bodies will be like, Paul explains that there are different types of bodies among different created things—angels, animals, and humans. Our mortal body is planted in the ground like a seed, and it rises up immortal. Adam was made from the dirt, then the Spirit was breathed into him, and he came to life. We are all made of dirt, like him. When the Day of the Lord comes, the Spirit will breathe life into us again, and we will come alive. In the same way that we were like Adam, we will be like the Messiah. There is no reason, then, for Christians to fear death. Jesus the Messiah has defeated it.

Supporting the Jerusalem Community

Paul ends his letter by making specific mention of the collection that he has been taking up from all the Christian communities for the mother community in Jerusalem. This was a request made of Paul during his first visit to Jerusalem by the apostles there, and he endorsed it as good and right. Compared to most of the more metropolitan communities scattered through the empire, the community in Jerusalem had a higher rate of poverty. Holding everything in common provided for everyone but did not make everyone affluent. The temple was still utilized by Christians but was not the center of Christian religious life in the same way. It was, to a certain extent, displaced by the Eucharist and its sacrificial nature. Nonetheless, the apostles in Jerusalem were seen as the leadership of the whole gathering of the Christian communities and the hub around which the lives of Christians rotated.

CHAPTER FOURTEEN

Imprisonment in Ephesus:
Philippians, Colossians, Ephesians & Philemon

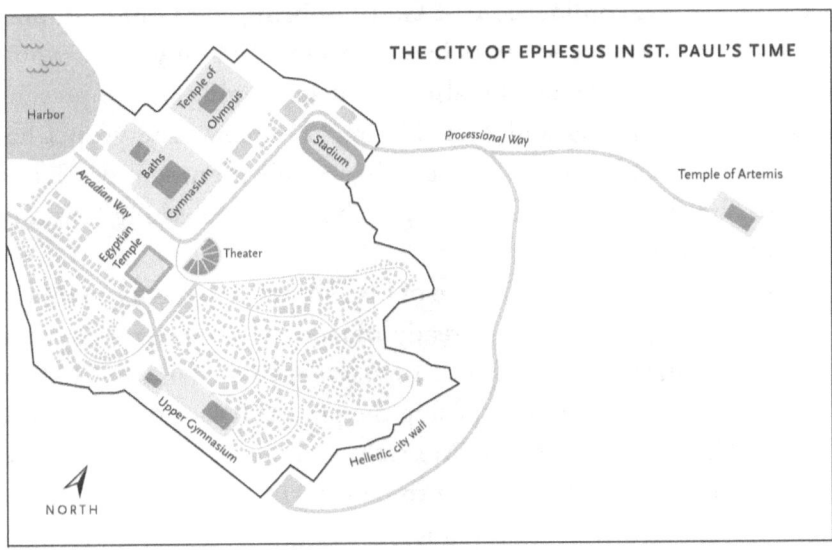

For some portion, or perhaps portions, of the time St. Paul spent in Ephesus during his third missionary journey, he was imprisoned. This is reflected in the text of four letters that he clearly wrote during that time, which refer to and show other signs of having been written during a period of imprisonment in Ephesus. Two of these letters are commonly questioned by contemporary scholars as to whether they are, indeed, of Pauline authorship. More will be said on this in terms of the specifics of the letters themselves.

The Epistle to the Philippians

The first of these letters is not contested. The Epistle to the Philippians is clearly the work of St. Paul in its themes and even in particular turns of phrase. That said, this letter is from an older Paul who has been through considerable hardships, including at the time of writing. The major theme of the letter is joy, but it is a joy that comes from God through difficult circumstances. There is a bittersweetness in his expressions of love for the community in Philippi that is unusual, compared to other letters.

Paul has great confidence that God can bring good out of human evil, out of suffering, and out of bad situations. Not only is this a possibility for the future, but he also sees it happening in the present. Through his suffering and even his imprisonment, the gospel has spread further and into new places. He sees his imminent death as a real possibility, but Paul sees that possibility as something that ultimately would be positive.

In Philippians, Paul makes one of his clearest statements about the preexistence of Jesus. He had already alluded to this understanding in various ways in this epistle: He had spoken of God having created the world through the Lord Jesus, using the phrase "Word of God," *logos theou* in Greek, to refer to the Messiah. Paul is not innovating here. Judaism in this period had come to believe, in various forms, in the existence of a divine being often identified as the *memra* in Aramaic or *logos* in Greek—the Word. This Logos preexisted the creation, and God created the world through the Logos.

It was also commonplace for Jewish groups in this period to identify the coming of the Messiah with the return of Adam, Melchizedek, or David. Saint Paul's understanding of Jesus as the embodiment of the Logos, then, is not a massive stretch. He shared this understanding of Jesus' messianic identity with the other apostles, such as St. John, who makes it even more explicit. Here in Philippians, Paul describes the divine Logos being made man then humbling Himself even to the point of being crucified—a painful and humiliating death. After this humiliation, Jesus the Messiah has been exalted to the heavens.

Paul sees this kind of humility as the path of salvation that he and the members of the Christian community in Philippi must follow. He strongly emphasizes that salvation in the Messiah is not something already achieved, even for him. Faithfulness is a lifelong process of dedication and steady pursuit. Paul writes, "Work out your own salvation with fear and trembling, because God is working in you to desire and to do the good things that He desires" (Phil. 2:12–13). The community in Philippi must continue to recommit itself to following the Messiah, to loving one another, and to being united.

This unity is important in the face of those who still were seeking to compel non-Jewish Christians to enter the Jewish community. Paul points out that his Jewish bona fides are second to none. Salvation, however, is not about achieving some kind of status in the Jewish community. It is about a life of faithfully following God in Jesus the Messiah. This is the path of salvation for anyone, Jewish or not.

The Epistle to the Colossians

The authorship of St. Paul's epistle to the Colossians is more controversial. Certainly, when one turns the page in a Greek New Testament from Philippians to Colossians, one enters a different world in terms of grammar and style. The Epistle to the Ephesians, which will be discussed next, is likewise different from many of Paul's other epistles in these ways but is very similar to Colossians in style and themes. Concluding from this that Paul was not involved in the composition of either of these epistles, however, is premature.

The uncontested epistles of Paul are not a sufficient amount of text to form a conclusive writing sample. This is doubly so when we remember that these texts were actually written down by different secretaries who were fully intended to make grammatical and stylistic contributions to the final product. Additionally, both these letters include St. Timothy as a listed coauthor, although the precise extent of his contributions is not entirely clear. With no conclusive evidence to set aside what these letters claim to be, the most logical option is to assume that they are exactly what they claim: letters written by Paul and Timothy, through a secretary, to particular communities in Asia Minor.

Colossae was first evangelized by Epaphras, an associate of Paul. Paul sees his role in writing to the community as helping them to continue to grow in knowledge and understanding. He is trying deliberately to educate and build the community rather than organize it himself or govern it. He is perhaps even more explicit than in Philippians regarding the divine identity of the Messiah as the Son of God. While in his Epistle to the Romans Paul dealt with Jesus as the firstborn in terms of inheriting the promises given to Abraham, in Colossians this Sonship has more to do with authority and with Him being the image of God sine qua non.

Paul also returns to familiar themes regarding purification with the blood of the Messiah's sacrifice, which now allows non-Jewish Christians, who once were far off from God, to draw near. Drawing near is not a one-time decision or something accomplished by a procedure; it is an ongoing movement with a beginning, a middle, and a conclusion that Christians must press on toward. This conclusion Paul calls being "perfect" or "mature."

Colossae is another community in which some teachers sought to cause non-Jewish Christians to be circumcised and become Jewish. Paul argues in response that Jesus the Messiah has set them free from their former idolatry and the demonic rulers who had enslaved them. They now belong to the Messiah. Jesus, as the Jewish Messiah, was circumcised and fulfilled the whole Torah. He is the firstborn who inherits the promises of Abraham. As long as the non-Jewish Christians of Colossae are faithful followers of Jesus, then through Him they receive a share in those promises. If they go and become circumcised themselves, then they are not seeking those blessings in the Messiah but on their own in another way. Why give up what they already have in the hope of reacquiring it?

All those in the community in Colossae who have been baptized have ended their old life and begun a new one. Every Christian in Colossae needs to live this new life. All the sin and wickedness of their old life need to be killed off and left behind, and they need to pursue in this life all the good things of the life of the world to come—things like love, holiness, compassion, kindness, and humility. Being united together in love will bring them peace. Forgiving one another will bond them together in love.

The Epistle to the Ephesians

The Epistle to the Ephesians, as mentioned, deals with many similar themes to Colossians. It may seem odd that an Epistle to the Ephesians was written from Ephesus itself, but it has the character of a circular letter. It is not intended for a single community as its audience but to circulate throughout an area and a region. This means that Paul's method of teaching in this letter is one level more abstract than is typical. When writing to a single community, in particular one that Paul helped organize or with whom he spent time, Paul writes in a way that is very direct and specific. As a circular letter, Ephesians is more general and broadly applicable. While he was imprisoned, Paul's letter visited the local community gatherings in his place.

Familiar themes are addressed in the way in which Paul presented the gospel in non-Jewish circles. The Ascension of Jesus the Messiah into heaven places Him above all angelic and demonic powers, including the demonic powers the nations used to serve through idolatry. This has allowed the Messiah to set them free. They were previously dead in sin and wickedness, but they have been brought back to a new life. This new life is a gift they have received from Jesus the Messiah by remaining faithful to Him.

As in Philippians and Colossians, Paul presents the Messiah as a heavenly being who was made human. In Ephesians, Paul emphasizes that Jesus' humanity had the effect, in His Ascension into heaven and sitting at the right hand of God, of bringing our humanity with Him. Jesus the Messiah transforms our common humanity, shared with Jewish and non-Jewish people; the non-Jewish Christians of Ephesus who were far off have been brought near and united to Jewish Christians in the Messiah. Now they are one people serving the living God, each in their own way.

Their salvation is a gift, but they have also received their own individual gifts to use faithfully in the community. This requires that the unity of the community be maintained in peace and love. It also requires that they all press on toward maturity and the fullness of understanding and living out their faithfulness to the Messiah. For non-Jewish Christians, this means a clean break from the way of life they practiced in the nations with all its violence, sexual immorality, idolatry, lies, and treachery. These sins not only will lead them away from God but also will break apart the community in which they are working out their salvation.

In the Epistle to the Ephesians, Paul speaks about the social and cultural structures of the world in which the Ephesian Christians find themselves. Paul does not thereby endorse all these structures, but he certainly reimagines how a follower of the Messiah will live within them. What Paul will never do is call for destruction, overthrow, or revolt against these structures. By this point in his life, Paul had repudiated his former zealotry, seeing it as the grave source of error in his past. In his mind, he has returned to being a Pharisee and returned to Gamaliel, as well as returning to the experience of Tarsus. Living within the structures of the time as much as possible without compromising faithfulness to God and the authorities will, for the most part, leave followers of Jesus in peace to pursue their salvation in godliness and sanctity.

Wives, therefore, are called to submit to their husbands—not that they had much choice within the Roman Empire. What is radical, however, about Paul's statements on marriage for this era is his command that husbands love their wives and do so self-sacrificially. Marriages in that era were arranged. Some men did not even see their wives until their wedding day. Many men who were later success-ful would divorce their wives and seek someone they thought better suited to them. It was commonplace among Greek and Roman men to see marriage purely as a duty to reproduce the species while seeking romantic and sexual fulfillment elsewhere. But Paul demands that a husband be as faithful to his wife as the Messiah is to His people.

Likewise, Paul reminds children that they should honor and obey their parents. Again, however, he places the commandment of God on fathers, who, within the cultural structures, wield great power. A paterfamilias in a Roman household literally had the power of life and death over his children. For Paul, this power brings responsibility for men to educate their children, particularly in the knowledge of the Lord. They should not embitter and anger their children and stoke rebellion. They must be the kind of father that God the Father is to His children. Slaves, likewise, must not revolt against their masters. At the same time, the masters—those with the power—must remem-ber that they too have a master in God, who will hold them to account.

Epistle to Philemon

Paul's shortest letter, written to Philemon, reveals more about his understanding of slavery. To argue based on what he says elsewhere that Paul endorses or even condones slavery betrays a lack of nuanced understanding. Violent revolt was off the table for Paul, and abolishing slavery within the Roman Empire could not be done short of that. To that point in history, additionally, no slave revolt had ever been suc-cessful. The abolition of slavery would have required a complete over-haul and transformation not just of social conditions in the empire, but of the mode of economic production. No replacement system of trade and production had yet been envisioned.

Onesimus, an enslaved man who had become a member of the Christian community, escaped and fled from his master, Philemon, and came to Paul seeking sanctuary. Philemon was also a member of the same Christian community meeting in the same house. Paul felt compelled to tell Onesimus to return to Philemon—not only because Paul rejected rebellion but also for Onesimus's safety. Escaped slaves could be punished by death.

In his short note, part of which was handwritten, Paul nevertheless points out how things must change. He so buries his command in pleasantries that he doesn't seem to be giving an order to Philemon. Yet Paul is clear: Onesimus is now not only an enslaved person; he is Paul's brother, and he is Philemon's brother. All three of them belong to Jesus the Messiah. None of them can treat the other as anything less. Philemon cannot treat Onesimus in any way that he wouldn't treat Paul, whom he respects as an apostle and leader in the community.

CHAPTER FIFTEEN

Second Epistle to the Corinthians

As already mentioned, Paul wrote several letters back to the community in Corinth that he had helped to found and in which he had ministered for two years. One of these letters, written early in Paul's time in Ephesus and now known as the First Epistle to the Corinthians, has already been discussed. That letter appears to have been the second one that Paul sent, with the first now being lost. Before what we now call the Second Epistle to the Corinthians, Paul had sent at least one more letter to the Christians in Corinth. He refers to this now-lost third letter as "sorrowful," as he had apparently received a report about a great many problems and negative developments in the community. He had addressed these forthrightly, but it had not been pleasant.

Thinking back on that letter, Paul was preparing to continue his journey and eventually come to Corinth in person. This motivated him to write another letter. He wanted his time with the community in Corinth to be joyful and helpful to them and to him. He was aging, and his ministry had forced him to endure more and more persecution and suffering. This left him with ongoing physical difficulties as well as the practical problems of imprisonment. As much as Paul needed his pastoral visits to be restorative, he had to be faithful to his calling to address serious issues in the community in Corinth if they were not yet resolved. He hoped a letter could help bridge that gap.

A number of signs in the structure of what is now 2 Corinthians suggest that this epistle may actually be a compilation of that fourth letter, as well as a fifth. Within academic scholarship, of course, theories abound in direct proportion to the need to publish. Some scholars have argued that content from as many as half a dozen letters is present here in this single text, pointing to individual sentences and ideas that are split off from the flow of the letter and thus suggest additional sources. While this is of interest to those of a particular scholarly bent, it does not help readers interpret the text or understand St. Paul. For more than nineteen centuries, the text of the Second Epistle to the Corinthians has functioned as a textual unit. This is the best, and only meaningful, way to address it.

Comfort in Suffering

Paul's major theme in this letter is comfort. He begins with the comfort that he has received from God in his suffering. As great as that suffering has become recently, God's comfort has always been greater. He wants to help bring God's comfort to the community in Corinth in light of the difficulties they have suffered and the tough love that Paul has had to show to them. When he addresses the fact that he has been wanting to visit but hasn't been able to, he states that that is likely a good thing, given the situation, as his visit would likely not have been pleasant.

The apostle seeks reconciliation with the community if anyone feels estranged from him after the previous letter. The community has experienced pain, with tears being shed not only among the Christians there but by Paul as well. Paul, however, declares that whatever harm needs to be redressed, there is no harm against him. He has forgiven anything that might have been said or done against him. He needs no apologies and no mediation. He is eager to be reconciled to anyone who wishes reconciliation.

In the First Epistle to the Corinthians, Paul had to push the community at Corinth to deal seriously with gross sexual immorality taking place. Believers there did not like to confront issues or to be confronted. Paul needs them to learn that this is necessary. He makes an extended comparison to aspects of the life of Moses. When Moses came down Mt. Sinai with the tablets of the Torah, he confronted and condemned those worshiping the golden calf. Many people were killed. And basic to Paul's understanding of the gospel is the fact that the sinful people who we were must be killed so that we can have new life in the Spirit. But this necessity doesn't make the confrontation of our sin pleasant.

Paul continues his analogy in the life of Moses. Moses spoke to God face to face atop Mt. Sinai after being sent there because the people feared God's presence. Even the slowly fading, reflected glory of God that shone from the face of Moses was more than they could bear, and they made him wear a veil over his face. Paul says that the Christian community in Corinth is like this. They fear to look at the Torah, at the teaching of God, at the way of life that is pleasing to Him, because of how it will confront their own way of life. They want a veil to cover it. But Paul says that we can no longer hide. We must remove the veil and look squarely at the face of the Torah. When we do, though it may be painful, we will be transformed by the Spirit of God to become more like Him.

Looking to the Day of the Lord with Hope

Paul's message is also a message of hope in the midst of suffering and difficulty. He can see in his own body that on the outside, he is breaking down and decaying, and the time will come when he passes away. But in his heart, he is made alive again and again by the Spirit of God. The miraculous power of God sustains him, and the weaker and more broken he becomes in the eyes of other people, the more obvious it is that the wonder-working power of God is at work in him. He clearly is no longer operating under his own strength.

The imminent coming of the Day of the Lord, when Jesus the Messiah will be revealed from the heavens and come to judge the living and the dead, was always an integral part of Paul's gospel. It gave urgency to his appeal to those of the nations who had now been given an unknown window of time to embrace Jesus the Messiah and escape the wrath of God coming upon their wickedness. By this point in his life, Paul is, more and more, looking to the Day of the Lord with hope. As he sees the time of his departure from this life drawing nearer, Paul begins more and more to look forward to passing from this age, in which there is death and sorrow and suffering, to the age to come, where there is comfort, joy, and immortality in the Messiah.

Paul continues to gather his monetary collection for the community in Jerusalem, and he urges the community in Corinth to contribute to it willingly and joyfully. He does not see this as a burden or a duty he is imposing on them to support others whom they don't know. He sees it rather as a manifestation of a real unity that exists among the Christian communities scattered throughout the whole world. His understanding here parallels the solidarity of Jewish communities throughout the world who also saw Jerusalem as the mother and head of them all.

Paul's Authority as an Apostle

In Paul's absence, other teachers have come to Corinth, apparently seeking to lead them in different directions or to reshape the community in their own image. It seems that part of their approach has been a criticism of Paul. Paul concedes that he is not the most winsome and handsome individual; he is not the greatest orator or gifted with the most perfect rhetoric. He had always approached the community in Corinth humbly, supporting himself, asking them for nothing. Now this has become the source of criticism.

While Paul is loath to boast about himself in any respect, he condescends to do so in this letter under the guise of playing the fool. Paul repeats his credentials as a Jewish teacher, but then he goes further:

What marks him out as a true apostle is not a list of glorious accomplishments, but a list of what he has suffered and endured. He's been beaten. He's been imprisoned. He's been shipwrecked. He's been robbed. He's been persecuted by different groups of people. He's been hungry, thirsty, and naked. Those who come to the community in Corinth seeking the members' allegiance have been through none of these things. That they wouldn't endure these hardships is the mark of their falsehood.

Here, Paul speaks more clearly than anywhere else about his own visionary experiences. Not only has he studied the Torah and the Hebrew Scriptures at the highest and deepest level, but God has also seen fit to reveal the mysteries of creation to him. Even in admitting to these experiences, he treats them less as a boast than as a confession as he recounts how God has aided him in maintaining his humility. Paul has received a persistent thorn in his flesh, a physical problem—likely related to his eyes—that has troubled him and given him difficulty for years. He prayed repeatedly that God would heal him and take it away but learned that what God had given him was sufficient. Paul saw even this persistent problem as a means to his repentance and humility.

Paul speaks, finally, of his upcoming visit to Corinth. Anything not resolved by the time he arrives will be resolved then. Following the guidance of the Torah, every issue, every case, will be decided by the testimony of two or three witnesses. Even though his last letter, and some of the things that will happen at this impending visit, will bring sadness to the community, Paul does not regret it. There is a kind of sorrow that brings about repentance and transformation, not despair. If Paul must inspire sorrow, he wants it to be a bright sorrow.

CHAPTER SIXTEEN

Epistle to the Hebrews

Questioning whether or not the Epistle to the Hebrews is the work of St. Paul is not merely a modern phenomenon. Beginning in the third and fourth centuries AD, people began to question his authorship. While there was a broad agreement that the themes and ideas and even many of the expressions used in Hebrews are Pauline, the Greek style seems too different. That said, in any extant manuscript, the text was never known and has never been labeled as anything other than St. Paul's Epistle to the Hebrews.

By AD 100, the epistles of Paul were circulating together as a collection. Every manuscript we have of any of his letters is actually a copy of the collection containing all of them. The earliest known manuscript of Paul's epistles is labeled p46. The *p* abbreviates papyrus, the form of the manuscript, while the manuscripts are numbered in the order they were discovered. This particular handwritten copy of Paul's epistles dates to somewhere between AD 125 and 150, and it contains the Book of Hebrews. Not only is it included, but Paul's letters are arranged by length, meaning that Hebrews is the second letter in the collection after Romans and before 1 Corinthians. This shows that the earliest copyists either were unaware of the differences that seemed so apparent later or knew something that later readers did not.

The Question of Genre

While this text is part of a collection of St. Paul's epistles and is referred to as the Epistle to the Hebrews, it lacks any of the usual introductory material in Paul's letters—or in any formal letter from the ancient world, for that matter. However, the conclusion of the text features greetings and statements that are similar to the conclusions of his epistles. This makes it worth asking whether this text is an epistle in terms of genre. Reading the text reveals rhetorical features such as multiple comments about how long the implied speaker is taking. There are comments about repetition, and some comments seem to indicate skipping over certain topics because of time considerations. None of these features make sense in what is fundamentally a written text.

These features do, however, make sense in a text that represents an oral presentation. Oratory in the ancient world was frequently recorded in writing. Disciples recorded their teachers, and onlookers took notes on public discussions and debates. Hebrews shows all the signs of being recorded preaching. Once this genre consideration is established, the text can be reassessed in terms of how it relates to Saul of Tarsus.

When compared to the preaching and public speaking of Paul as recorded in the Acts of the Apostles, there are a striking number of similarities in style. Scholars have long noticed the differences in phrasing and style between those sermons in Acts and the Pauline epistles. This is suggestive of the hand that may have been involved in recording the homily now known to us as the Epistle to the Hebrews: St. Luke. The text of Hebrews reads very much like an extended sermon of Paul recorded by his companion Luke. The written homily was likely broadly circulated, explaining the epistle-like ending appended to the text.

In particular, Hebrews is a sermon preached on Psalm 110/109, which is the portion of the Hebrew Scriptures most often quoted in the New Testament. The Epistle to the Hebrews, however, is an extended meditation on it in detail. This psalm is viewed in the New Testament—as it was widely understood across multiple forms of Judaism in the first century—as speaking of the Messiah. The New Testament, of course, identifies the Messiah in this psalm as Jesus of Nazareth. Hebrews makes a positive argument that the details regarding the Messiah in the psalm accurately describe the person of Jesus of Nazareth and the particulars of Paul's gospel concerning Him.

Based on comparisons to the material in the Acts of the Apostles, Hebrews appears to be a sermon preached in a synagogue setting. This was something Paul commonly did, and we know that at various points in his missionary journeys he preached for weeks in a single synagogue to the same community. The homily assumes the audience's high degree of familiarity with the Hebrew Scriptures, even more than in his usual epistles. It also assumes great familiarity with certain Jewish practices of the contemporary period. All these factors likely account for the traditional ascription "to the Hebrews."

Jesus as King and Priest

Jesus, the Messiah, is identified as the Son of God from the beginning of the sermon, and His divine preexistence is presupposed. Paul's initial concern is to demonstrate that the Son of God whom we come to know as Jesus is superior to every created being—including all the angelic and demonic powers. He refers to passage after passage of Hebrew Scripture, which he reads as describing the Son in terms that are never used to describe angelic beings or human kings. In being made human, the Son of God has elevated our humanity to the heights, above the angelic powers, and given humanity a share in His rule over the age to come.

Psalm 110/109 uniquely combines the Messianic prophecy of the son of David, the king, with the promise of a new high priesthood. As Messianic king, He is enthroned beside God. He also is made a priest forever after the pattern of Melchizedek. Melchizedek—as he appears in the Torah—is both a priest and a king. His priesthood also has no beginning and no end in the text, while the Levitical priesthood is bound by the mortal men who serve in it. They live and die and are succeeded in their ministry. That is not the case with Melchizedek.

Hebrews sees Jesus fulfilling both the Jewish traditions regarding a Messianic king and those regarding a priestly Messiah who would restore the worship of the temple. In this latter case, however, it is not the earthly sanctuary that Jesus purifies as a high priest but the heavenly one. Moses received the pattern for the earthly sanctuary after being in the presence of the heavenly sanctuary atop Mt. Sinai. The Levitical high priest needed to purify the sanctuary every year on the Day of Atonement so that sinful people could continue to live safely in the presence of God. The Messiah, with the blood of His self-offering, has purified the sanctuary in heaven so that everyone, everywhere can have the Holy Spirit dwelling within them.

Faithfulness to Jesus the Messiah

As always, the primary issue for St. Paul in this preaching is faithfulness. Throughout Hebrews, he repeatedly warns against apostasy and faithlessness and warns of the destruction that will result from turning away from God. He compares his hearers, as he had in 1 Corinthians, to the Israelites in the wilderness after leaving Egypt. Those who were faithless fell there in the desert. He warns that the Messiah's sacrifice has purified them and given them a new life. If they squander that new life in further sin, He will not die again. Remaining faithful to God in Jesus the Messiah is a matter with eternal consequences.

In addition to repeated warnings against faithlessness, Paul also turns to praising faithfulness. Faithfulness, he says, gives substance to the hope we have. When hope seems far off, remaining faithful makes that hope real. He turns to the Hebrew Scriptures and the great holy ones of old. Despite all these great role models and patrons of the past living very different lives, they all pleased God through their faithfulness to His calling. As is usual with Paul's preaching, Abraham looms large as the father of all the faithful. This is not just a matter of history for Paul or a theological point. These faithful people of old show us the way and cheer us on as we seek to follow their example and remain faithful to our callings. The Day of the Lord is coming when every one of them and of us will receive the reward for the life we have lived.

Paul concludes his preaching with specifics of how believers should press on together as a community bound together by love. They must continue to show hospitality to each other. They must continue to gather in worship, to offer the Eucharist, to offer a sacrifice of praise to God. They must honor their leaders, who are shepherding them in their faithfulness. They must put off all sin. They must avoid even temptations that come through greed or not properly honoring one's marriage. They must remain faithful until the end.

CHAPTER SEVENTEEN

Return to Jerusalem

As St. Paul prepared to leave Troas at the end of his third missionary journey, he knew that more of his days lay behind him than ahead. He suffered the physical effects of all that had befallen him—the beatings, the stoning, the shipwrecks, hunger, thirst, and imprisonment. He had seen opposition arise at some point nearly everywhere he went. Through it all, he remained faithful and was unafraid. But he was also realistic. He was preparing to sail back to Jerusalem, and he anticipated more conflict and problems of the kind he had recently been facing. Opposition from leaders in Jewish communities who rejected Jesus as the Messiah was one thing in Greek and Roman cities. Jerusalem, however, was a different matter—a Jewish community whose leadership, even those leaders who weren't hostile to the Christian movement per se, were certainly hostile to Paul.

Paul didn't know if he would ever get another opportunity to return to visit the communities that he had established in Asia Minor. Chief among these, of course, was Ephesus, where he had recently spent so much time. He summoned the presbyters there to come and meet with him so that he could encourage them and give them a farewell if this was, in fact, to be their last face-to-face encounter. He pointed them again to his own example of living among them. He warned them that once he was gone, false teachers would come, and the leaders would need to be vigilant in protecting the community. They would now need to lead the faithful in Ephesus without him.

Journey to Jerusalem

The journey back to Jerusalem by sea was more than eight hundred and thirty-five miles. Paul wanted to be in Jerusalem by the Feast of Pentecost, but he also made significant stops at various ports of call along the way. Ship travel in the first century was made in short hops down the coast, carrying passengers and cargo. When the ship docked at a place with a Christian community, Paul would make a short visit. Paul and his companions spent a week in Tyre, in what is now Lebanon. They spent a day in Ptolemais. When they reached the major port of Caesarea, they stayed for a short time with Philip, one of the seven original deacons from Jerusalem.

At each of these stops, members of the Christian communities warned Paul in more and more striking terms that arrest and imprisonment awaited him in Jerusalem. The prophet Agabus publicly and dramatically bound himself with Paul's belt to predict imprisonment. But Paul was undeterred. He had faced hardship, including imprisonment, before. For Jesus to go up to Jerusalem had meant death. How could Paul be faithful to his calling without being willing to do likewise?

When he finally arrived in Jerusalem, Paul went to stay with Mnason of Cyprus, a Jewish Christian who had joined the movement in Jerusalem early on. Paul then went the very next day to see James, the brother of the Lord, and to deliver the collection he had taken up from all the Christian communities he had visited. He told St. James and the other apostles everything that had happened on his journeys, including how many non-Jewish people had been coming to know Jesus the Messiah and had turned away from idolatry and immorality. James showed Paul, in turn, how greatly the community of Jewish Christians in Jerusalem had grown and how zealous they were for the Torah.

There was also bad news for St. Paul. Rumors had come to the Jewish communities of Jerusalem from those who were opposed to him and his work in the cities of Asia Minor and Greece. Though Paul had everywhere taught that the Torah was good and right and given to the Jewish people, his opponents claimed that he was telling Jewish Christians to abandon it and not circumcise their children. Paul had preached clear, sometimes even intense, messages against requiring non-Jewish Christians to be circumcised or to keep other elements of the Torah that were directed only to the Jewish people. But his words were misinterpreted as him calling for even Jewish Christians to abandon Moses and the traditions of their fathers. This was far from the truth.

James had a plan, however, about how to correct this error and debunk these rumors. Paul had taken a Nazirite vow at the end of his second missionary journey. In Jerusalem, several other Jewish Christians also had recently completed such a vow. As Paul had, they were now preparing to go to the temple to make the sacrificial offerings, including a sin offering, that accompanied the end of the vow. James suggested to Paul that he sponsor those offerings and accompany them to the temple as a way of publicly showing that he still kept the Torah and encouraged other Jewish people to do the same.

When the time came for Paul to follow through on this plan, he and the Nazirites entered the temple, and everything went wrong. A group of Jewish people from the cities of Asia Minor, who were in Jerusalem for Pentecost, spotted him and believed that he was bringing Greeks into the temple, where they were forbidden. The desecration of the temple by pagan Greeks under Antiochus IV Epiphanes, the Seleucid emperor, still loomed large in the collective memory of the Jewish people. These called out to the crowds that Paul was the one who preached against the Jewish people, the Torah, and the temple.

Arrest and Trials

A mob quickly formed. They dragged Paul out of the temple and began to beat him. They likely would have killed him if Roman soldiers hadn't arrived to restore order. They arrested Paul and had to physically carry him to get him away from the crowd. The soldiers served under Claudius Lysias, the tribune in charge of the Roman forces in Jerusalem at this time. He was a chiliarch, or the "leader of a thousand," with ten centurions and their forces under his command. They operated out of an expansive barracks near the temple complex in the city.

Despite the vehemence of the crowd, Paul asked the tribune for an opportunity to address them and attempt to defuse the situation. Lysias suspected Paul might be a Jewish man from Egypt who had recently attempted to start an insurrection in the desert. The Roman garrison had likely been put on alert for that criminal. But after he understood that Paul was not that person, he allowed him to speak.

Paul addressed the crowds in Hebrew and told them his story. He told them of coming from Tarsus to study with Gamaliel. He told them of being radicalized and going from synagogue to synagogue seeking to oppress and end the Christian movement. He told them what happened on the road to Damascus and about his baptism. He concluded by speaking of something that had happened during his first visit to Jerusalem after his baptism. While praying in the temple, Jesus had appeared to him and told him to leave the city and travel to the nations to spread the gospel because Jerusalem would not receive him. At this point, the mob's patience ended, and the tribune had him brought into the barracks.

Lysias, for his part, assumed that the uproar was some kind of intra-Jewish conflict. He ordered Paul to be beaten until he explained how he had caused so much trouble. Before the centurion could carry out the tribune's order, however, Paul informed him that he was a Roman citizen. The tribune was dubious at first, but upon learning that Paul was, in fact, a citizen, he had a problem on his hands. He had

158

already failed to follow through on his duty to protect a citizen from a mob of noncitizens, although Paul likely waited to inform the guard of his citizenship because of the possibility of violent Roman "protection" of a citizen.

Still seeing the problem as an intra-Jewish one, the tribune sent Paul for a hearing before the Sanhedrin. If the Jews could resolve this matter themselves, then it would be removed from the tribune's plate, and he could get on with more important matters. As the hearing began, Paul detected immediate hostility. This would not be an evenhanded and fair hearing. Paul also noted, however, that the council as it currently stood was divided between the Pharisees and the Sadducees. Proclaiming his identity as a Pharisee, he stated that the whole reason he faced opposition was his devotion to the resurrection of the dead. A debate thus broke out with at least some of the Pharisees then seeing Paul as a brother—one who perhaps had some strange visions, but a brother nonetheless. Before this situation could turn into another riot, the tribune brought Paul back to the barracks.

A small band of zealots in Jerusalem made a pact to assassinate Paul and attempted to get the Sanhedrin to ask for him again so they could spring their trap. Paul's nephew was in the city at the time and learned of the plan. He brought news to his uncle and then to the tribune. This development allowed Lysias to get the problem off his hands. He sent Paul to the city of Caesarea, where Antonius Felix, the Roman procurator of Judea, was presiding. He also sent along a letter saying that he was protecting Paul, a Roman citizen, from a bloodthirsty Jewish mob. The tribune let Paul's accusers know that if they wanted to pursue their dispute, they would need to go to Caesarea and make their case before the governor.

Paul was imprisoned in Herod's palace and awaited the arrival of those accusers. Five days later the high priest Ananias, some members of the Sanhedrin, and a lawyer named Tertullus arrived to make the case against Paul to Felix. Paul essentially was accused of disturbing the peace. The Roman peace, for a Roman procurator, was sacrosanct. Felix's job, even his life, depended on maintaining the peace in Judea.

He had broad powers, mostly violence and the sword, to allow him to do that. Accusing Paul of being the ringleader of some sect who stirs up riots from city to city meant Paul would face the death penalty under Roman law.

Paul's defense was simple. He was, indeed, a leader in the Christian movement. He was also, however, a Pharisee. He worshiped the God of Abraham, Isaac, and Jacob. He was faithful to everything in the Torah and the Prophets. He believed in the coming resurrection of the dead. After being away from Jerusalem for years, he had come to give financial assistance to his people there and to go to the temple and make offerings. He had entered the city peaceably, and some Jewish people from another province—who, suspiciously, were not in attendance at the trial that day—stirred up the mob. Felix declined to rule at that time.

The wife of Felix, Drusilla, was Jewish and was familiar with teaching about Jesus the Messiah. Likely she had encountered Philip the deacon and others in the overlap of the Jewish and Christian communities in Caesarea. Paul took opportunities to speak to both her and her husband about Jesus the Messiah, a good that Paul always sought to bring out of his imprisonments and trials. Felix was primarily looking for a bribe to release Paul, and when it didn't come, the apostle ended up imprisoned, albeit able to receive visitors, for two years.

In AD 59 or 60, Porcius Festus became procurator of Judea, and Felix was recalled to Rome. There he stood trial before Nero for deliberately causing unrest in his province to enrich himself but was not punished any further. Upon Festus's first official visit to Jerusalem, he was approached by Jewish opponents of Paul who wanted him finally eliminated. Festus agreed to hear the case when he returned to Caesarea. Those who came to present the case against Paul at this point, two years after the initial fervor against him, did so in lackluster fashion. Paul simply stated that he had not sinned against the Torah, nor against the temple, nor had he committed any offense against Caesar's laws.

Festus sought to send Paul to Jerusalem anyway, where potentially he could be assassinated, to ingratiate himself to his new subjects. Paul knew, by this point, the games that were being played with his life, and so he used the ultimate right of a Roman citizen: he appealed to Caesar. Paul did not primarily do this to save his own life. He was willing to die for the gospel's sake. But in addition to preserving his life temporarily, this appeal might give him the opportunity to preach the gospel to the emperor himself. This had long been a goal of Paul's, and he dreamed of how the whole known world might be transformed if its ruler became a faithful follower of Jesus the Messiah.

While Paul's right of appeal could not be denied, Festus was unsure what letter to send the emperor about the case. Like Tribune Lysias earlier, he thought this conflict was an intra-Jewish dispute about religious matters that he neither understood nor cared to understand. When he summarized the whole affair, he stated that he believed it to be about a certain Jesus whom the Jews said was dead, but Paul said was alive (Acts 25:19). Festus certainly did not want to ask the emperor to formally weigh in on that matter.

Soon after, Herod Agrippa II, the last of the tetrarchs, and his sister Bernice made an official visit to the new procurator. When they indicated to Festus that they wanted to hear what Paul had to say, he gave Paul a public platform. Festus hoped that this might give him some way to address the matter to Rome. Paul again presented his own personal history as a Pharisee and a former persecutor of the Christian movement, and recounted the vision he had received of Jesus the Messiah on the road to Damascus. Since that day he had been calling those among the nations to repent and turn to God. Finally, he said that he was teaching what Moses and the Prophets had foretold: that the Messiah would suffer, he would be the first to rise from the dead, and he would be preached to both the Jewish people and the nations.

To Festus, this was so much madness and nonsense. Clearly Paul was a learned man, but none of what he said made any sense to a Roman completely unfamiliar with the religion of the Jewish people. Paul, however, continued to address Agrippa, who was familiar with the Jews and understood what he was saying—to the point that Agrippa wondered if Paul sought to convert him. Agrippa did not, in fact, join the Christian movement. He was fated to be the final ruler of the Herodian dynasty before the Jewish revolt led the Romans to end that experiment. Nonetheless, Festus saw no crime of which he could possibly find Paul guilty. But since Paul had appealed to Caesar, he had to be sent to Rome.

The Journey to Rome

Paul was ultimately given into the custody of Julius from the Augustan Cohort, which was stationed in Syria and named for the emperor at the time of its formation in AD 6. A cohort was a tenth of a legion, and Julius was one of six centurions within the cohort. A detachment of soldiers set sail with Paul for Italy and ultimately Rome. Luke and Aristarchus, a Christian from Thessalonica, were allowed to join Paul for the difficult voyage. Paul sensed more difficulty was on the horizon, but his voice on matters of sailing didn't carry much authority. As they moved from port to port, sometimes changing ships, they faced unpredictable weather and seas. Winter was approaching, and they hoped to make port for the season in Crete.

The bad weather intensified, and the boat was lost at sea for two weeks before shipwrecking. In the midst of the boat's wandering, Paul received a vision of an angel who assured him that no one on the ship would die, which Paul used to encourage the sailors. Other prisoners besides Paul were on board, and in the confusion of the shipwreck, some soldiers prepared to kill the prisoners to prevent escape. Julius, however, having been charged with Paul, a Roman citizen bound for the emperor, put a stop to the plan.

Stranded on Malta, the soldiers, prisoners, and sailors connected first with the natives. Paul was bitten at one point by a poisonous snake but suffered no ill effects. Later they found the most respected Roman citizen on the island, a certain Publius. Paul healed Publius's father and then many of the sick on the island, giving him yet another opportunity to preach the gospel of Jesus the Messiah. Publius and many others converted, and Publius became the first overseer of Malta's Christian community. Later in life, Publius would travel to Athens and then be martyred there.

After wintering on Malta, they connected with members of local Christian communities on the way to Rome, where they completed their journey. Paul awaited his hearing before the emperor while under house arrest in Rome, meaning that he generally had his freedom except for a soldier being posted with him as a guard at all times. In this way he was able to receive visitors and help organize and build up the Christian communities in Rome and other nearby cities. Paul also called the Jewish community of Rome to come and meet with him, explaining his situation. Many more Jewish Christians also joined the community in Rome through his preaching, and he remained under house arrest for two years.

CHAPTER EIGHTEEN

Fourth Missionary Journey

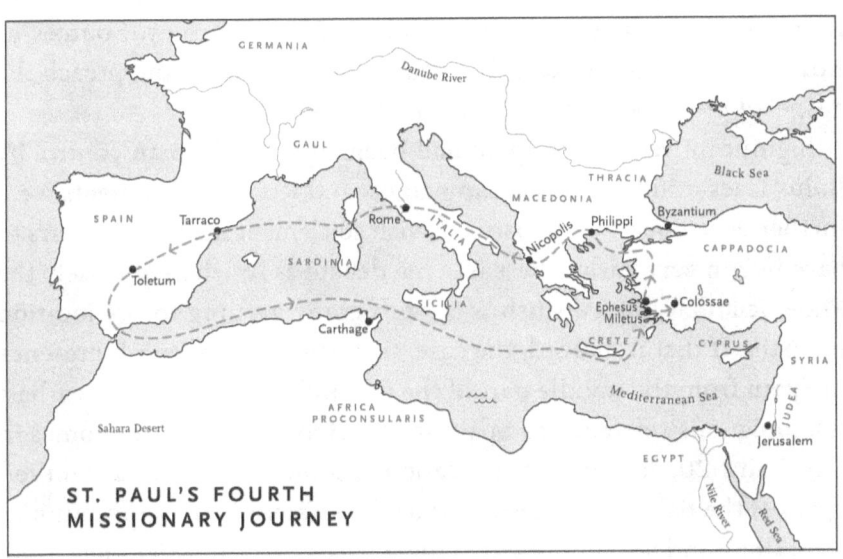

**ST. PAUL'S FOURTH
MISSIONARY JOURNEY**

The narrative of the Acts of the Apostles ends with St. Paul under house arrest in Rome for two years, awaiting his hearing before the emperor. For the remainder of Paul's life, as for his early years, we are dependent on history and on historical traditions preserved by ancient Christian communities. The end of Paul's house arrest brings us to AD 62. Based on references in both the Scriptures and the earliest

Christian writings outside the Bible, Paul did indeed stand before the emperor and make his case. Though there were some in Nero's household and a handful of ranking imperial officials who joined the Christian community in Rome, Nero himself was anything but a convert. Nevertheless, he set Paul free.

Journey to Spain

When he had written his Epistle to the Romans, Paul had indicated that he hoped to travel to the farthest-flung Jewish community that he knew of at the extreme west of the known world. This meant traveling to the province of Baetica in what is now southern Spain. Originally, he had planned to stop in Rome on the way. Now finding himself in Rome, he had already completed much of the journey. Sources as early as 1 Clement indicate that Paul did indeed reach and preach the gospel of Jesus the Messiah in Spain.[33]

Significant regions of Spain had been added to Roman control by Julius Caesar in his various campaigns, and Roman settlements were further developed by Augustus. Jewish settlement in Spain appears to have begun very early. There is some debate as to where precisely the Phoenician city of Tarshish was, with many arguing for its location in Spain. If that is, indeed, the case, then there was a Jewish presence in Spain from the middle part of the first millennium BC. The earliest unambiguous reference to Spain in the Hebrew Scriptures comes in Obadiah 1:20, describing the location of some of the most distant refugees of the Babylonian destruction of Jerusalem. These communities were small and not prominent in the Roman cities in which they lived. Nevertheless, Paul knew they were there—a western endpoint for his mission to preach the gospel to the nations.[34]

---

33 1 Clement 5:5–7; written c. AD 95. The Acts of Peter and the Muratorian Fragment, both written in the second century, also give testimony to Paul's trip to Spain.

34 A decade later, these Jewish communities would begin receiving many more refugees after the Roman destruction of Jerusalem. After Paul's life had ended, Jewish communities in Spain would go on to have a long and complex history.

One city in Spain with strong traditions of having been visited by Paul is Tarragona, known in the first century AD as Tarraco. The city lay along the northwestern Mediterranean coast. Its full name, given it by Julius Caesar, translates roughly to "the colony city Triumph of Julius Tarraco." The province was later named Hispania Tarraconensis after Tarraco was made the capital. In addition to being the capital of the province, Tarraco hosted one of the permanent Roman courts for the administration of justice in the region. Paul preached the gospel in Tarraco to its small Jewish community and then to the broader city. He made Prosperus, one of his first non-Jewish converts, the first overseer of the Christian community in the city.

It is unclear exactly how long Paul spent in Spain. Four years after his Roman release, Paul would again be imprisoned in Rome. It is possible that he spent four full years traveling and preaching in Spain, with a significant amount of that time in Tarraco. Saint Prosperus would later be presented as the successor of St. Paul in the region, implying a mentoring relationship of some length. The other possibility is that after some amount of time in Spain, Paul left to revisit the Christian communities he had helped establish.

Any information on these visits by Paul on his fourth journey comes from his epistles to Timothy and Titus. Paul mentions events in these epistles—in particular events that take place in Ephesus and Crete—that seem to have happened recently. Evidence is not conclusive, however, that these happened on a fourth missionary journey rather than some time earlier. Given the time he must have spent in Spain and the time required for voyaging back to the East, these visits to Ephesus and Crete would have been relatively short. If Paul indeed made these visits, he must have returned to Rome or been arrested somewhere near Rome and taken there by AD 66.

Final Return to Rome

It is considerably more likely that Paul journeyed to Rome deliberately, despite the persecution of Christians going on there that included the death of St. Peter. Though Nero was keen on killing leaders of the Christian movement, there is no record of him sending troops long distances in pursuit of these leaders. His arrests and executions were far more opportunistic. In either case, when Paul returned to Rome, he would have understood that he likely would not leave alive.

Once back in Rome, Paul was imprisoned in what is now called the Mamertine Prison. It had served as a prison since before the founding of the Roman Republic and was built over a large cistern with a spring of water at its base into which prisoners were lowered. This lowest level of the cistern was called the Tullianum. Every prisoner there was awaiting trial and/or execution. It was the place of confinement of important state prisoners. Conquered barbarian kings were taken there before their public humiliation and execution. So were rebels and leaders of popular revolts against Rome. Not long before Paul arrived there, it had been the place of imprisonment of St. Peter, who used the spring in the cistern to baptize some of his fellow prisoners.

Paul was abandoned here to await his fate in the cold, with nothing but the clothes on his back. He was now an elderly man; his body had been beaten and broken many times over in hardship. It was not any sort of pessimism but instead realistic discernment that caused him to believe that the end of the course of his life in this world was quickly approaching.

CHAPTER NINETEEN

Roman Imprisonment:
First Timothy, Second Timothy & Titus

D uring Paul's final imprisonment in Rome, he wrote the last of his extant epistles. These three letters, the First and Second Epistles to Timothy and the Epistle to Titus, are commonly grouped together as the Pastoral Epistles. They are also frequently considered by scholars not to be the work of St. Paul, although they could easily be the product of the author of the other epistles working with a different secretary.

The Pastoral Epistles, First and Second Timothy and Titus, are often considered not to be Pauline in the true sense because of their contents. There is a general presupposition among many scholars that the early Christian communities emerged in a very primitive state, beginning as a new religion. This is clearly not true. The Christian communities organized by Paul were heirs to the Jewish communities in those same places. The Christians were a group within Judaism, primarily within Pharisaic Judaism, parallel with any other Judaism in the first century AD. They had an equal claim to be the inheritors of the Jewish tradition, but they believed that the Jewish Messiah had come. The proclamation of Jesus of Nazareth as the

Messiah was responsible for early Christianity's sectarian distinctions from other Judaisms.

Until some disruption or break happened, early Christians remained active in their local synagogues, with the Christian gathering for the Eucharist as an added meeting on the Lord's Day. They continued to read, study, reason, and argue from the Hebrew Scriptures, though sometimes in Greek translation. The Eucharist is a sacrificial activity that incorporated elements of temple worship, but this use of temple practices also was not unheard of among scattered Jewish groups of that period. At Qumran, the community that produced the Dead Sea Scrolls, rejection of the Jerusalem temple as corrupt led them to adapt certain temple rituals for their own community. In Alexandria, Egypt, the Jewish community still embraced the Jerusalem temple as the center of sacrificial worship, but they also had a temple in Leontopolis where certain elements of sacrificial worship took place.

The particular issue taken with Paul's authorship of the Pastoral Epistles is a certain scholarly understanding of the *ekklesia*, the Christian community—in modern terms, the Church. The purported problems are twofold: Paul's understanding of the connectedness of Christian communities throughout the world and the structure of leadership in this supposedly primitive era of Christian history.

A Universal Christian Community

First, Paul is thought to have died too early for him to have had a conception of the Church as a whole, as opposed to individual churches or individual communities. But Paul's collection taken for Jerusalem shows that this is not actually a problem.

As a Jewish person, Paul belonged to a particular segment of Judaism, the Pharisees, and was part of the Pharisaic movement in Judea. Other subgroups and factions in Judaism disagreed radically with what he taught, even apart from the gospel of the Messiah. Nevertheless, Paul's conception of the Jewish people and Jewish religion encompassed the whole, not just the particular. He could speak about the Jewish community in a given place. He could also speak of the Jewish people scattered throughout the world in their various communities.

Jerusalem and its temple were major factors in the understanding of this unity. Even groups that saw the temple and its priesthood at that time as hopelessly corrupt understood what the temple ought to be. Though Jerusalem was languishing under foreign domination, it was a symbol as the City of David. Rome understood this significance, and they destroyed the temple and city to try to break the unity of the Jewish people scattered through the empire.

Paul's monetary collection, as well as the way he speaks of Jerusalem and the other apostles, shows that he shared this conception of unity vis-à-vis the Christian communities. While Paul de-emphasizes the temple—at least, the physical one on the earth—Jerusalem is the place to which the Messiah came, the place where He died, and the place where He rose again. The Christian community in Jerusalem was overseen by Jesus' immediate disciples, including His brother, James, whom He had appointed to lead it. Many members of that community in Paul's lifetime had encountered and followed Jesus during His earthly life. Jerusalem remained the mother of all communities. Therefore, Paul could speak of the Christian communities scattered throughout the world as one community.

Leadership Structures in Early Christianity

The second supposed issue with the Pastoral Epistles is that they give a picture of a structured leadership within these communities. Scholars somehow imagine that Christian communities sprang up in a kind of happy anarchy with no leadership, then these leadership structures developed over time. Aside from this thesis having no correspondence with reality, it is hard to think of a group in history that has emerged without leaders. This model sets aside the clear and uncontested account of the Acts of the Apostles. No one has any doubt that the immediate disciples of Jesus were the leaders of the early Christian community in Jerusalem.

More importantly, though, the early Christian communities began as subsets of local Jewish communities, which had authority structures in place and ways of functioning, adjudicating disputes, and maintaining community bonds. Christian communities, as they took on their own existence and life, were the heirs to these structures and mirrored them. For example, Jewish communities had elders. We read of many cases in which some of those elders became Christians and therefore served as elders in both communities until and unless some sort of definitive break took place. The structures that Paul describes in the Pastoral Epistles all existed, verifiably, within Jewish communities, within the Christian community in Jerusalem, or within both.

Paul's discussion of the relationship between these leadership structures and women has become controversial in recent times. In reality, Paul stakes out a position on the role of women within Christian communities commensurate with that of Jesus in His ministry. He emphasizes that women should practice silence and learn. This contrasts with the practice in many Pharisaic circles in which women were not allowed to study Torah. He has a place for deaconesses, for women serving the needs of other women and teaching them within the Christian community.

In 1 Timothy 2:13–15, Paul gives a standard argument for the calling of men to exercise leadership by pointing to the case of Adam and Eve. Adam failed to exercise the leadership to which he was called, Eve took over that leadership position, and his weakness led to disaster. Paul, however, points to the salvation of Eve. Paul argues in his epistle to the Roman community that Jesus the Messiah had redeemed Adam from his sin. Likewise, Eve, the woman, has been saved by an act of childbearing—namely by the woman, Mary, who gave birth to the Messiah. Salvation is not only a concern for men who bring along with them the women, children, and slaves under their authority. Salvation is for men and women and children and enslaved people who come to know God through Jesus the Messiah.

Timothy and Titus as Paul's Successors

Paul writes to St. Timothy as his intended successor. He knows that he is coming very near to the end of his life. Timothy has traveled with him, observed him, and helped him write several of his later epistles. Paul also knows that several of the other apostles have preceded him in death, including central leaders of the broad Christian community like St. Peter and St. James. A transition was taking place. Like Moses, the first generation of leadership in the Christian community had been chosen by God. When Moses knew that his life was drawing to an end, he designated Joshua as his successor. Paul followed this model, and other apostles did likewise.

Paul speaks to Timothy about the opposition he is going to face. Paul himself had continually faced opposition, and his successor would likewise. Unlike Paul, Timothy was still a young man. He didn't have some of the credentials that Paul and his opponents could enlist to shore up their authority. While he was still young, Timothy would have to exercise Paul's authority through the authority of the gospel itself. It was really the authority of the Messiah that would work through Timothy if he remained faithful.

Timothy's own life must focus on two things: the Hebrew Scriptures and prayer. Despite his youth and early lack of reputation, if Timothy can marshal the Scriptures, they will help him become a faithful worker and allow him to withstand his opponents. Prayer will aid him in avoiding the snares of sin, and praying for all people will allow him to love others and manifest the unity he will try to give to the communities. Both tools will help him both to do his work and to be content in the life to which God has called him.

Timothy's responsibility to the community is in large part to organize them. The community being in good order will ensure that their worship is acceptable to God and help members resolve the disputes that will inevitably arise in their life together. He, as a leader, will also be in a position where he needs to judge and resolve disputes without favoritism or anger. Preserving the bonds of peace and love in a community is beautiful but difficult work.

Part of the good order of the community is its leadership. Communities in cities of significant size had an overseer—*episkopos* in Greek. This word is frequently used in Greek translations of the Hebrew Scriptures to translate a word that refers to a herdsman who watches over flocks. This is the office that St. Timothy would exercise in Ephesus for a time and that St. Titus would exercise in Crete. Every community of every size had elders, or *presbyters*, who led the people. If a community didn't have an overseer—later called a bishop—or he wasn't present, the presbyters presided at the Eucharistic gathering.

The first deacons had been appointed by the apostles to care for certain ministry tasks within the Jerusalem community. Though other Christian communities were not structured in exactly the same way, they likewise had deacons who cared for some of the same ministries to the sick and the needy. Women deacons played a somewhat analogous, though not identical, role in ministering to the needs of women as was socially appropriate. Deaconesses overlapped heavily with those officially enrolled as widows. Widows past a certain age were encouraged not to remarry but to serve the broader community, especially in mentoring and assisting younger women. In return for this service, the community supported them.

The Pastoral Epistles seek to guide both Timothy and Titus in finding the right sort of faithful men and women to fulfill these different roles. Many Christian communities that hadn't received an apostle in person had sprung up somewhat organically from within Jewish communities. When this happened, people gravitated into leadership roles, but this does not mean that these people were the best leaders for the health of the community. Paul sees that pastoral leadership cannot be allowed to be a matter of chance or of human ambition or other desires. Selecting leaders forms an important part of Timothy's and Titus's oversight in the communities in which they will exercise their ministry.

Paul understands the calling that he received on the road to Damascus as a sacred charge to which he has struggled to be faithful. He conveys to Timothy and Titus that they must see the charge that he is giving to them in the same way. They have been given this ministry as a gift. They must prove themselves worthy of it. From Paul's passing until theirs, faithfully living out this calling to ministry will be the way in which they find salvation.

CHAPTER TWENTY

Martyrdom

St. Paul's second imprisonment in Rome proved to be his final one. He had previously been found innocent and released by a Roman tribunal. Those previous trials had been an inquiry into certain accusations made against Paul, a Roman citizen, by Jewish noncitizens in Jerusalem. But this imprisonment was the result of direct persecution of the Christian community in Rome by Nero. No trial or appeal was necessary. Paul was, incontrovertibly, a leader within the Christian community.

By the latter part of Nero's reign, the growth of the Christian community in Rome, especially in non-Jewish circles, had differentiated it in the eyes of the Roman government from the Jewish community. While the Jewish community had longstanding privileges in Rome, albeit sporadically honored, the Christian community as such had none. Further, though still essentially Jewish in character at this point, the Christian community had more difficulty claiming antiquity for at least some of their beliefs and practices. This allowed Nero to brand Christianity as a dangerous new cult and use it as a convenient political scapegoat.

Nero's Legacy

In recent times, some doubt has been cast on the extent of Nero's persecution and on some of historians' more florid stories of executions. Certainly, reading purely Christian sources will give an impression of Nero as a cackling villain. He became the paradigm by which Christian communities for centuries understood the figure of the coming man of Belial. At the same time, part of the reason for that identification by Christians was pagan Romans' belief that, despite his death, Nero would return as a god to save Rome from various future plagues and difficulties. Christians saw in popular Roman devotion to Nero a dark reflection of the Messiah.

Madness, tyranny, and open villainy would not produce this kind of veneration of Nero among the Roman citizenry. The unpopularity of Nero's uncle and predecessor, Caligula, and the rejoicing at his assassination by his own bodyguards attests to this. In July of AD 64, a massive fire broke out in Rome that destroyed significant temples, the forum where the Senate met, and Nero's own palace. There were accusations at the time that Nero had set the fire himself for purposes of urban renewal or that he was otherwise responsible. It seems more likely that the population density of Rome and the state of waste management in the first century simply resulted in a fire that quickly burned out of control.

As the emperor, especially with accusations in play of his own culpability, Nero's immediate move was to find someone on whom to pin the blame. The burgeoning Christian community in Rome was ready at hand. The refusal, especially of non-Jewish Christians, to honor the city's gods was enough, in the Roman mind, to lead those gods to visit all manner of misfortune and calamity upon the city.

The majority of Rome's Christians, Jewish or not, were from the lower classes. Women, slaves, and noncitizens were not entitled to trials and were subject to any available form of execution. Crucifixion, burning, and feeding to wild animals before spectators were the most common forms of these executions. Near the end of the first year of persecutions, Nero achieved his first real public victory against the Christian community and her leaders. On June 29, AD 65, St. Peter was publicly crucified before a Roman audience. Even the death of such a major leader was not enough, however, to break and disperse the community of Rome's Christians. Rather, Peter's remains were reverently taken and buried, and the site of his burial became a gathering place for the Christian community's worship.

St. Paul's Execution

As a Roman citizen, Paul's execution required a few more formalities. At minimum, show hearings would occur, though not necessarily hearings at which Paul would be allowed to speak. As already mentioned, his alleged crime was "being a leader among the Christians." Very little could be said by anyone to contravene that Paul eminently filled that role. These legal procedures added to Paul's time in prison, allowed him to receive more visitors to whom he could preach, and allowed him to write his final letters. Eventually, however, his execution was scheduled for June 29, the same date as Peter's to make a symbolic point, in the year AD 67.[35]

Paul's status as a Roman citizen also meant that he could not be executed in the humiliating and tortuous ways that so many of his fellow Christians were. The execution of Romans was carried out by beheading. This was seen as a quick, relatively painless, and therefore merciful death. Government officials and generals were executed above the steps leading down to the Tiber so that their heads would bounce downward into it. Paul did not have this rank and was likely publicly executed elsewhere in order to send a further message to the Christian community. Stories later emerged from those who saw the beheading that indicate that they saw even Paul's martyrdom as something miraculous from God. Some said that blood and milk flowed

---

35   As reflected in the Synaxaria of the feasts of Ss. Peter and Paul. These liturgical texts summarize the historical memory of the Church regarding the death of these saints.

when his head was severed. Others said that his head bounced three times, producing three springs of water.[36]

Members of the Christian community in Rome, despite potential for further persecution, reclaimed the head and body of Paul and took them for burial outside the walls of the city. The place of his burial was remembered and became a gathering site for Christian worshipers there. Even later pagans in the second and third centuries indicate that the location of the burial of the Christian leaders Peter and Paul were still well and publicly known. Recently, scientific dating techniques have been applied to the remains of Paul and his clothing, revealing them to be the remains of a Jewish man from the first century AD wearing clothing from Palestine.[37] One year later, Nero himself died hiding from his enemies during a tax revolt, ending both the Julio-Claudian dynasty of emperors and the first persecution of the Christians in Rome.

36   These stories first emerge in late antiquity along with the identification of a particular site on the Via Ostia as the location of St. Paul's execution. Unlike the place of Paul's burial, there is no evidence of veneration of the site between the time of Paul's death and the fifth century AD.

37   Associated Press, "Pope Says Tests 'Seem to Conclude' Bones Are the Apostle Paul's," *The New York Times,* June 28, 2009, https://www.nytimes.com/2009/06/29/science/29vatican.html.

St. Paul the Apostle

The earliest physical description that we have of St. Paul comes from outside the Scriptures. He was bald, with large, moist eyes. The latter is likely a description of the condition that afflicted his vision throughout his life. His eyebrows pointed downward. His nose was large and hooked. For most of his life, his posture was permanently stooped, and he was bow-legged. He was not very tall. These details come from a sympathetic Christian source. This is not the description of a hero of the Roman world. This is a man who spent much of his life being mocked or ignored because of his unassuming appearance.

As Paul said regarding himself, his traits made the demonstrations of God's miraculous power through him and his preaching stand out all the more. It is much easier to envision this man spending his life squirreled away somewhere devoted to Torah study than traveling thousands of miles, crisscrossing the world, and bringing non-Jewish people into a sect of Pharisaic Judaism. It is hard to imagine anyone enduring the kind of suffering that Paul endured yet continuing forward.

For the first thirty-odd years of his life, Paul was on a path. He studied the Torah. He became a Pharisee. He took what he could from the learning of the nations and used it to further understand the traditions of his fathers and his people. He traveled to Jerusalem to study with one of the greatest rabbis of his day. During his youth and education, he became zealous and radicalized, and he rode out to do battle against what he saw as heresy and a betrayal of his beloved traditions. He was wise. He was righteous.

But in his last thirty-two years, Saul of Tarsus experienced a radical change of course. He joined those whom he had formerly sought to eradicate. He devoted himself to constant travel, covering thousands of miles. Everywhere he went, he faced rejection. Even in the places where he experienced some success in organizing Christian communities, he would end up leaving town under bad circumstances. If that didn't happen, after he was gone his opponents would come in and seek to lead the community he loved and cared for in a different direction. He was beaten. He was robbed. He was imprisoned. By the end of his life, his body was badly broken and never fully or correctly healed. He spent his final days at the bottom of a cistern before being publicly executed.

From Paul's own perspective, in his own words, as he looked back he ultimately did not see a radical disjunction in his life. Rather, he came to see his whole life as an ongoing interaction between himself and God through Jesus the Messiah. Through everything that he endured, he learned, and he grew. He was able to use his great learning in the Torah to do good and build, rather than destroy and tear down. He learned contentment and endurance. He grew up and became mature. He came to know Jesus in a deep way by sharing in His life. Through coming to know the Messiah, he came to better know God Himself.

Not many people today, from the outside, would look at St. Paul and declare that they wanted to be like him. But Paul knew deep in his heart that through it all, he had become the person whom God had created him to be.

Saint Thekla

The most important extrabiblical book bearing traditions related to St. Paul is the Acts of Paul and Thekla. This text was written at some point early in the second century AD. These Acts are part of a larger Acts of Paul that was composed of several different pieces, though the first part, with St. Thekla, was by far the most popular.

Within that larger work, roughly half consists of what are intended to be two epistles of Paul to the community in Corinth. The missing letters described in 1 and 2 Corinthians gave occasion for attempted reconstructions, and these present themselves as the "lost" epistles. These two letters condemn certain heretical ideas from the second century. Certainly, Paul would have rejected the teachings in question because they are counter to his gospel. Nevertheless, there is very little of Paul per se in those letters, even with all the possible qualifiers in terms of his authorship. The final portion of the Acts of Paul presents the cause of Nero's persecution of Christians as Paul raising one of Nero's servants from the dead. Nero fears Paul's power and has him and the other Christians killed. While likely containing bits and pieces of tradition surrounding the end of Paul's life, again, there seems to be little connection to history.

Saint Thekla, however, as a person seems incontrovertibly to be a historical companion of Paul, regardless of what one thinks of the details of her life as recorded in this or other texts. The earliest Pauline traditions outside the Bible testify to her and her ministry: a major historic monastery dedicated to her in Maaloula, Syria, the earliest traditions about Paul's visit to Spain mentioning her as his companion, a fresco of Thekla with Paul near Ephesus, and iconography in a Roman catacomb.

Women were involved with Paul's ministry throughout its course. Saint Phoebe the deaconess and St. Lydia the seller of purple feature prominently in the Acts of the Apostles, and St. Priscilla is often listed before her husband, St. Aquila. A number of important women in various cities helped fund Christian communities and hosted their Lord's Day gatherings to celebrate the Eucharist. Paul's female companions and associates in ministry represent a continuation of the women disciples of Jesus the Messiah Himself. The Christian movement distinguished itself from most other Jewish movements by openly accepting and encouraging female disciples.

As has been seen, in neither Paul's ministry nor the early Christian movement as a whole did women hold the same leadership positions held by men in the communities. But that is not to say that they had no roles or that they exercised no leadership. Much of St. Thekla's behavior in the Acts conforms to the duties performed by deaconesses in the early Church. She participates in baptisms, and she preaches and teaches with Paul, especially ministering to other women. She assists Paul in every way.

At the same time, because she is a woman, Thekla faces unique challenges in the Acts that differentiate her from Paul and his ministry. Thekla is portrayed as receiving the kind of resistance from women in communities that Paul faced broadly. More centrally, however, St. Thekla faced opposition due to her intent to remain chaste. Before the rise of Christianity, the Roman world did not have a concept of female consent in sexual matters. Fathers married off their daughters to men they might never have met. The husband was legally entitled to use his wife sexually as he saw fit. For a woman to refuse a marriage, let alone all marriage, was considered perverse.

Thekla's greatest trial in the Acts is her escape from would-be suitors turned would-be rapists. They were ready to have her executed if she would not accept her place as a woman in the world at the time. This is a fate from which she was ultimately protected by God Himself when a mountain swallowed her to protect her from a mob. On this site her monastery in Syria was built.

Saint Thekla, as a disciple of St. Paul, is an important image of a female leader in the early days of the Christian movement. She made no attempt, at any time, to usurp a traditionally male role in any community. She served as she was called, assisting as she was asked. She taught and she baptized. Most importantly, she became a disciple herself. She learned Paul's gospel and was able to teach it. She was able to give guidance to her fellow women. She took charge of her own morality and chastity. She spent her life faithfully following God and seeking to fulfill the calling that He had given her in life.

Select Bibliography

The following books have shaped the thinking of the author in various ways and make significant recent contributions to our understanding of St. Paul and his writings. Inclusion here is not an endorsement of any or all of the ideas contained in any given work. As these books represent radically different viewpoints, endorsing them all together would be impossible in that regard. Nevertheless, the texts listed here contain ideas worth consideration, even if the end result of that consideration is the rejection of those ideas.

Crossan, John Dominic, and Jonathan L. Reed. *In Search of Paul*. San Francisco: HarperOne, 2004.

Eisenbaum, Pamela. *Paul Was Not a Christian: The Original Message of a Misunderstood Epistle*. San Francisco: HarperOne, 2009.

Keener, Craig S. *The Mind of the Spirit: Paul's Approach to Transformed Thinking*. Grand Rapids, MI: Baker Academic, 2016.

Penna, Romano. *Paul the Apostle*. 2 vols. Translated by Thomas P. Wahl. Collegeville, PA: Liturgical Press, 1996.

Sanders, E. P. *Paul and Palestinian Judaism*. London: SCM Press, 1977.

Thomas, Matthew J. *Paul's "Works of the Law" in the Perspective of Second-Century Reception*. Downers Grove, IL: InterVarsity Press Academic, 2020.

Thompson, James W. *Moral Formation According to Paul: The Context and Coherence of Pauline Ethics.* Grand Rapids, MI: Baker Academic, 2011.

Wright, N. T. *Paul: A Biography.* San Francisco: HarperOne, 2018.

Wright, N. T. *Paul and the Faithfulness of God.* Christian Origins and the Question of God 4. Minneapolis: Fortress Press, 2013.

SAINT PAUL'S EPISTLES
An Interpretive Translation

TO THE

GALATIANS

Paul, the apostle not from men or because of a man but because of Jesus the Messiah and God the Father who raised him from the dead, and all the brothers with me.

To the Christian communities in the province of Galatia,

Grace to you and peace from God our Father and the Lord Jesus the Messiah, who gave himself for our sins so that he might free us from this present, evil age according to the will of our God and Father. To God be glory unto ages of ages. Amen.

I am amazed at how quickly you are falling away from the One who called you in the grace of the Messiah into another gospel. There is no other gospel. There are some people troubling you who desire to twist the gospel of the Messiah. If even we ourselves, or an angel from heaven, come to you and preach a gospel to you other than what we preached, let him be accursed. As we said before and now, I say again: If anyone preaches a gospel to you other than what you received from us, let him be accursed. Am I trying to get people to praise me or God? Am I trying to make people happy? Because if I try to make people happy, then I am not a servant of the Messiah.

I brought you the knowledge, my brothers, of the gospel that I preached, that it is not a human teaching. Because neither did I receive it from any human, nor was I taught it. It was revealed to me by Jesus the Messiah. You have heard about how I lived within Judea before, that I attacked the assembled people of God viciously and tried to destroy them. I was advancing in the religion of my people beyond many of my contemporaries and countrymen because I was more zealous for the traditions of my fathers. But when God decided the time was right, God, who had chosen me when I was in my mother's womb and called me by his grace, revealed his son to me so that I would preach his gospel to the seventy nations.

I did not immediately consult with flesh-and-blood people, nor did I go back to Jerusalem to the ones sent as apostles before me, but I went to Arabia and then again returned to Damascus. After three years I went to Jerusalem to meet Peter, and I remained with him for fifteen days. I did not see any of the other apostles except for James, the Lord's brother. What I am writing to you know, I swear before God, I am not lying. Then I went to the provinces of Syria and Cilicia. The communities of the Messiah in Judea did not know me at that time. They only heard that the man who had been persecuting them before was now preaching the gospel of faithfulness to the Messiah, which he was trying to destroy beforehand, and they gave glory to God over my transformation.

After another fourteen years, I went to Jerusalem again with Barnabas and also took Titus with me. I was directed to go by a vision, and I laid out for them privately the gospel that I am preaching to the seventy nations, to those who were considered the leaders of the community there. I wanted to make sure that I was not traveling and working for nothing. But Titus, who came with me, a Greek man, was required to be circumcised because of false brothers who snuck in to try to understand our freedom that we have in Jesus the Messiah. They wanted to enslave us. I did not give in to their demands for even an hour so that the truth of the gospel could remain with you. Even the people there who were considered leaders didn't change anything about what I preach. Their reputation doesn't bother me; God is no respecter of persons.

Rather, they eventually changed their view, after seeing I had been entrusted with preaching the gospel to the uncircumcised peoples, just as Peter had been entrusted with preaching it to the circumcised people. Because the One who is working through Peter, sending him to the circumcised, is also working through me, sending me to the seventy nations. Once they knew the grace that was working in me, James, Peter, and John, who are considered the pillars of the community, offered Barnabas and me their right hands in community. We would go to the seventy nations; they would go to the Jewish people. The only request they made was that we take up a collection for the poor of Jerusalem, which I was more than happy to do.

Later, however, when Peter came to Antioch, I had to confront him face to face because he did wrong. Before certain people came from James, Peter was sharing the Eucharist with non-Jews. But when they came, he pulled back and separated himself from the non-Jewish members of the community because he was worried about how it would appear to these circumcised, Jewish brothers. He was being a hypocrite, and the other Jewish members of the community were following his lead. Even Barnabas joined him in this hypocrisy. But when I saw that they were not doing right, according to the truth of the gospel, I said to Peter before everyone, "If you, being Jewish, live like a foreigner, why do you want to force these foreigners to become Jewish? We are Jewish from birth and not sinners from the nations. But we know that it is not the Jewish way of life that makes us pleasing to God, but being faithful to the Messiah. That is why we are also faithful to the Messiah, so that we can please God through our faithfulness to the Messiah. No person is pleasing to God simply because they follow Jewish practices."

But if we, in seeking to please God in the Messiah, are found ourselves to be sinners, does that mean that the Messiah leads people into sin? Of course not. If I rebuild something that I tore down before, then I show that I am a violator of the Torah. Because through the Torah, I died to the Torah, destroying my past transgressions so that I could live to God. I was crucified with the Messiah. Now I no longer live, but the Messiah lives in me. My current life in the flesh I live faithfully to the Son of God who loved me and gave himself up for me. I don't set aside God's grace, because if I had been able to please God through my keeping of the Torah, then the Messiah would not have needed to die to give me a new beginning.

Oh, you foolish people in Galatia, who tricked you into not obeying the truth after I showed you before your eyes Jesus the Messiah crucified? Answer this one thing for me: Did you receive the Spirit of God by keeping a particularly Jewish way of life or by faithfulness to what you heard from me? How foolish are you? Having started your new life in the Spirit of God, are you now going to bring it to completion through your own abilities? You've suffered so many different struggles; was all of that for nothing? God gave you his Spirit, and he is working miracles among you. Is this because you practice a Jewish way of life or because you are living faithfully to the Messiah about whom I preached to you?

Remember that Abraham was faithful to God, and God considered him to be a righteous man. You should know, then, that those who are faithful to God are the sons of Abraham. The Scriptures knew in advance that the seventy nations would be made pleasing to God through faithfulness, so it spoke about the gospel to Abraham saying, "All the nations will be blessed in you." So, all those who are faithful to God are blessed along with faithful Abraham.

Those who keep a Jewish way of life suffer under the effects of sin in the world as much as anyone else, because the Scriptures say,

"Everyone who does not continue in all the things written in the book of the Torah, doing them all, is cursed." But in the Torah, it is clear that no one is pleasing before God, because "the righteous man will live faithfully." But the Torah way of life given to Jews is not identical to faithfulness for everyone. The Jewish person who does these things will live by them. The Messiah has freed us from the curse described in the Torah by having become accursed for us. The Scriptures say, "Cursed is everyone who hangs on a tree." This is so that the blessing of Abraham might come to the seventy nations in Jesus the Messiah. This is so that we could receive the promise of the Spirit together through faithfulness.

Brothers, let me speak to you using a human metaphor. A human who signs a covenant agreement is not able to then set it aside or add things to it. The promises were spoken to Abraham and to his descendant. It doesn't say, "and to his descendants," as to many people, but speaks of one: "and to your descendant," who is the Messiah. I say to you now, the covenant with Abraham had already been confirmed by God when the Torah was given to Israel 430 years later. The Torah given through Moses does not void or overwrite the promises made to the seventy nations in Abraham. If the promised inheritance comes to the nations through their keeping Torah, then it is not through the promise to Abraham, but God granted it as a promise to Abraham.

Why was the Torah given later, then? It was added because of the people's transgressions until the promised descendant would come. The Torah was given in the council of the angels by the hands of a mediator. A mediator implies more than one, but God is one. The Messiah is also the mediator of the Torah. Is the Torah opposed to the promises of God? Of course not. But if the Torah had been given as the means of giving new life, then it would be the Torah that made all people pleasing to God. But the Scriptures of the Torah contained and controlled all those things affected by sin until the promise that comes through faithfulness to Jesus the Messiah would be given to those who are faithful.

Before faithfulness came, the Torah was our custodian, containing our sin until the promises that come by faithfulness would be revealed. So, the Torah became our teacher, leading us to the Messiah, so that by following him faithfully we could become pleasing to God. Now that faithfulness has brought us the Spirit of God, we no longer need a teacher to know what is pleasing to God.

All of you are sons of God through faithfulness to Jesus the Messiah. As many of you as were baptized into the Messiah have been clothed with the Messiah. In your standing before God, there is no Jew or Greek, enslaved or free person, male or female, because you are all one in Jesus the Messiah. If you belong to the Messiah, then you are Abraham's descendants and heirs to the promises God gave him.

As long as an heir is a child, he is no different from any of the servants, even though technically he is going to be the owner of everything in the estate. As a child, he is under guardians and housekeepers until the time that his father decides. In the same way, when the people of the nations were children, they were held in slavery to the demonic forces active in the world. When the proper time came, God sent forth his son. He was born of a woman. He was born under the Torah so that he could redeem those under the Torah and so that everyone might be adopted as the sons of God. Because you are now sons and heirs of God, God sent the Spirit of his son into our hearts who cries out, "Father, Father." You are no longer a slave, but a son. If you are a son, you are also an heir of God.

Back before you knew God, you were enslaved to forces of nature that are not truly gods. Now that you know God, or better, now that you are known by God, how could you turn back to the weak and poor beings to be enslaved to them all over again? You observe holy days and seasons and years and feasts. I am afraid for you; maybe I have worked so hard for you for nothing. I want you to become like me, as I have become like you, my brothers. I will be honest with you. You haven't done any wrong by me. You know that I came and preached the gospel to you, from the beginning, with all my obvious weaknesses. My weakness was a test for you. You didn't hate or reject me despite my failings. Instead, you received me like an angel of God, or like Jesus the Messiah himself. How blessed are you? I testify that if you could have gouged out your own eyes and given them to me to replace mine, you would have. Am I now your enemy because I tell you the truth?

They are not pursuing you for good reasons, but to separate you from us. They want you to pursue them. It is good to zealously pursue good things, not only when I'm there with you in person. My children, I feel like I am in labor with you until you are transformed in the Messiah. I wish that I could be there in person and to speak to you in a different tone, but I am concerned for you.

Tell me, those of you who wish to start keeping Torah as Jewish people, do you listen to what the Torah says? The Scriptures say that Abraham had two sons, one by a slave woman and one by a free woman. The son born from the slave woman was the firstborn according to nature, but the one born from the free woman was the one who received Abraham's promises. Here is an allegory: There are two covenants. One covenant is from Mt. Sinai, giving birth to slavery, which is Hagar. Hagar is Mt. Sinai in Arabia. She corresponds to the present Jerusalem, who is in slavery with her children. But the heavenly Jerusalem is free and is our mother.

The Scriptures say, "Rejoice, barren woman who cannot give birth. Burst forth and rejoice, you who are not in labor, because the one who was abandoned has many more children than the one who has a husband." Brothers, you are like Isaac, children who receive the promises. Just as back then the one who was born first according to the flesh persecuted the one who was firstborn according to the Spirit of God, it is the same now. What do the Scriptures say? "Throw out the slave woman and her son. The son of the slave woman will not inherit along with the son of the free woman." Brothers, we are not children of the slave woman, but of the free woman.

The Messiah set us free so that we would be free. Don't get tangled up in a yoke that will make you a slave again. I, Paul, say to you that if you get circumcised, you will be giving up the benefits that the Messiah has given you. I can testify to you that if a man is circumcised, he must then keep the whole Torah. You will cut yourself off from the Messiah because whoever tries to be pleasing to God through keeping the Jewish way of life is giving up on the inheritance given to him by the Messiah. We, because of the Spirit of God, through our faithfulness, await the hope of being found pleasing to God. Because the Messiah has come, circumcision by itself has no power to make you pleasing to God, nor does being uncircumcised. Only through faithfulness working through love can we please God.

You were running well. Who cut you off so that you wouldn't obey the truth? You are being persuaded of something but not by the one who called you. A little bit of yeast leavens a whole lump of dough. I am confident about you in the Lord, that you won't have any other way of thinking. The person who comes and troubles you and tries to draw you away will face judgment, whoever they are. But as for me, brothers, if I try to get people from the nations to be circumcised, why are they coming after me? If I did that, maybe they would not be so offended by the gospel I preach about the crucifixion of the Messiah. I wish that those who were troubling you would just go all the way and castrate themselves.

Brothers, you were called to freedom, but not freedom that gives opportunities for your sinful desires. Instead, out of love you should serve one another. The whole Torah is summed up in this one commandment: "Love your neighbor as yourself." But if you bite and consume one another, you had better be vigilant, or you will be destroyed by one another. I say to you that you should walk in the way of the Spirit of God rather than try to gratify the sinful desires of your flesh. Our sinful flesh has desires that are opposed to the Spirit of God, and the Spirit leads us away from the desires of the flesh. They are opposed to each other, and your sinful desires will try to stop you from doing those things that you know you should do. If you follow the lead of the Spirit, you do not have to be taught by the Torah.

The sinful works of the flesh are obvious: things like sexual immorality, uncleanness, sensual indulgence, idolatry, sorcery, holding grudges against enemies, strife, jealousy, anger, contentiousness, dissensions, the forming of factions, envy, drunkenness, and lasciviousness. I warn you again, as I have before, that those who do these things will not inherit God's kingdom. But the fruit brought forth by the Spirit of God are love, joy, peace, patience, kindness, goodness, faithfulness, gentleness, and self-control. There is no commandment in the Torah that you will break if you do these things. Those of us who belong to Jesus the Messiah have crucified the sinful flesh with its passions and desires. If we live following the Spirit, we need to walk following the Spirit. We should never boast, provoking or envying other people.

Brothers, if a person is overcome by some sin, those of you who follow the Spirit should help restore him to the community in the Spirit of gentleness. Watch yourselves, though, so that you are not also tempted. Carry each other's burdens, and you will fulfill the Torah in the Messiah. If someone thinks they are something, but really, they are nothing, they are lying to themselves. Each of you judge your own works, and then boast to yourself rather than to others. Each of you must carry your own burden also. Let the person who is being taught the Word share the good things he has with his teacher. Don't be misled; God is not mocked. Whatever a person sows, that is what he will reap. The one who sows according to the sinful desires of his flesh will reap the decay of his flesh. The one who sows according to the leading of the Spirit will reap eternal life. Do not get weary in doing good; at the right time, we will reap a harvest if we don't give up. Every opportunity we get, we should do good toward everyone and especially toward our fellow faithful in God's household.

Look at the big letters in which I now write to you with my own hand.

Those who want to look good to their fellow humans want to force you to be circumcised. This is because they don't want to face any hardship for being faithful to the crucified Messiah, Jesus. These circumcised people don't keep the Torah themselves, but they want you to be circumcised so they can brag about getting converts. Far be it from me to ever boast except in the cross of our Lord Jesus the Messiah. Because of him, the world has been crucified to me, and I have been crucified to the world. I am cut off from this present world. Neither circumcision nor lack of circumcision count for anything, but a renewed creation, a new faithful follower of the Messiah does.

If you walk according to this rule I've laid out, peace be to you and mercy, and also to the Israel of God. From now on let no one trouble me, because I have the marks of Jesus' suffering on my body. The grace of our Lord Jesus the Messiah be with your spirit, brothers. Amen.

TWO LETTERS TO THE
THESSALONIANS

The First Letter

Paul and Silouan and Timothy,

To the Christian community in Thessalonica in God the Father and the Lord Jesus the Messiah,

Grace to you and peace from God our Father and the Lord Jesus the Messiah,

We give thanks to God all the time concerning all of you. We remember you in our prayers. Specifically, we remember to God our Father your faithful work and loving labor and your endurance in the hope that we have in our Lord Jesus the Messiah. Brothers whom God loves, we know that you are His chosen because our gospel came to you not only in the Word, but also in miraculous works and in the Holy Spirit of God. We know this just as certainly as you know us from when we were there with you. You follow our way of life and the Lord's. You received the Word in great struggles and difficulty, but also with the joy of the Holy Spirit of God. In that way, you became an example for all the faithful in Macedonia and in Achaia, the entirety of the provinces around you. In fact, in every place I go, your faithfulness to God is being talked about already. We don't need to tell them about it. They tell us about how well you received us and how you turned away from worshiping idols to worship the living and true God. Now we await his son from the heavens. He raised his son Jesus from the dead and delivered us from the wrath that is coming against sin in the world.

Brothers, you know that we didn't come to you for no reason. After we had suffered and been mistreated in Philippi, we still had boldness in our God to speak the gospel of God to you in the midst of a lot of struggle and difficulty. We do not preach error or uncleanness or treachery, but God has entrusted us with his gospel. So, we speak not to please people but instead to please God, who knows our hearts. We never came to you and flattered you, as you saw, nor did we use our preaching as a pretext for greed, to take money from you. God is our witness, we were not seeking to be praised by people, even you, or anybody else. We have the authority to be taken seriously as those sent by the Messiah, but we were very gentle with you, like a nursing mother with her children. We are happy that we not only shared the gospel of God with you, but we also shared our lives with you, and we love you.

Brothers, remember how we worked and struggled when we were there. We worked night and day to provide for ourselves so that we wouldn't be a burden to anyone while we preached the gospel of God to you. You saw, and so did God, the holy and just and blameless way that we treated you who are faithful, just as a father treats his own children. We exhorted you, we comforted you, and we testified to you that you should live your lives in a way that is worthy of the God who calls you to his kingdom and glory.

We never stop thanking God that when you heard about the Word of God from us, you accepted him not as the human ideas of some people, but as he is, the Word of God who is working in those of you who are faithful. Brothers, as a community you became just like the communities of God in Jesus the Messiah that are in Judea. You suffered difficulty at the hands of your own countrymen just as they did from the Judeans. Those who now oppose the communities of God in the Messiah are the same ones who killed the Lord Jesus and the prophets. They drive us out and they do not please God. They are really the enemies of humanity. They don't want us to bring the gospel to the seventy nations so that they might find salvation, and they keep filling up their sins. When that happens, God's wrath will come against them.

Brothers, we are saddened that we are separated from you in person, though not in our hearts. We are very eager to see you again face to face. We wanted to come to you multiple times. I, Paul, myself wanted to, but Satan hindered us. What hope or joy or proud crown do we have? Is it not going to be you when you stand before our Lord Jesus at his appearing? You are our glory and our joy. Eventually I decided to stay in Athens alone, and I sent Timothy, our brother and coworker for God in the Messiah's gospel. I sent him to strengthen and encourage you in your faithfulness so that no one would be shaken by the troubles and difficulties you have faced. You know that these struggles are going to come. Remember, when we were there with you, I told you beforehand that you would soon suffer difficulties, and it happened just like I said. This is why I decided to stay alone and send Timothy so that I could hear about your faithfulness in case someone had come and tempted you. I did not want all the work we did with you to come to nothing.

When Timothy came back from visiting you, he brought us a good report about your faithfulness and love. He said that you remember us fondly and want to see us in person again just as much as we want to come and visit you. Brothers, we were very encouraged by your faithfulness as we deal with our own struggles and difficulties. We can go on because we know that you are standing firm in the Lord. What can we do to thank God in return for all the joy we have received because of you before our God? Night and day we pray that we might get to see your faces again and try to help with anything you need in terms of your faithfulness. May our God and Father himself and our Lord Jesus direct our way to you. May the Lord cause you to grow and overflow with love for each other and for all people, like the love we have for you. May he strengthen your hearts and make you blameless and holy before our God and Father at the appearing of our Lord Jesus with all of his holy ones.

Brothers, finally, we want to strongly encourage and remind you in the Lord Jesus that, in the same way you heard and saw with us, you also live the same way in order to please God. You are already doing this, but you must continue to pursue it. You remember the instruction we gave you from the Lord Jesus. This is the will of God: that you be holy. You must avoid all sexual immorality. Each of you needs to control your own body and act in a way that is holy and honorable, not in a way that is lustful and passionate like those in the nations that don't know God. You must not be grasping and competing with your brothers to their detriment, because the Lord will avenge and correct all things in justice, just as we told you and warned you about. God has not called us to impurity but to holiness. The person who rejects this is not rejecting me or my opinion but is rejecting God, who gives his Holy Spirit to you.

I don't need to write to you about the love shared by brothers because you have been taught by God to love each other. You are showing love not only to your brothers in your community but also to all of Macedonia. We encourage you to do this more and more and to seek to live a quiet life, care for your families, and work with your hands as we told you when we were there. This will set an example for those outside your community, and no one in your community will have unmet needs.

Brothers, we don't want you to be ignorant about the members of your community who have fallen asleep in the Lord. We don't want you to grieve for them the way people grieve when they don't have any hope.

We know that Jesus died and rose again, so we also know that God will bring with him those who have fallen asleep in Jesus. We declare to you the Word of the Lord. We who remain alive at the appearance of the Lord do not have any advantage over those who have fallen asleep in the Lord by that time. The Lord himself will appear with a loud command, the voice of an archangel, and God's trumpet. He will descend from heaven, and the dead in the Messiah will rise first. Then immediately we who remain alive, together with them, will be caught up in the clouds to meet the Lord in the air as he descends, and then we will all be together with the Lord. Encourage each other with these words.

In terms of when all this will happen, what day and what time, we don't need to write to you. You already know that the Day of the Lord is like a thief that comes at night. When people are saying that there is peace and they are safe, then suddenly destruction comes upon them. It is like labor pains that come suddenly upon a woman with a baby in her womb. They will not escape. Brothers, you are not in the dark. The Day of the Lord shouldn't sneak up on you like a thief. You are sons of the light and of the day. We are not sons of the night or of darkness. We shouldn't be asleep the way other people are but should be prepared and ready when it comes. People who sleep, sleep at night, and people who get drunk, get drunk at night. Since we are people of the day, we should be sober. We should put on the breastplate of faithfulness and love and the helmet of salvation. God doesn't have wrath waiting for us but wants us to obtain salvation through our Lord Jesus the Messiah who died for us. Whether we watch or sleep, we should live with Him. Continue to encourage each other and support each other the way you have been.

Brothers, we encourage you to appreciate those who work among you and who are your leaders in the Lord, even when they have to correct you. Honor them greatly with love because of their work. Be at peace with each other. Brothers, correct the unruly, encourage those who are weary, help the weak, be patient with everyone. No one should pay back evil when evil is done to him. Everyone should always pursue what is good for each other and for everyone. Always be joyful. Don't stop praying. Give thanks to God for everything. This is what God wants for you in Jesus the Messiah. Do not put out the fire of the Spirit. Do not ignore the messages brought to you from God. Rather, test everything you hear. Keep what is good; throw away what is bad.

May the God of peace make you completely holy. May he preserve your spirit and your soul and your body blameless until the appearance of our Lord Jesus the Messiah. He is faithful, the God who has called you, and he will do it. Brothers, pray for us as well. Greet all the brothers with a holy kiss. In the name of the Lord, read this letter to all the brothers.

The grace of our Lord Jesus the Messiah be with you. Amen.

The Second Letter

Paul and Silouan and Timothy,

To the community of God our Father and the Lord Jesus the Messiah in Thessalonica,

Grace to you and peace from God our Father and the Lord Jesus the Messiah,

Brothers, we give thanks for you at all times. We're right to do so, because your faithfulness continues to grow, blossoming into the love that each and every one of you has for each other. As for us, we brag about you in all the communities of God. We talk about your perseverance and faithfulness in all the attacks you face and in all the struggles you're dealing with.

This is a sure sign of God's just judgment that he considers you worthy of God's kingdom, for which you are suffering. It will be just for God to repay those harming you with harm, and for you who have suffered to have rest with us when the Lord Jesus is revealed from the heavens with his mighty angels, in flaming fire. He will take vengeance on those who do not know God and who do not obey the gospel of our Lord Jesus. They will be judged to be destroyed in the age to come, away from the Lord's face and his glory and strength. When he comes to be glorified with his holy ones, he will be looked at with awe by those who have been faithful, who have been faithful to the testimony we gave to you until that day. We also pray that he will consider you worthy of our calling from God and that he will give you a good will and the power to work faithfully. Then the name of our Lord Jesus will be glorified because of you, and you will be glorified in him, through the grace of our God and the Lord Jesus the Messiah.

Brothers, we pray in light of the appearing of our Lord Jesus the Messiah, when we will be gathered together with him, that you not quickly be shaken up or troubled in your mind. Neither the Spirit nor the Word nor a letter that is really from us will tell you that the Day of the Lord already happened. Don't let anyone trick you. The Day of the Lord will not happen until first there has been a great falling away from faithfulness. Then the lawless man will be revealed, the son not of God but of destruction. This person will place himself above everything that is called a god or that is worshiped by people. He will sit down in the temple of God and claim that he himself is a god.

Don't you remember when I was there and told you these things? And you know what it is that is restraining him from appearing and that he will be revealed only at the proper time. That said, the mystery of lawlessness that he represents is already working in the world. There is one thing holding it back right now until the time comes that it is removed. When he is finally revealed, the Lord Jesus will kill him with the breath of his mouth, and he will be ended by his appearing. The lawless man's appearance is a manifestation of the works of Satan in all manner of miracles and signs and phony wonders and wicked deceit to those who are dying. They are dying, and they will be deceived because they rejected the love of God in the truth that was offered to them so that they could be saved. Because of this decision, God will send them a strong delusion, and they will live according to lies. They will be judged for not having lived according to the truth. Instead, they delighted in injustice.

Brothers, we should always thank God for you, whom the Lord loves, because God chose you from the beginning to find salvation in the Spirit of God, who makes you holy by your being faithful to the truth. He called you to this faithfulness through the gospel we preached to you so that you might ultimately receive the glory of our Lord Jesus the Messiah. Brothers, stand firm in the traditions you received from us, both in person and in letters. May our Lord Jesus the Messiah himself and God our Father, who loved us and gave us comfort regarding the age to come and good hope in his grace, encourage and strengthen your hearts to perform every good work and word.

Brothers, lastly, pray for us that the Word of our Lord may come quickly and be glorified, just as you also pray for yourselves. Pray that we would be rescued from perverse and evil people, because not everyone is faithful. But the Lord is faithful, and he will strengthen you and protect you from evil. We know regarding you that the things we preached to you in the Lord, you are doing them and will continue to do them. May the Lord direct your hearts toward the love of God and to the steadfastness of the Messiah.

Brothers, we urge you in the name of our Lord Jesus the Messiah to keep away from every brother who is living an idle life and is not living according to the tradition you received from us. You know how important it is that you live as we did. We were not idle when we were there with you. We didn't live off anyone's charity. Through hard work and struggle, working night and day, we made sure we were not burdens on anyone there. It's not that we didn't have the right to be supported by you, but we wanted to set a good example for you to imitate. When we were there with you, we told you that if someone refused to contribute to the community, then they should not live off the community. We hear that there are some people there in the community who live in an idle way, not working but getting involved in other people's business. For people like this, we urge and preach in the name of the Lord Jesus the Messiah that they work quietly and peacefully and support themselves.

Brothers, do not get tired of doing good. If anyone refuses to listen to these words of ours in this letter, take note of this person and don't associate with him so that they will be embarrassed and change their ways. But don't treat him as your enemy; correct him as your brother.

May the Lord of peace himself give you peace through everything you face in life in every way. May the Lord be with all of you.

Here is a greeting written with my own hand: Paul. This is the mark of my letter. Look at how I write.

The grace of our Lord Jesus the Messiah be with you all. Amen.

TO THE
ROMANS

Paul, a servant of Jesus the Messiah, called and sent out into the world with the gospel of God, the gospel being his promises made through his prophets in the holy Scriptures: The gospel about his son who came from the line of David the king according to human descent and was shown to be the son of God through miracles and signs by the Holy Spirit and by rising from the dead. This son is Jesus the Messiah, our Lord. From him we received grace, and by him we were sent to faithfully obey him among all the seventy nations bearing his name. Jesus the Messiah has also called you,

To all of you who are in Rome, whom God loves and whom he calls to be holy ones,

Grace to you and peace from God our Father and the Lord Jesus the Messiah,

First, I thank my God through Jesus the Messiah for all of you because your faithfulness is talked about all over the world. God is my witness, the God whom I serve with the Spirit and the gospel of his son which were given to me, that I always remember you in my prayers. I pray that I may finally get to come to see you if it is God's will. I am eager to come see you so that I can give you a blessing in the Spirit that would strengthen and encourage you in the faithfulness that you all share together. It would also be a blessing to me.

Brothers, I want to make sure that you know that there have been many times when I wanted to come and visit you in person, but I was prevented from doing it, even up until now. It would be good to be blessed by you as I have been by people from other nations. Both Greeks and barbarians, wise and foolish cultures have blessed me alike in sharing with me. I am ready to come to you who are in Rome to preach the gospel.

I am not embarrassed about the gospel I preach. The gospel contains the power of God to save everyone who is faithful to it, both Jewish people and Greeks. God reveals his justice in it, from our first believing it is true to our ongoing faithfulness. As the Scriptures say, "The just person will live faithfully."

The wrath of God is being revealed from the heavens on all the impiety and injustice of humanity. Humanity has hidden the truth from themselves to justify their wickedness. Everything that needs to be known about God they have been able to know because God has revealed it to them. Even though he is invisible, from the time when he created the world it has shown his character. His immortal power and divinity are shown in the things that he made, so they have no excuse. Humanity knew who God was, but they did not worship him as God, and they did not thank him for his creation. Rejecting God made all their thinking and their arguments empty and worthless. Their hearts became dark, and they became foolish. They claimed that they were wise, but they became foolish. The worship that they should have given to the immortal God they gave instead to idols carved to look like humans and birds and animals and reptiles.

So, God gave them what they wanted: their hearts' desires. Their bodies became unclean and dishonored, and they dishonored each other with them. They traded God's truth for a lie. They worshiped and served things that were created rather than the Creator of everything, who is blessed unto the ages. Because God gave them what they thought they wanted, their dishonorable passions, even women traded the good things for which they were created for unnatural acts. Their sexual desire burned toward each other, as also did men with other men. They continued to behave shamefully, and they received the consequences of following these lies among themselves.

Since they didn't want to know God, God let their minds know depraved things and do depraved things. They became full of injustice, evil, greed, malice toward other people, jealousy, murder, strife, lies, maliciousness, gossip, slander, hubris, arrogance, and bragging. They invented new kinds of evil. They were disobedient to their parents and other authorities God had placed over them. They became foolish, untrustworthy, heartless, and merciless. They knew what behavior was right before God and that the things they were doing were worthy of death, but they did them anyway and gave approval when other people did them.

So, no human has an excuse to judge others. When you judge someone else you are only condemning yourself, because you do the same things. But God will judge everyone who does these things according to the truth. If you judge others for things that you yourself do, do you think you won't be judged by God? Do you reject the kindness of God and his patience with you, because his kindness should cause you to repent? If your heart is hard and you don't repent, there will be wrath waiting for you on the day of wrath when the just judgments of God are revealed. God will give to each person according to what he has done in this life. To those who have continued to do good he will give glory and honor and immortality in the life of the age to come. To those who are selfish and disobey the truth, who choose instead injustice, he will give wrath and anger. Trouble and distress will come upon every human soul that does evil, first to the Jewish person and then to the Greek person. But glory and honor and peace will be given to every person who does good, first to the Jewish person and then to the Greek person. God shows no partiality.

Those who have sinned without having the Torah will perish without the Torah. Those who have sinned despite having the Torah will be judged according to the Torah. It is not those who hear the Torah who are pleasing to God. It is those who do what the Torah requires of them who are pleasing to God. When the people from the nations who didn't receive the Torah do the things the Torah requires of them based on what they see in creation, they are a Torah for themselves. They show that the things required by the Torah are written in their hearts. Their conscience is a witness to them and between them. On the day that God judges the things that people try to hide through Jesus the Messiah according to my gospel, they will be judged according to their thoughts and intentions.

But if you are Jewish and you put your trust in the Torah and take the name of God for yourself, you know the will of God. Because you have been instructed in the Torah, you should praise those things that are better. You should be a guide to those who are blind and light in the darkness of the world. You should be an instructor of the foolish and a teacher of children. In the Torah, you have the embodiment of knowledge and truth. But while you are teaching others, do you teach yourself? You preach not to steal, but do you steal? You say not to commit adultery, but do you commit adultery? You hate idolatry; do you rob the temple? You boast of your knowledge of Torah; do you dishonor God by violating the Torah yourself? The Scriptures say, "The Name of God is blasphemed among the nations because of you."

Being circumcised is valuable if you do the things the Torah requires. But if you violate the Torah, then your circumcision becomes uncircumcision. So, if someone who isn't circumcised does the things that the Torah requires, won't God consider that person to be circumcised?

Will you, a circumcised person with the knowledge of the Scriptures but who violates the Torah, judge a person who is uncircumcised but keeps the commandments of the Torah? A person is not Jewish on the outside or circumcised on the outside. A person is Jewish when their heart is circumcised. They are Jewish when they have the Spirit of God living within them, not just possessing the written Scriptures. These people don't look for praise from their fellow humans, but they seek to please God.

How is it better to be Jewish then? What is the benefit of being circumcised? It is much better, and it benefits in every way. First off, the Jewish people were entrusted with the Scriptures by God. So, what if some of them were faithless? It is not their faithlessness but God's faithfulness that wins in the end. God is true, and every human is a liar. The Scriptures say, "You will be justified in your words, and your judgments will be victorious." But if God brings about good things from the evil things we do, why does He condemn us for doing the evil things? This is a human way of thinking, but it is ridiculous. If that were true, how could God restore justice in the world? But someone might argue, if my lies end up revealing the truth of God to people more clearly, leading them to worship him, why would I be considered a sinner? Some people even claim that this is what I am teaching— that people should go out and do evil things in order to bring about good things. These people will rightly be condemned.

So then, are we Jewish people really better? No, because as we have already shown, both Jewish and Greek people have all fallen into sin. The Scriptures say, "No one is just, not even one person. There is no one who understands. There is no one who seeks after God. All of them have turned away from him, and they have all become worthless. There is no one who is doing good, not even one person. Their throat is like an open grave. Their tongues lie. Their lips are full of snake poison. Their mouth is full of cursing and bitterness. Their feet run quickly to do violence. Their ways produce ruin and misery.

They don't know the way of peace. They don't see the fear of God." We know that what the Torah says, it says to those who received the Torah so that every mouth will close and the whole world will be put right by God. No one is pleasing to God just because they are Jewish, because the Torah brings us knowledge of our sins.

Besides the Torah, God's justice has now been revealed to everyone. The Torah and the prophets witness the fact that pleasing God comes through faithfulness to Jesus the Messiah to all those who are faithful. There is no distinction. Everyone has sinned and fallen short of what God requires of them. But God sets them right as a gift of his grace through the freedom from sin that comes in Jesus the Messiah. God gave him as a purifying sacrifice. When we are faithful, we are purified from sin by his blood. This shows God's justice. God was patient with sin for a long time, and now he has revealed his solution for sin. God is just, and he is the one who sets right those who are faithful to Jesus.

So, who is there who can brag? It isn't possible. By what part of the Torah? The parts of the Torah that define what it is to be Jewish? No. What the Torah requires of everyone is faithfulness. It's right to say that a person pleases God through faithfulness, without reference to whether they are Jewish. Or are you going to say that God is only the God of the Jewish people and not also of the nations? Of course he is also God of the nations. There is one God who finds circumcised people pleasing for their faithfulness and also uncircumcised people for their faithfulness. Does this undermine the Torah and replace it with faithfulness? Not at all. This upholds what the Torah itself teaches.

Let's look at Abraham, who is our father as Jewish people, according to genealogy. If Abraham was pleasing to God because of something he did, he would have something to brag about, though not to God, of course. But what do the Scriptures say? "Abraham was faithful to God, and God considered him to be pleasing in his sight." If someone is an employee, then when they are paid, that isn't considered a gift—it's something owed. But the one who is not an employee, who is faithful to the God who sets right those who are not godly, that person's faithfulness is considered pleasing to God. Remember what David says about how blessed a person is whom God finds pleasing apart from working: "Blessed are those whose lawlessness is forgiven and whose sins are covered. Blessed is the man whom the Lord does not consider sinful."

Is this blessing just for Jewish people or also for people from the nations? We are saying that Abraham's faithfulness was considered pleasing by God. When did God say this? Did he say it when Abraham was circumcised or before he was circumcised? He said it when Abraham was still uncircumcised. God gave him the sign of circumcision as a marker of the faithfulness that made him pleasing to God before he was circumcised. This makes Abraham the father of all those who are faithful. His circumcision was the mark that he had been found pleasing by God. He is the father not only of those who are circumcised, but also of those who follow his path of being faithful while being uncircumcised. Abraham is the father of us all.

The promise made to Abraham and his descendants that they would become heirs of all the nations was not based on keeping Torah but based on faithfulness, which makes them pleasing to God. If these promises were only for those who received the Torah, then faithfulness would be unimportant, and the promises regarding the nations would not be true. The Torah brings judgment because before the commandments were given, they could not be violated. Pleasing God comes through faithfulness, so it is a gift. This makes the promises certain for all Abraham's descendants, not only to those descendants who received the Torah. The promises are for all those who are faithful like Abraham, who is the father of all of us. The Scriptures say, "I have made you a father of many nations."

Abraham faithfully followed the God who makes the dead to live again and who speaks and causes things to come into being. Abraham was faithful even when he lacked hope that he would become the father of many nations because God had said, "So many will your descendants be." His faithfulness did not weaken or waiver, even though he was a hundred years old, and his body was virtually dead already in his mind and his wife Sarah's womb was lifeless. Because of the promise of God, he did not fall away into faithlessness but rather was strengthened in his faithfulness, giving worship to God. He was completely confident that God could do what he had promised. Because of all this, his life was considered pleasing to God. This isn't written in the Scriptures just to tell us something about Abraham, but to tell us how we can please God: by being faithful to the one who raised the Lord Jesus from the dead, who was offered as a sacrifice for our wickedness and was raised to set us right before God.

Since we are pleasing to God through our faithfulness, we have peace with God through our Lord Jesus the Messiah. Through him we receive, by our faithfulness, the gift that we now hold to ourselves. We boast in the hope that we have of the glory of God, and we also boast in our struggles. We know that our struggles help us develop perseverance in our faithfulness. When we develop perseverance, we develop character. When we develop character, we have hope. We will not end up being embarrassed about our hope, because God's love has been poured into our hearts through the Holy Spirit who has been given to us.

The Messiah, while we were still weak and sick, at the right time died for the ungodly. It is rare that someone will die for a good man, but maybe for a good man someone might be willing to sacrifice his life. But this shows God's love for us that when we were still sinners, the Messiah died for us. So, we know that since we have been cleansed by his blood from sin, we will be saved by him from the judgment that is coming on the world for sinfulness. Back when we were God's enemies, we were reconciled to him by means of the death of his son. How much more, now that we're reconciled, will we be saved by his son's resurrected life. So now we rejoice in God through our Lord Jesus the Messiah, who gave us this reconciliation.

Through one person, sin came into the world. Through sin coming into the world, death came into the world. Because of this, death comes for every human: every human sins. Before the Torah, sin was active in the world, but without the Torah, sin was not recognized as sin. Death reigned over humanity from Adam until Moses—even over those who hadn't broken a commandment the way Adam did. Adam is an image of the Messiah who was coming, but the gift we receive is not exactly like Adam's sin. Because of the one sin, many people died. But many more people will receive the grace of God, his gracious gift, which is the one man, Jesus the Messiah. The gift is also different from Adam's sin in another way. The judgment received for Adam's one sin was condemnation, but the gift purifies those who receive it from many sins.

Through that one man's sin, death reigned over all people. But now through grace and the gift of purification that we have received, life will reign forever through the one man, Jesus the Messiah. Just as through one man's sin, all men fell prey to death, so also by one purifying sacrifice, all men can receive a new, purified life. Through the disobedience of one man, many people were made sinners, so also through the obedience of one man, many are purified from sin. The Torah was given so that sin could be identified as the breaking of commandments. When these many sins were identified, God's grace came even more overwhelmingly. In the same way that sin reigned in death, so also will the grace of God rule over a new, purified life that extends into the age to come, which we receive through Jesus the Messiah, our Lord.

So, am I saying that we should just go on sinning because God will give his grace to forgive our sins? Obviously not. Our sinful self died, so how can we make it live again? Don't you realize that all of you who were baptized into Jesus the Messiah were baptized into his death? Our old self was buried with him when we were baptized into his death. Then in the same way that the Messiah was raised from the dead by the Father's glory, we also were raised to live a new life. If we were united to the Messiah in the symbol of his death, we will also be united to him in his resurrection. We know that the person that we were was crucified with him, so we left our old sinful body behind and we are not slaves to sin anymore. The person who dies is liberated from sin. If we died with the Messiah, we are faithful to him so that we will live with him.

The Messiah was raised from the dead; he won't die again. Death doesn't rule over him or us anymore. His death was for the purification of us from sin, once and for all. The life he lives, he lives with God. In the same way, you should consider your sinful self to be dead, and you should live faithfully with God in Jesus the Messiah. Do not let sin reign in your mortal body by obeying its desires. Do not let yourself be a tool that sin uses for injustice. Instead, give yourself to God who gives life to those who are dead, and give yourself to him as a tool to bring justice to the world. Sin will not reign over you, so you are not judged by the Torah but by what you do with God's gift to you.

Since we are not judged by the Torah but by what we do with God's gift, should we go ahead and violate the Torah? Of course not. Don't you know that whatever you serve, whatever you obey, you will become that thing's slave? You can be a slave of sin and death, or you can be an obedient and pleasing servant of God. Give thanks to God because you used to be slaves of sin, but now your heart is obedient to God through the teaching that has been passed on to you. You have been set free from sin; now you serve to please God. I am speaking in human terms because of the weakness of your flesh. In the past, you were slaves, used as tools of uncleanness and lawlessness to create more lawlessness. Now, serve God by offering yourself to him as tools pleasing to him in order to become holy.

When you were slaves of sin, you were free from trying to please God. But what was the result of those things you did, the ones that you are now ashamed of? At the end of that road lies death. Now that you've been set free from sin, you are now slaves to God; the result you receive is holiness. At the end of this road is the life of the age to come. The wage of sin is death. The gift of God is the life of the age to come in Jesus the Messiah, our Lord.

Brothers—and now I am talking to those of you who know the Torah—are you not aware that the Torah governs a person during the time they are alive? A married woman is bound by the Torah to her living husband. If her husband dies, she is freed from the Torah's commandments regarding marriage. If her husband is alive, she is an adulteress if she is with another man. If her husband dies, she is free from the Torah's commandments on marriage and is not an adulteress if she marries another man. My brothers, in the same way, through the body of the Messiah, you have died with respect to the commandments of the Torah. You belong to the Messiah who has been raised from the dead so that you would live a life pleasing to God. While we were living our old lives, the sinful passions that we knew about through the Torah worked through us to bring about the result of death. Now we have been set free from the sins we committed under the Torah. We died to those sins that bound us so that we can serve God in a new life through the Spirit, not in the old way according to identifying sins and trespasses through the Torah.

Are we saying that the Torah is sinful? Of course not. I wouldn't have known what sin was if not for the Torah. I wouldn't have known what covetousness was if I had not read, "Do not covet." Sin used this commandment as a way to cause all kinds of covetousness in me. Without the Torah, sin is dead. I was alive once, without the Torah. Once I knew the commandments, sin came to life in me, and I died. The commandment that was meant to bring life ended up bringing me death. Sin in my life used this commandment to trick me and then to kill me. The Torah is holy, and the commandments are holy and right and good. Did something good become death for me? Of course not. But sin was working death in me, and the Torah, which is good, showed sin to be sin. Through learning the commandments, I became aware of how incredibly sinful I was.

We know that the Torah comes from the Spirit of God. But I was living from my flesh, which had been sold as a slave to sin. I didn't know what I was doing. What I didn't want to do, I did. What I hated, I did. I acknowledged that the Torah was good, and I wanted to keep it, but I didn't. At that point, I wasn't doing anything; it was the sin that was living in me that was acting. There was nothing good living in me, in my flesh. I was able to desire good things, but I couldn't do them. I wanted to do good, but the evil things I didn't want to do, I did over and over again. When I did what I didn't want to do, it wasn't really me doing it; it was the sin living in me doing it through me. The Torah showed me how to desire to do what is good and that evil was present in me. I delight in God's Torah in my inner person. But I saw another principle working in my body, warring against the Torah in my mind and making me a captive of the principle of sin. I was a wretched man. Who could set me free from my dead body? Thank God, I was set free by Jesus the Messiah, our Lord. With my mind I served the Torah of God, but with my flesh, the principles of sin.

In Jesus the Messiah, we no longer stand condemned. We do not live in the old way, according to the flesh, but according to the Spirit of God. The Messiah Jesus has set you free to follow the Torah in the life of the Spirit rather than the principles of sin and death. The Torah was powerless to give life because of the weakness of our flesh. God, by sending his son in what looked like sinful flesh, dealt with sin by judging sin in the flesh. So, the ability to please God in the Torah was given to those who do not follow the sinful desires of the flesh but who follow the Spirit of God. Those who follow the sinful desires of the flesh think about satisfying those desires, but those who follow the Spirit of God think about how to please the Spirit. Satisfying the desires of the flesh brings death. Pleasing the Spirit brings life and peace. Seeking to please the desires of the flesh means opposing God, because those desires don't care about God's Torah. They can't care about God's commandments. So those who follow the desires of their sinful flesh can't please God.

You are not living to satisfy the desires of the flesh, but to please the Spirit if the Spirit of God dwells in you. If someone does not have the Spirit of the Messiah, then he does not belong to the Messiah. If the Messiah is in you, then your old self is dead because of its sin, but the Spirit has made you alive through the purification of your body. If the Spirit who raised Jesus from the dead dwells in you, then Jesus who was raised from the dead will make your mortal body alive again through his Spirit, who dwells in you.

Brothers, we don't owe our flesh anything such that we would need to satisfy its desires. If you live seeking to satisfy your sinful flesh, you are about to die. If the Spirit in you puts the sinful flesh to death, then you will live. Whoever follows the leading of the Spirit of God is a son of God. You have not received a Spirit who would make you a slave to fear. You have received the Spirit who makes you a son, by whom we cry, "Father, Father." The Spirit testifies within us that we are children of God. If we are children, then we are heirs. If we are God's heirs, we are coheirs with the Messiah. We suffer like he did so that we will be glorified together with him. But the sufferings that we deal with now simply don't compare to the glory that will soon be revealed in us.

The whole creation waits impatiently for the sons of God to be revealed. Creation was subjected to emptiness and suffering not on its own, but because of Adam, who subjected it. Creation hopes to be set free from slavery to death and decay. This freedom will come with the glory of the children of God. All creation groans and struggles up until this very day. We also groan, because we have the Spirit as the beginning and first taste of the glory that is coming. We who are adopted sons of God wait for our bodies to be set free. We have been saved for this coming glory for which we hope. But if we see something, it is no longer hoped for. Who hopes for something that they already have? Because we hope for something that hasn't come yet, we wait patiently.

The Spirit works with us to help us in our weakness. We don't even really know what we should pray for, but the Spirit knows and prays within us with the yearnings that we can't express in words. God, who knows our hearts, knows our mind through the Spirit. The Spirit intercedes with God for the holy ones.

We know that for people who love God, God works everything that happens to be ultimately for their good. He has called them for a particular purpose, those whom God knew beforehand. God set things in order in advance so that they could be shaped after the likeness of his son, so that he would be the firstborn among many brothers. Having set things in order, he then called them. Those he called, he also set them right. Once he had purified them and set them right, he shared his glory with them. What more can we say? If God is on our side, who can oppose us? God didn't spare his own son but offered him as a sacrifice for all of us. If he was willing to do that for us to be saved, what will he refuse to offer us?

Who can make accusations against those whom God has chosen for a purpose? God is the one who sets people right, so who is it who would condemn them? The Messiah, Jesus, who died and was raised from the dead, is at the right hand of God, advocating on our behalf. What can separate us from the love of the Messiah? Trouble or strife or persecution or famine or nakedness or danger or violence? No. The Scriptures say, "For your sake, we face death all day. We are treated like sheep to be slaughtered." But even when we face all these things, we are completely victorious over them because Jesus loves us. I am convinced that neither death nor life, neither angels nor demons nor principalities, neither things in the present nor things in the future, nor powers, neither anything in the heights of the heavens nor the depths of hell, nor anything created on earth will ever be able to separate us from the love of God shown to us by the Messiah Jesus, our Lord.

What about the Jewish people who haven't accepted the Messiah? Have they been separated from the love of God? I tell you the truth about the Messiah, and I have two witnesses, my conscience and the Holy Spirit, that this issue causes me great pain. My heart is continually sorrowful. I would rather be cursed myself and separated from the Messiah myself if it would mean that my brothers, who are my people according to heredity, the Israelites, would all embrace him. The Jewish people were the first to receive the promises of being adopted as sons of God and of the glory of the age to come. They received the covenants. They were given the Torah. They were taught the correct way to worship God. They received the promises of Abraham, Isaac, and Jacob. The Messiah, who is God over all people, comes from the Jewish people according to his genealogy.

The Word of God didn't fail. Not everyone who is an Israelite by birth is really part of the Israel of God. Not everyone descended from Abraham is really a child of Abraham. From the very beginning, it says, "Your descendants will be counted through Isaac." This isn't talking about biological descendants, but about those who are considered the children of God. It is the children who inherit the promises to Abraham who are really his children. The Word promised this: "When the right time comes, Sarah will have a son." The same is true with Rebecca, who bore children with our father Isaac. Before her twins were born or had done anything good or evil, God chose one of them to inherit the promises. This wasn't because Jacob was somehow better than Esau, but it was based on God's own purposes. Rebecca was told, "The older will serve the younger." The Scriptures say later on about the nations descended from them, "Jacob I have loved, and Esau I have hated."

Is God unjust for having chosen one particular line to receive his promises rather than giving them to every descendant of Abraham? Of course not. God told Moses, "I will have mercy on whom I want to have mercy, and I will have compassion on whom I want to have compassion." It is not about what human people want or try to get God to do, but the mercy of God. The Scriptures say to Pharaoh, "This is why I brought you to power in Egypt, so that I could reveal my power to the world and my Name would be spoken all over the earth." God shows mercy to whomever he wants, and he hardens whomever he wants. God is free to give people different purposes and callings in their lives.

Why would God judge someone like the wicked Israelites then? If God knew they would reject him, why would he call them, and why would he blame them for not answering? Who is a human to judge God? Can someone who is made by God demand to know why he was made the way he was instead of the way someone else was? A potter will take a lump of clay and make two pots. One he will set on the shelf and decorate, and another one he will use for a toilet. What we really see is God's patience. He created people and gave them different gifts and blessings, even those who were wicked and whom he knew would come to destruction. He did this out of his kindness and to make it even clearer how abundantly he loves those on whom he would end up having mercy, in preparing things in advance for them to share in the glory of the age to come. This is who we are, not only those of us who are Jewish but also those who are from the seventy nations.

Hosea says, "I will call those who are not my people, my people. She who hasn't been loved, I will love her. And in the very time and place when it was said, 'You are not my people,' they will be called sons of the living God." Isaiah also spoke out about Israel: "Although the number of the sons of Israel are like the sands of the sea, only a small remainder will be saved. God will quickly bring this to a conclusion on the earth." Isaiah said in advance, "If the Lord of the heavenly hosts had not left us any descendants, we would have been like Sodom and Gomorrah."

What are we saying? Are we saying that those from the nations who were not trying to please God have been found pleasing to God in their faithfulness? Are we saying that Israel, who sought to please God by keeping Torah, did not succeed in pleasing him by Torah keeping? Why would that happen? The Jewish people who failed were not being faithful to God but thought their identity as Jewish people would make them pleasing to God. Because of this, they tripped over a block that made them stumble. The Scriptures say, "I am placing in Zion a stone over which people will stumble and a rock that will offend people. But the person who is faithful to him will not ever be ashamed."

Brothers, what I want in my heart and what I pray for to God is the salvation of the Jewish people. I can testify to you that they are very zealous for God, but they lack knowledge. They don't know how to please God, and so they try to find ways to please him themselves. They won't submit to the means he's given them to please him. The purpose of the Torah is to point to the Messiah. Everyone who is faithful to him is pleasing to God. Moses writes about the way to please God in the Torah, "The person who does these commandments will live because of them." He says this about faithfully pleasing God: "Do not say in your heart, 'Who will go up into the heavens?'"—that is, to bring the Messiah to earth—"or, 'Who will go down into the abyss?'"—that is, who will raise the Messiah from the dead? What does Moses say?

"What you need to do is right at hand. It is in your mouth and in your heart." What we need to do is to be faithful, as we preach.

If you confess the Lord Jesus with your mouth and you are faithful in your heart to God, who raised him from the dead, you will be saved. A faithful heart is pleasing to God, and the mouth that confesses will be saved. The Scriptures say, "Everyone who is faithful to him will not ever be ashamed." There is no difference in this regard between a Jewish person and a Greek person. The same Lord is the Lord of both of them, and He bestows bountiful blessings on all those who worship him. Everyone who worships the Lord will be saved. But how can you worship him if you haven't been faithful to him? And how can you be faithful to him if you've never heard of him? And how can anyone hear of him unless he is preached? And who will preach about him if no one is sent out? The Scriptures say, "How beautiful are the feet of those who preach the gospel of peace, those who preach the gospel of good things."

But not everyone in Israel obeyed the gospel. Isaiah says, "Lord, who has been faithful to what they heard from us?" So, faithfulness comes from hearing—specifically, hearing the news about the Messiah. But had they really not heard? The Scriptures say, "Their voice has gone out into all the earth and their words to the ends of the inhabited world." Did Israel really not know? First, Moses says, "I will provoke you using a nation that isn't really a nation. I will use an ignorant nation to make you angry." Isaiah boldly says, "Those who weren't seeking me found me. I revealed myself to those who weren't asking about me." As for Israel, he says, "All day long I have reached out my hands to a people who are disobedient and rebellious."

So, I ask, did God reject his own people? Of course not. I am an Israelite myself. I am a descendant of Abraham from the tribe of Benjamin. God did not reject his people whom he knew beforehand. Don't you remember what Elijah says in the Scriptures when he pleads with God about Israel? "Lord, they have killed your prophets and torn down your altars. I am the only one left, and now they want to kill me." But what was the answer Elijah was given? "I have seven thousand men remaining who have not worshiped Baal." The same is also true now. There is a remnant who has answered God's call and received his gift. But if this is a gift, then it is not based on their Jewish identity. If it were, then it wouldn't be a gift to the remnant that receives it. If it was based on their Jewish identity, it would not be a gift, and they all would have received it.

What Israel as a whole was seeking, they have not found as a whole. But those who answered God's call have received it, and the rest are now hardened in their hearts. The Scriptures say, "God gave them a spirit of drunkenness, eyes that don't see, and ears that don't hear until this very day." David says, "Let their table be a trap and a snare and a stumbling block. This is the wages of their rebellion. Let their eyes be dark and not see. Let their backs be bent over."

So, since they have stumbled, have they fallen completely so that they can't get back up? Of course not. God is using the gospel of salvation going to the nations to make them jealous so that they will repent of their sins. If God is bringing such wonderful things to all the people of the world because of the Jewish people's sins, and their failure has given these blessings to the nations, how much more will God bless the whole world when they repent and return to him?

Now I am talking to those from the nations since I am the one who was sent by God to the nations. I increase my ministry if, by bringing the nations to worship the true God, I make some of my own people jealous, and they find salvation. If their rejection of the Messiah has led to the whole world being reconciled to God, then what will their reconciliation to God bring about if not the resurrection of the dead?

If the first portion of a lump of dough is holy, then the whole lump is holy. If the root of a tree is holy, then the branches are also holy. But imagine that some branches were broken off this holy tree and other branches from a wild olive tree were grafted in their place. You who are from the nations are these branches, and you are fed by the root of the olive tree. You have nothing to brag about regarding the branches that were cut off for you to be grafted in. It is the root that feeds and supports you, not the other way around. You may say, "Those branches were broken off so that I could be grafted in." That's true. But they were broken off because of their own faithlessness, and you were grafted in because of your faithfulness. Don't get too full of yourself. If God didn't spare those natural branches, why would he spare you if you don't remain faithful? God is kind, but he can also be harsh. He was harsh with those who were cut off. He is kind to you who were grafted in, provided you continue faithfully in that kindness. If not, you will be cut off, too. As for them, if they don't continue in their faithlessness, they will be grafted back in. God is certainly able to graft them in again. If you, who were wild olive branches from another tree, could be grafted in, how much easier would it be to graft branches back in that belonged to the tree originally?

Brothers, I don't want you to be ignorant about what is happening with Israel. I want you to use wisdom to understand this. Part of Israel by birth has been hardened so that people from all the seventy nations can come in and fill up Israel. Once this has happened, then all of Israel will be saved. The Scriptures say, "The deliverer will come from Zion. He will remove godlessness from Jacob. This will be my covenant with them: I will take away their sins." Because they reject the gospel, you may think of them as your enemies. But in terms of their calling, they are loved by God because of Abraham, Isaac, and Jacob. The gifts and the calling of God are never taken away. You were once disobedient to God, but now he has shown you mercy for that disobedience. A part of the Jewish people is now disobedient, and that resulted in you being shown mercy, but they will also have mercy shown toward them when they repent. God allows all of us to fall into disobedience so that he can show mercy to all of us.

How deep are God's knowledge and his wisdom? Who can figure out his plans or comprehend all that he does for us? Who knows the Lord's mind or can try to offer him advice? Who has done something for God so that God would owe him something? Everything comes from him. Everything is accomplished through him. Everything is ultimately for him. To him be glory unto the ages. Amen.

Brothers, I encourage you because of God's compassion to offer your bodies to him as a living sacrifice that will please him. This is the worship that he expects of you. Don't conform yourself to the ways of this age, but be transformed by God by having your mind made new. This new understanding will allow you to understand what God's will is, what is good, what pleases him, and what will bring you to maturity. I say to you because of the gift given to me, none of you should think more highly of yourself than you ought. Think in a clear and sober way as God has gifted you, and be faithful.

One body is made up of many different parts. The parts are not all the same and don't all do the same thing. In the same way, all of us make up the body of the Messiah. Each of us is one of the body parts. We each have different gifts as they have been given to us by God. Some have the ability to teach and direct others in so far as they themselves are faithful. Others have gifts to use to help others. Others preach the gospel. Others are able to give to the community generously of their finances. Others are able to lead the community diligently. Others are able to resolve problems and reconcile people with gentleness and joy.

Your love for each other must not be fake. You should hate evil and cling to what is good. Love each other, be devoted to each other, and honor each other. Don't stop being diligent. Serve the Lord in the new life given by the Spirit. Rejoice in hope. When you face troubles, be patient. Pray continually. Contribute to the needs of God's holy ones. Pursue hospitality. Bless those who attack. Bless them—don't curse them. When someone is rejoicing, rejoice with them. When someone is weeping, weep with them. Try to see things the same way. Don't try to fit in with lofty and important people, but try to be with lowly people and the poor. Don't think that you yourself are very wise. When someone does evil to you, don't do evil to them in return. Give every person what they are due. As much as you can, live at peace with everyone.

Beloved, don't take revenge, but wait for God's judgment. The Scriptures say, "Revenge belongs to me. I will repay, says the Lord." If your enemy is hungry, feed him. If he is thirsty, give him something to drink. If you do this, it will be like dumping hot coals on his head. Don't try to fight evil with more evil. Instead, defeat evil by doing good.

Everyone should be obedient to the authorities that God has put over them. There is no one who has authority who wasn't given that position by God. All existing authorities were instituted by God. If you resist these authorities, you are resisting the authority God has ordained. If you rebel, you will bring judgment on yourself. People who do good should not be afraid of authorities; those who do evil should. Do you want to not be afraid of the authorities? Then do good, and the authorities will praise you. Everyone in authority is a servant of God appointed for your good. But if you do evil, you should be afraid because the authorities have the ability to use violence against you. The authorities are servants of God to bring his wrath to those who do evil. You should be obedient not only because you fear wrath, but also because you want to have a good conscience. So, pay your taxes. The authorities are God's public ministers, and this is what they attend to. Pay everyone what they are due. If they are due taxes, pay the taxes. If they are due tolls, pay the tolls. If they are due respect, give them respect. If they are due honor, honor them.

Do not owe anyone anything except the love you owe each other. If you love others, you fulfill all the Torah. You will not commit adultery. You will not murder. You will not steal. You will not covet. You can name any other commandment in the Torah; all of them really require just one thing: "Love your neighbor as yourself." The person who loves his neighbor doesn't do evil, so love fulfills the whole Torah.

Remember that our time in this age is short. It is time for you to wake up from your sleep. Our salvation is closer every day. The night is almost over, and the dawn is coming. We need to throw away the things that are done in the darkness and put on the armor of the light. We need to walk at all times the way we do in public, in the daytime. Don't party and get drunk. Don't be sexually immoral and yield to your sinful desires. Don't argue, and don't be jealous. Put on the Lord Jesus the Messiah, and don't do anything to satisfy the sinful desires of the flesh.

You should receive a person who is wobbly in their faithfulness, not judge him or demand reasons for his behavior. One person can remain faithful to God while eating whatever is put in front of him; another person needs to eat only vegetables. The person who eats anything should not judge the person who doesn't. The one who doesn't also shouldn't judge the person who does. God has received both of them. You don't criticize someone else's servant. It is only the master's opinion of his servant that is important. The Lord is able to support and strengthen all of his servants.

Jewish members of your community observe the Sabbath day. Those of you from the nations consider every day the same. This way of life is good for each of you. The Lord honors the Sabbath day for the one who observes the Sabbath. The Lord does not demand that the one who doesn't observe the Sabbath keep it. The one who eats anything, the Lord eats with him in fellowship when he gives thanks to God for the food. The Jewish members of your community who follow a careful diet also give thanks to God when they eat. No one really lives by himself. No one really dies by himself. While we live, we live before the Lord. When we die, we die before the Lord. Whether we live or die, we still belong to the Lord. This is why the Messiah died and then lived again—so that he would rule the dead and the living.

But as for you, why do you judge your brother? Why do you sometimes even hate your brother? Every one of us will stand before the throne of God to be judged. The Scriptures say, "'As surely as I live,' says the Lord, 'every knee will bow to me, and every tongue will confess to God.'" Each of us should be more concerned with the account that we will have to give to God on that day.

We must stop judging each other. Instead, we need to focus on making sure we don't do anything that might cause our brother to fall into sin. I know and I am fully convinced that because of the Lord Jesus, nothing is unclean in and of itself. But if someone considers something unclean, that thing is unclean for him. If you cause pain to your brother over food, you aren't loving anymore. Why would you harm someone, for whom the Messiah died, over food? Don't let something you think is good become something evil. The kingdom of God is not about eating well and drinking well. The kingdom of God is about pleasing God, about peace and joy that comes from the Holy Spirit. The one who serves the Messiah in these ways is pleasing to God and will receive a good report from his fellow men also.

We need to pursue peace and help build each other up rather than tear each other down. Don't destroy the work that God is doing over food. Everything is clean, but if eating will lead him into sin, eating is wrong for that person. It's better to just not eat meat or not drink wine or to give up anything else that causes your brother to fall into sin or become sick. Be faithful before the eyes of God. Blessed is the person who doesn't condemn himself by what he gives his approval to. The person who sees that it is wrong but who eats will be condemned because it is not an act of faithfulness. It is an act of rebellion for him. Anything you do that you don't do out of faithfulness, to please God, is sin.

We who are stronger need to help carry the weakness of our weaker brothers and not try to please ourselves. We should each try to please our neighbor for their good and to help strengthen them. For the Messiah himself didn't try to please himself. The Scriptures say, "The insults of those who insult you have fallen on me." All the things that were written in the past were written to teach us. Through our endurance in hard times and the encouragement we receive from the Scriptures, we have hope for the future. May God who endures and encourages help you to see things the same way the Messiah Jesus does. Then with one heart and one mouth you will worship the God and Father of our Lord Jesus the Messiah. Receive each other the way the Messiah received you, and give glory to God.

I say to you that the Messiah came as a servant to the Jewish people to attest to God's truth and to confirm the promises given to Abraham, Isaac, and Jacob. He also came to the people of the nations to give them mercy so that they would come to worship God. The Scriptures say, "This is why I will praise you among the nations and I will sing your name." They also say, "Rejoice, all of you nations, with your people." They also say, "Praise the Lord, all you nations, and praise him, all you peoples." And Isaiah says, "The Messiah will come from the root of Jesse, and he will rule over the nations. In him, the nations will be given hope." May the God of hope fill you all with joy and peace through your faithfulness so that you will have abundant hope in the power of the Holy Spirit.

Brothers, I am convinced concerning you that you are full of goodness and knowledge, and you are able to correct each other when you need to. But I have written to you anyway, partly to remind you of the gift that God has given to me to be his minister of Jesus the Messiah to the nations. He has given me the gift of serving as a priest of the gospel of God, bringing him a pleasing offering from all the nations who have been made holy by the Holy Spirit.

If I wanted to, I could boast about the Messiah Jesus and things related to my calling from God. But I wouldn't dare to speak in this way. I only speak of what the Messiah has done through me in bringing the nations to obey God, in my words and my deeds, in miraculous signs and wonders, in the miraculous Spirit of God. I have gotten to proclaim the gospel of the Messiah from Jerusalem all the way around Illyricum. I don't want to go and preach the gospel in places that have already heard about the Messiah because I don't want to take over what someone else has worked to build. The Scriptures say, "People will see him without him being announced, and people who have not heard of him will come to understand." This is part of what has stopped me from coming to visit you in person.

Since I don't really have a place in these regions anymore, I have wanted to come and visit you for many years. When I eventually go to Spain, I hope that I will get to pass through Rome and visit you. I hope that seeing you will equip me for the rest of my journey. But now, I am on my way to Jerusalem to minister to the holy ones there. Macedonia and Achaia gave contributions to the poor people among the holy ones in Jerusalem. They realize that in certain ways they are in their debt. The people of the nations have gotten to share in the Spirit who first came in Jerusalem, so it is only fair that they ought to share their material things with them. Once I have finished this journey and handed over the collection to them, I will leave to head to Spain, passing through Rome first. I know that when I come to you, I will come full of the blessings of the Messiah.

Brothers, I encourage you by our Lord Jesus the Messiah and by the love of the Spirit of God to make an effort with me in prayer for me to

God. I hope that he will deliver me from those people in Judea who refuse to be persuaded about the Messiah. I also hope that when I get to Jerusalem, the holy ones there will find my service acceptable. If it is God's will, I will come to you joyfully to be refreshed by you. May the God of peace be with all of you. Amen.

I recommend our sister Phoebe to you. She is a deaconess in the community in Cenchrea. Receive her in the Lord in a way that is worthy of holy ones and help her with anything she might need. She has been a patroness of many people, including myself.

Greet Priscilla and Aquila, my coworkers, in the Messiah Jesus. They would lay down their lives for me. Not only do I thank them, but the communities in all the nations do also. Also greet the community that meets at their home.

Greet Epenetus, whom I love. He is one of the firstfruits of the region of Asia for the Messiah.

Greet Mary, who has worked very hard for you.

Greet Andronicus and Junias, who are family to me and prisoners like me. They are notable among those sent out before me by the Messiah.

Greet Ampliatus, whom I love in the Lord.

Greet Urbanus, our coworker in the Messiah, and Stachys, whom I love.

Greet Apelles, of whom the Messiah approves.

Greet the whole extended family of Aristobulus.

Greet Herodion, who is family to me.

Greet the whole extended family of Narcissus, those who belong to the Lord.

Greet Tryphena and Tryphosa, who are working hard in the Lord.

Greet Persis, whom I love, who has worked hard in the Lord.

Greet Rufus, who was called by the Lord, and his mother, who is like a mother to me as well.

Greet Asyncritus, Phlegon, Hermes, Patrobas, Hermas, and the brothers who are with them.

Greet Philologus and Julia, Nereus and his sister, and Olympas and all the holy ones with them.

Greet each other with a holy kiss. All the Messiah's communities greet you.

Brothers, I encourage you to watch out for divisions and causes of sin that go against what you have been taught. Turn away from them. The kind of person who causes these things doesn't serve our Lord the Messiah, but their own desires. They speak well, and they flatter people to trick people whose hearts are naïve. Word of your obedience has spread all over, and so I rejoice. I want you to be clever concerning what is good and innocent about evil. The God of peace will crush Satan under your feet very soon. The grace of our Lord Jesus the Messiah be with you.

Timothy, my coworker, greets you, as well as Luke, Jason, and Sosipater, who are family to me.

I, Tertius, the one who is writing down Paul's words in this letter, also greet you in the Lord.

Gaius, my host, greets you and all his community. Erastus the steward of the city and his brother Quartus greet you.

To the one who is able to make you strong as I teach in my gospel and my preaching of Jesus the Messiah, who was a mystery in ages past and is now revealed, and also in the writings of the Prophets according to the commandment of the God of the age to come, and for faithful obedience, who has been made known to all the nations, to the only wise God through Jesus the Messiah, whose glory is unto the ages of ages, Amen.

TO THE
CORINTHIANS

Paul, who was called and sent by the Messiah Jesus by God's will, and his brother Sosthenes,

To the community of God in Corinth that has been made holy in the Messiah Jesus and is called to be holy, and also all those who worship our Lord Jesus the Messiah in every place, whether gathered by another apostle or by us,

Grace to you and peace from God our Father and the Lord Jesus the Messiah,

I constantly thank God for you and for the gift God has given you in the Messiah Jesus. You have gained so much knowledge through him, and he has transformed the way you speak. The testimony I give about the Messiah is confirmed by how you live. I don't want you to be lacking in even one of the gifts of God while we await our Lord Jesus the Messiah being revealed from the heavens. He will also provide for you until the end so that on the day of our Lord Jesus the Messiah, you will be blameless. God is faithful. He has called you to have communion with his son, Jesus the Messiah, our Lord.

Brothers, I encourage you in the name of our Lord Jesus the Messiah that you all speak with one voice and that there not be divisions among you. I want you to be brought together in the same mind and in the same way of thinking. Brothers, Chloe's family told me that there are arguments happening within your community. I am told that some of you say, "I am a follower of Paul" or "I am a follower of Apollos" or "I am a follower of Peter," and only a few, "I am a follower of the Messiah." Is the Messiah divided up? Was Paul crucified for you? Were you baptized in the name of Paul? I thank God that I didn't baptize any of you except for Crispus and Gaius, so that none of you claim that you were baptized in my name. I did baptize Stephanas's family, now that I think of it. I don't remember if I baptized anyone else. But the point is, the Messiah didn't send me just to baptize people and make followers. He sent me to preach the gospel. I didn't preach the gospel with brilliant rhetoric, but I trusted in the power of the Messiah's cross.

The message about the Messiah's cross seems foolish to those who are dying, but to those of us who are being saved it is the miraculous power of God. The Scriptures say, "I will destroy the wise men's wisdom, and the great ideas of the intellectuals I will set aside." Who is wise? Who is an expert in the Scriptures? Who is the great debater of our time? Hasn't God made all the world's wisdom look foolish? For all the world's wisdom, they didn't know God. So, God, in his wisdom, used preaching that seems foolish to save those who are faithful. Jewish people want to see miracles. Greek people want philosophical arguments. But we preach that the Messiah has been crucified. This is scandalous to Jewish people and seems foolish to Greek people, but to Jewish and Greek people who are called by God's Messiah, it is the miraculous power and wisdom of God. God's foolishness is wiser than human wisdom. God's weakness is stronger than human strength.

Brothers, think about the calling that you received from God. Not many of you were brilliant scholars. Not many of you were powerful people. Not many of you were born from noble families. But God called you nonetheless so that you, being "foolish," could put the wise men to shame. He called you who are weak, in terms of how the world looks at things, in order to embarrass the powerful. He chose those of you who are from the lower classes to shame those who are of noble birth. He chose you even though some of you were despised by society. God called you who were nothing in the sight of the world to abolish the way the world currently is. This is why nobody can brag in the presence of God. But you have now received the Messiah Jesus who has given us wisdom from God. He has purified us, made us holy, and redeemed us. The Scriptures say, "If someone is going to boast, he should only boast about the Lord."

Brothers, I didn't come to you with profound rhetoric or philosophical arguments. I preached to you the testimony of what God has done. I decided not to preach or teach anything to you when I was there except for Jesus the Messiah, that he was crucified. You saw while I was with you that I often had to deal with weakness, fear, and illness. What I had to say, as well as my preaching, were not persuasive, rousing speeches, but you saw the miraculous power of the Spirit of God. You are not called to be faithful to some human philosophy but to be faithful to what God has done among you.

We talk about deeper and more complicated things with those who are mature members of the community. But these things that we talk about are also not the philosophy of our time or of the rulers of this time who are collapsing and failing. Even in these cases, we talk about God's wisdom. The gospel was a mystery that was hidden by God from before the world was created and is our glory. None of the rulers of this world knew or understood it. If they had, they would not have crucified the glorious Lord. The Scriptures say, "Something that no one has seen or heard or considered in their heart has now come. God prepared it for those who love him." This mystery has now been revealed by God through his Spirit to us. The Spirit of God knows everything, even the deep things of God. A human person's spirit knows everything about them. In the same way, no one knows the fullness of who God is except the Spirit of God.

We haven't received the spirit of this world or this age. We have received the Spirit who is from God so that we can come to know God as he reveals himself to us. You can't teach someone who God is with human words or philosophical arguments. You must be taught by the Spirit, who can bring your spirit to know God. People don't just naturally understand what the Spirit of God has to teach. They think it is foolish, and they don't understand them. They are discerned only through the Spirit. If you have the Spirit of God, you can understand all these things, but other people will not be able to understand you. Who can claim to understand God's mind? Who can try to teach him something? We have the mind of the Messiah.

Brothers, when I was first there, I couldn't speak to you about the things of the Spirit; I had to speak in human terms because you were newborn babies in the Messiah. I gave you milk to drink, not solid food, because you weren't ready for it yet. Many of you are still not ready for it because you still think in human terms. There wouldn't be jealousy and disputes in your community if you weren't still thinking and living in a human way. Why would someone say, "I follow Paul" or "I follow Apollos" if you weren't thinking about your community as a human organization?

Who is Apollos, anyway? Who is Paul? We are servants of God who taught you how to be faithful to what you received from the Lord. I planted seeds, Apollos came and watered them, but God caused you to grow. The person who planted the seeds and the person watering them aren't who you should thank, but God, who causes you to grow. As for Apollos and myself, we will receive our reward from that same God for our work. We are workers in God's fields. You are the building that God is building. I use the gifts God has given me like a wise builder. I laid a foundation, but other people are building on it. Each of you should be careful, though, what you build, because there will not be any other foundation that gets laid in the future. Jesus the Messiah is the foundation. Some of you are building on that foundation with gold and silver and precious gems. Others are building on it with wood and hay and straw. When the day of the Lord comes, fire will be put to it, and everyone will know what it was that was built. Gold, silver, and gemstones will survive the fire. Wood, hay, and straw will be burned up and leave nothing left. Everyone who is saved will pass through this fire.

You are God's temple, and so the Spirit of God lives in you. If someone destroys the temple of God, God will destroy him. God's temple, the temple that you are, is holy. Don't be fooled. If someone there thinks that he is wise by the standards of this world and this time, he needs to become foolish with us so that he can become truly wise. This world's wisdom is foolishness to God. The Scriptures say, "He catches the wise in the subtleties of their own arguments." The Scriptures also say, "The Lord knows the thoughts of the wise. He knows that they are worthless." None of you should be proud of anything human. Everything is yours now. Paul, Apollos, Peter, the world, life, death, things right now, things in the future—these things are all yours now because you belong to the Messiah, and the Messiah belongs to God.

When thinking about people, you should think of them as servants of the Messiah and caretakers of God's mysteries. In examining caretakers, you want to find a faithful one. I don't care if you or some other people or even a court judge me. I don't even judge myself. I don't know of anything that I could be charged with, but that doesn't mean that I am innocent either. The Lord is the one who judges me. Don't judge things in advance. One day the Lord will come and will shine a light on things hidden in the darkness and will reveal the desires of human hearts. Then a judgment will come to each one from God.

Brothers, I have said these things about Apollos and me for your sake so that you can learn. I'm not going beyond what the Scriptures say. No one in your community should think that he is better than anyone else. What makes you so special? What do you have that wasn't given to you by God? And if God just handed it to you, how can you brag about it? You act like you are already well fed and full. You act like you are rich. You act like you were rulers of the world without us. I wish that you had been the rulers of the world because then we would already be ruling with you.

I think God chose who he did to be apostles in these last days to display this. We are like people sentenced to death. We are displayed before all the world, to angels, and to humans. We look like fools because of the Messiah, but you are wise because of the Messiah. We apostles are weak, but you have been strengthened. You are honored; we are without honor. Right now we are hungry and thirsty; we wear ratty clothes. We are beaten, and we wander around homeless. We work hard, working with our own hands. People insult us, and we bless them. We are attacked, and we endure the attacks. We are slandered, and we speak comfort in return. We are the scum of the earth. We've become trash for the present time.

I'm not writing these things to you to embarrass you, but to correct you as my children. You may have a thousand people teaching you about the Messiah, but you don't have very many fathers. In the Messiah Jesus, I gave birth to you. I encourage you to imitate me as your father. This is why I sent Timothy there, who is my son whom I love and who is faithful to the Lord. He will remind you of the way that I live in the Messiah Jesus just as I teach in every community. Because I haven't come to see you in person, some of you are becoming proud. Soon I will come in person, Lord willing, and show those who are speaking proudly my strength. The kingdom of God is not just talk. It is miraculous power. What do you want? Do you want me to come to discipline you or for me to come to you in the Spirit of love and be gentle with you?

I have received word that there is sexual immorality going on in your community. The report is of a kind of sexual immorality that even the pagans know is wrong. Someone there is having sex with his father's wife. Some of you are proud of how tolerant and understanding you are. Instead, you should mourn and weep over what's happening. You should want it to stop. If it comes down to it, you need to remove the person doing it from the community. Even though I am not there in person, I am there in the Spirit. The Spirit who is present has already judged the one who does this. In the name of our Lord Jesus, who brings all of you and me together in the Spirit and with the power of our Lord Jesus: Hand this man over to Satan for the destruction of his sinful flesh so that his spirit might find salvation on the day of the Lord.

Your bragging is not good. Don't you know that just a little yeast will leaven a whole lump of dough? You need to clean away the old yeast so that you may be a new lump of dough, an unleavened lump of dough. The Messiah is our Passover lamb, and he has been sacrificed for us. We need to celebrate the feast not with the old yeast, the yeast of evil and wickedness, but with the unleavened bread of sincerity and truth.

I wrote to you in a letter before that you shouldn't associate with sexually immoral people. I am not talking about people out in the world who are sexually immoral or greedy or swindlers or idol worshipers. You would have to leave the world to avoid them. But I am writing to you now that you need to not associate with anyone who calls himself a brother in the Messiah who is sexually immoral or greedy or an idol worshiper or a slanderer or a drunkard or a swindler. Don't share the Eucharist with someone like this. It's not my job to judge people outside the community, but you need to correct those within your community. God will judge those who are outside. You need to remove that evil man from your community.

Why would any of you who has an issue with another member of the community take him to a court that is unjust rather than resolving it among yourselves, who are holy? Do you not know that the holy ones of God will govern the world? If you are going to govern the world, why can't you handle the smallest issues? Don't you know that we'll even govern angels? How much more should we be able to govern things in our lives in this world? Why would you take these issues to judges who despise your community? You should be ashamed of this. Is there no one there who is wise enough to be able to settle these issues for his brothers? Instead, a brother takes his brother to a court that is faithless.

If you take these issues to court, you have already lost. Why not just allow yourself to be wronged instead? Why not just allow yourself to be defrauded? Instead, you wrong and defraud your brothers. Don't you know that those who are unjust will not inherit God's kingdom? Don't be fooled. Sexually immoral people, idol worshipers, adulterers, male prostitutes, those who have sex with other men, thieves, the greedy, drunkards, slanderers, and swindlers will not inherit the kingdom of God. Some of you used to do these things, but you were washed, you were made holy, you were purified in the name of our Lord Jesus the Messiah and by the Spirit of our God.

I can do anything I want, but not everything is beneficial. I can do whatever I want, but I will not let anything take control of me. Food is for the stomach and the stomach is for food, but someday God will allow both to decay. Your body is not for sexual immorality; it is for the Lord. And the Lord is for your body. God has raised the Lord and will raise us by his miraculous power. Don't you know that your bodies are part of the Messiah? If you know that they are parts of the Messiah, will I take those parts and unite them with a prostitute? Of course not. Don't you know that the one who is united with a prostitute is one body with her? The Scriptures say, "The two will become one flesh." The one who is joined to the Lord is one with him in the Spirit.

Run away from sexual immorality. Every other sin a person does outside his body. A person who is sexually immoral sins inside his body.

Don't you know that your body is a temple of the Holy Spirit, who dwells in you? The Spirit whom you received from God? You do not belong to yourself. You were purchased at a price. So, in return, you should use your body in a way that brings glory to God. Glorify God in the Spirit of God.

To answer some of the questions that you wrote to me about: It is good for a person to be celibate if that is his calling. But otherwise, everyone should be married to help prevent sexual immorality. Every husband has a duty to his wife, and every wife has a duty to her husband. A wife does not have sole ownership of her body, and neither does her husband have sole ownership over his. Do not refuse each other sex except for an occasional short time so that you have time for prayer. Then the two of you should come together again so you don't leave an opening for Satan to tempt you through a lack of self-control. This next thing I say not as a command to you, but I offer it to you as my opinion: I wish that everyone could be like me and be unmarried, but each person has their own gift from God. These gifts are different.

To people who aren't married or are widows, it is good for them to stay that way, as I do. But if they don't have strong self-control and might fall into sin, they should remarry. It's always better to marry than to give in to the passions. To those who are married, I say this—really, the Lord says it—a wife should not separate from her husband. If she does end up separated from her husband, she should either stay unmarried or, if possible, reconcile with her husband. A husband must not divorce his wife. To everyone I say—again, really, the Lord says it—if a brother has a wife who is not a part of the Christian community, but she agrees to stay with him, he should not divorce her. If a woman has a husband who is not part of the community, she should not seek divorce from her husband. The faithless husband will be made holy by the wife and the faithless wife by the husband. If this weren't true, then your children would be unclean, but they are holy. If a faithless person separates himself from his wife, let him go. The brother or sister who is faithful is not bound to them in that case. God has called you to peace. Wives, how do you know if you might save your husband? Husbands, how do you know if you might save your wives?

The Lord has given a role to each person, and God has called them to fill that role. Each person should answer their calling from God. This is what I say in every community. When you received the call of God, were you living a Jewish way of life? Continue to live it. When you received the call of God, were you not Jewish? You should not try to become Jewish. Being Jewish or not being Jewish is not what is important. Keeping the commandments of God is what is important. Each person should answer their particular calling from God and continue living in that way.

If you received the call of God as a slave, do not try to revolt, but if you have an opportunity to be free, take advantage of it. A slave who answers the Lord's calling is a freeman in the eyes of the Lord. The free person who answers the call of God is a servant of the Messiah. You were bought for a price by God; no human can claim to own you. But whatever way of life you had when you received the call of God, continue that way of life.

Concerning unmarried young people, I don't have a commandment given by the Lord, but I will give an opinion, and because of the mercy the Lord has shown me, I think my opinion is worthwhile. I think it is a good idea, because of our present difficulties, for a person to likewise stay as they are. If you are married, you should not try to leave the marriage. If you are divorced, you should not remarry. But if you did get remarried, you didn't sin. If you married someone previously unmarried, they did not sin. But not remarrying will spare you a lot of difficulties within your family.

Brothers, the time is short, and we shouldn't be focusing on trying to find spouses, or worrying about the cares of the world, or rejoicing over our accomplishments in the world, or accumulating wealth, or accumulating power. The present form of this world is passing away. I don't want you to be burdened with the worries and cares of the world. An unmarried man can focus on the Lord—on how he can please the Lord. The man who is married has to care for the things of the world to care for his family. His attention is divided. The unmarried woman or not-yet-married girl can focus on the Lord and on being holy in her body and in the Spirit. A married woman has to care for the things of the world so that she can care for her family. I say this for your benefit, not to make some demand of you. It is good to be able to be devoted to the Lord without distractions.

If a man has behaved improperly toward his betrothed, or if she is past the age at which she can find another husband, or if he has strong desires, or if marrying her is just the right thing to do, he should do it. If a man has a firm and committed heart and doesn't need to get married, if he is self-controlled and has contemplated in his heart and decides to remain unmarried, this is also good for him to do. Marrying one's own betrothed is good, but, in some cases, not being married can be better. A wife is bound to her husband for as long as he lives. If her husband has died, she is free to marry whomever she wants as long as they are faithful members of the community. She will be even more greatly blessed, though, if she remains unmarried, in my opinion. I think the Spirit of God says the same thing.

You asked about food that has been sacrificed to idols. We think we know everything. Knowledge can make someone arrogant, but love builds up others. People who think they know everything often don't know anything that is truly important. People who love God are known by him in return. So, concerning eating food that has been offered to idols, we know that an idol is not just a thing in the world. We also know that there is only one God. There are many things that are called gods in the heavens and on earth. There are many gods and many lords. But for us, there is one God, the Father, who created all things and created us for himself. There is one Lord, Jesus the Messiah, through whom he created all things, and he created us through him.

Not everyone has this knowledge. Some of you are in the habit, even up until now, of eating food that has been sacrificed to idols. Their ability to discern what is right is weak, and so they end up being defiled. Eating meat doesn't make us pleasing to God, and God will not condemn us for not eating meat. Eating meat doesn't give us some kind of advantage. So, don't let your eating meat cause your brother who is weaker in discernment to fall into sin. If someone sees you, who has all this knowledge, eating in an idol's temple, this is not going to help the person whose ability to discern what is right is weak. He will just start eating things offered to idols. Brother, your so-called "knowledge" will destroy this weak brother for whom the Messiah died. When you sin against your brothers and harm them because their ability to discern what is right is weak, you sin against the Messiah. If eating meat is going to lead my brother into sin, I will not eat meat until the age to come. I do not want to lead my brother into sin.

Does this mean I'm not free? Aren't I an apostle who is a leader? Did our Lord Jesus not appear to me? Aren't you my work in the Lord? Maybe others don't accept me as someone sent by God, but you must. You are the evidence that God sent me in that you have come to know the Lord. How do I defend my way of life? Don't we have the authority to eat and drink what we want? Don't we have the authority to take a sister as our wife when we travel the way the other apostles, including the brothers of the Lord and Peter, do? Do only Barnabas and I lack the authority not to work with our hands as we travel to support ourselves? What soldier in the army pays his own expenses? Who plants a vineyard and doesn't eat the fruit that grows there? Who shepherds a flock and doesn't drink the milk from the flock?

Am I just saying these things as one person, or does the Torah also say these things? In the Torah, Moses says, as the Scriptures say, "You will not muzzle an ox while it is treading your grain." Does God only care about oxen? Is he not speaking about all of us? This is in the Scriptures for our sake. The person who plows ought to plow, hoping for the harvest. The one who threshes out the grain works, hoping to partake of the grain at the end of the day. If we have sown the things of the Spirit with you, is it out of line to expect help with the things of this world from you? If other people in positions of authority over you get to partake, don't we have even more right?

While we were there, we did not use this authority. Instead, we took care of ourselves so that it wouldn't hinder you from hearing the gospel of the Messiah. Don't you know that those who work in the temple eat the bread in the temple? Those who serve at the altar in the temple partake of the food sacrificed at the altar. In the same way, the Lord has arranged it so that those who preach the gospel can live from preaching the gospel. I haven't used this authority. I haven't written things now to say that you need to provide for me. I'd rather die than have someone be able to make an accusation that I preach the gospel for money. I preach the gospel and get nothing in return but difficulties. But if I don't preach the gospel, I will be accursed.

This is the choice I've made, and I have my reward. I have had a position of authority placed upon me. What is my reward? I am able to preach the gospel without payment. I can offer everyone the gospel, and nothing compromises my authority in the gospel. Even though I am free in all respects, I serve everyone so that I may gain more people. When I am with Jewish people, I speak to them as a Jewish person so that I might win over more Jewish people. When I am with those who know the Torah, I speak concerning the Torah so that I can win over those who study the Torah. To those who don't know the Torah, I speak to them without reference to the Torah so that I can win them over. These last people are not without the Torah of God, but they have received the Torah through the Messiah. When I am speaking to weak people, I speak as if weak so that I can win them over. I become like every person so that in every way I can save some people. Everything that I do, I do because of the gospel, that I might be fully in communion with it.

When people run a race, they all run, but only one wins. You should run to win. The athlete who is running to win has to control himself in every way. They do this to inherit a prize that will someday decay and be forgotten. We are seeking to win an immortal prize. So, I don't run like someone who doesn't know where he's going. I don't fight like someone who is shadowboxing. I discipline my body and bring it under control so that, having preached all these things to other people, I don't end up failing myself.

Brothers, I don't want you to be ignorant. Our fathers were all under the cloud of glory, and they all passed through the Red Sea. All of them were baptized into Moses in the cloud and in the sea. All of them ate the same spiritual food, the bread from heaven. All of them drank the same spiritual drink because they were drinking from the rock that accompanied them in the wilderness. That rock was the Messiah. But God was not pleased with most of them. They ended up dead in the desert. This history has become symbolic for us. We should not indulge the same evil desires that they did. You should not be idol worshipers, the way some of them were. The Scriptures say, "The people sat down to eat and drink, and then they got up to play." So, you should not be sexually immoral as some of them were sexually immoral. At one point, twenty-three thousand of them died in one day.

We should not test the Messiah in the way that they tested God and were killed by poisonous snakes. We should not grumble the way some of them grumbled, and they died as a result of God's wrath. These things really happened to them, and they were written down so that we could learn from them now that we are at the end of the ages. The person who thinks that he is standing strong should be careful that he doesn't fall. All the trials you face in life are faced commonly by people all the time. God is faithful. He will not let you be tested beyond what you can stand. God will give you a way to pass the test so that you can endure it.

I love you, and I want you to run away from idol worship. I am speaking to those with discernment. Evaluate the message I am giving you. The cup of blessings that we bless in the Eucharist, is it not partaking of the blood of the Messiah? The bread that we break in the Eucharist, is it not partaking in the body of the Messiah? We are many different people, but there is one loaf and one body of the Messiah. We all partake of the one loaf. Think about the Jewish people. Aren't those who eat from the sacrifices in the temple partaking of the sacrifices on the altar? What am I saying? Is an idol, or what is sacrificed to an idol, something with power? No, but what the people of the nations sacrifice, they sacrifice to demons and not to God. I don't want you to partake with demons. You can't drink the Lord's cup and also drink from the cup of demons. You can't partake of the Lord's altar and the altars of demons. Don't you remember that God is a jealous God? Do you think you can challenge him?

You can do whatever you want, but not everything will be beneficial. You can do whatever you want, but not everything will build you up. No one should just seek his own benefit but should seek to benefit others. Whatever meat you find in the meat market you can eat without asking any questions or making any arguments. The whole earth is the Lord's and everything in it. If someone faithless offers you hospitality and you wish to accept it, eat everything they set in front of you without asking questions or arguments. But if someone says to you, "This was offered to an idol," do not eat it, for his sake. My freedom is not as important as a person keeping away from sin. On the other hand, if I give thanks to God for the food set in front of me, why would I be criticized for eating the things for which I gave thanks to God?

Whatever you eat, whatever you drink, whatever you do, do it all for God's glory. Then you will not offend either Jewish people or Greek people within the community of God. In the same way, I try to be pleasing to everyone not for my own benefit, but so that many people might be saved. Imitate me in the way that I imitate the Messiah.

I praise you that you remember all the things I taught you just as I taught them. And you are following those teachings. I want you to know that the head of every man is the Messiah. The head of a woman is her husband. The head of the Messiah is God. Any man who prays or preaches with a covering over his head as the pagans wear brings dishonor to his head, who is the Messiah. Every woman who prays or preaches with her head uncovered dishonors her head, who is her husband. It is the same thing with cutting her hair short. If she is not going to cover her head, she should also cut her hair short. If it is disgraceful for a woman to cut her hair short, then she should cover her head. A man should not cover his head, because he is the image and glory of God. A wife is the glory of her husband. Originally, a man was not created for a woman, but a woman was created for a man. So, women have someone in authority over them because of the angels.

Remember that a wife is not separate from her husband, nor a husband from his wife in the Lord. Originally a woman came from a man, but now every man is born from a woman. All people are ultimately from God. Judge for yourselves: Is it good for a woman to pray with her head uncovered? Even the natural science of your nation teaches that if a man has long hair, this is dishonorable. If a woman has long hair, it is her glory. Long hair is given to her for procreation, according to your medical texts. If someone wants to argue about this, they should know that the communities of God all around the world follow this custom.

I do not praise you but need to teach about when you come together to celebrate the Eucharist. You don't do this in a way that makes you better but in a way that makes you worse. In the first place, I hear that when you gather together to worship, there are divisions and factions among you, and I believe it. God allows these factions to develop because it helps make it more apparent who the faithful ones are in your community. But because of this, when you come together to worship, it is not the Lord's meal that you are eating. One person seizes food first, another goes hungry, and another person gets drunk. Can't you eat and drink in your own houses? Do you just not care about the house of God? Do you just hate the poor members of your community? What can I possibly say about this? Should I praise you for it? Obviously not.

The tradition that I received from the Lord I also passed down to you. On the night that the Lord Jesus was betrayed, he took bread and gave thanks. He broke the bread and said, "This is my body, which is for you. Do this as my memorial sacrifice." In the same way he took the cup after the meal and said, "This is the cup of the new covenant in my blood. Do this, and every time you drink it, it is my memorial sacrifice." Every time you eat that bread and drink from that cup, you preach the death of the Lord until the day he comes.

So, if someone eats the bread or drinks from the cup of the Lord in an unworthy way, he is guilty of the body and blood of the Lord. A person should consider his life and eat the bread and drink from the cup in a worthy way. A person who doesn't consider his life in the body will end up eating and drinking judgment on himself. This is how many of you have gotten weak and sick. Many of you have even died because of this. If we consider our own lives and repent, then we won't face judgment. When the Lord judges us, he disciplines us so that we won't end up being condemned with the world.

My brothers, when you gather together to worship and prepare to celebrate the Eucharist, wait for one another. If someone is truly hungry, let them eat at home so that there won't be judgment when you gather together. Once I am able to come there in person, we will take care of some other, related issues.

Brothers, I also don't want you to be ignorant about the gift of the Spirit of God. When you were in the nations, you were carried away, led into slavery by idols that do not speak. Here is how to tell the Spirit of God from those spirits you used to worship. No one who has the Spirit of God dwelling in them will curse Jesus. Not one is able to proclaim that Jesus is the Lord if he is not indwelt by the Holy Spirit. God gives us many different gifts, but he has given all of us one Spirit. We have been called to all different kinds of service, but we all serve the same Lord. There are many different activities we participate in, but these are the activities of God in which all of us participate.

The Spirit of God manifests himself in each of us in different ways to help the whole community. One person receives wisdom from the Spirit. Another person receives great knowledge from the same Spirit. Another one becomes renowned for their faithfulness through the same Spirit. Another person receives the gift of healing from that one Spirit. Someone else may work miracles, someone might preach, another one might be good at discerning between different spirits, someone else speaks many languages, and another person can translate many languages. All these things are the activities of one and the same Spirit of God, giving these gifts to each person as he chooses.

Your body is one body, but it is made up of many parts. All of them are parts of the one body. The same is also true of the Messiah. We were all baptized to receive the one Spirit to be one body. Whether we are Jewish or Greek, slaves or freemen, we all drink of the same Spirit of God. The body isn't just one part; it has many parts. If a foot said, "Since I'm not a hand, I'm not really part of the body," that would be ridiculous. If an ear were to say, "Because I am not an eye, I am not really part of the body," this would be bizarre. If your whole body was made of eyes, how would you hear? If you were all ears, how would you smell? God has put our bodies in order so that they each function properly. If every part were the same part, you wouldn't have a body.

There are many parts, but there is one body. An eye can't say to a hand, "I don't need you." A head can't say to its feet, "I don't need you." In most cases, those parts of the body that seem the least important are actually necessary. We are very careful with parts of our body that embarrass us, and we deal with them with manners and politeness. For other parts of us there is no such concern, and we display them openly. So, the parts of our body that might be seen as unclean or unpresentable we treat with honor and decency. The same thing should be true with the members of our community. We should honor those who do the difficult tasks that aren't glorious but are necessary. If one part of your body suffers, your whole body suffers. If one part of your body is honored, all the other parts of your body take part in the joy. Your community is the body of the Messiah, and you are parts of his body.

God has appointed certain people to be leaders in the community. In the first place are apostles, in the second prophets, teachers are third, then those who work miracles, those who have the gift of healing, helping others, administration, speaking different languages, etc. Not every one is an apostle. Not every one is a prophet. Not every one is a teacher. Not every one works miracles. Not every one has the gift of healing. Not every one can speak different languages. Not every one can translate. You should desire to have greater gifts from God.

But there is a higher way of life that I want to show you. If I could speak all human languages and even the language of the angels, but I didn't have the gift of love, I would be a banging gong or a clashing cymbal. If I had the gift of prophecy and I understood all the ancient mysteries and I knew everything, even if I were so faithful that I could move mountains, but I didn't have the gift of love, I would be nothing. I could give away everything I have and die as a martyr, but if I didn't have the gift of love, it wouldn't be any credit to me.

The love of God is patient. It is kind. His love is not jealous. His love doesn't brag. His love isn't full of itself. It doesn't do shameful things. It doesn't seek to gratify itself. It is not easily angered. It doesn't keep track of offenses. It isn't pleased with injustice. It rejoices at the truth. God's love bears everything, it is always faithful, it is always hopeful, and it endures all things. God's love never falls away. But prophecies? They are done away with. Languages? They cease being spoken. Knowledge? It gets lost in time. Our knowledge is partial. Our prophecies are partial. But when we have the gift of love, which is perfect, these "partial" gifts become unimportant. When I was a child, I talked like a child. I thought like a child. I solved problems like a child. When I became an adult man, I let go of childish things. We see things now as if we were looking through a smudged pane of glass. When we receive the gift of love, we will see God face to face. Right now I know partially, but then I will know God fully, in the same way that God has always fully known me. Now we live faithfully, with hope and love, these three things. But love is the greatest of all these gifts.

Pursue love. You should desire all the gifts of the Spirit, especially that you might preach and proclaim the gospel. A person who speaks in a language that nobody else knows isn't speaking to other people but to God in that language, because no one else understands it. The person who preaches and proclaims the gospel is speaking to all people to build them up, to encourage them, and to give them comfort. The person who can speak a foreign language has enriched himself, but the one who preaches and proclaims the gospel enriches the whole community. I wish that all of you could learn many languages, but I would rather that you all preach and proclaim the gospel. The one who preaches the gospel is more useful than the person who speaks languages, unless there is someone there to translate what he is saying so that the whole community can benefit from it.

Brothers, if I come to you speaking the different languages I know, how would that help you? Whether I gave you great revelations or knowledge, or prophesied or taught, you wouldn't understand. Even musical instruments like a flute or a harp, if you couldn't identify the notes that they were playing, how would you know what the music was? If someone blows a horn and it makes a strange noise, will the army know they're being attacked? In the same way, if you're speaking a language that the community doesn't know, how will anyone know what you're saying? You're just talking into the air. There are countless languages in the world, and all of them have meaning if you understand them. If I speak one language and another person another, then I am a foreigner to him, and he is a foreigner to me. Keep this in mind if you desire the gifts of the Spirit to help build up the community.

If a person is going to pray in a different language, he should have someone to translate. If I pray in a language, my spirit prays, but my mind isn't doing anything where I could translate for myself while really praying. Which is better? I pray with the Spirit; I also pray in a way that will be understood. I sing with the Spirit; I also sing in a way that will be understood. Otherwise, if I give a blessing with the Spirit in another language, how will the person in the community who doesn't know that language say "Amen" after I give thanks? He doesn't know what you're saying. It is good for you to give thanks, but the other people in the community don't benefit from it. I thank God that there are not more of you who speak different languages. Within the community, it is better to speak five words that are understood in order to instruct others than ten thousand words in another language.

Brothers, don't have childish minds. Regarding evil, be innocent like little children. But in terms of how you think about things, be adults. The Scriptures say, in the Torah, "'In other languages spoken by other lips I will speak to this people, but even then they will not hear me,' says the Lord." Being able to speak someone's language can be a miracle when preaching to the faithless, but not to the faithful. The preaching of the gospel is to the faithless, not the faithful. If your community gathers together in one place and everyone speaks in different languages, if someone who doesn't know about your community or someone faithless comes in, they'll think you're crazy. If all of you preach the gospel and someone faithless or a newcomer comes in, he will be convicted by everyone's preaching. Everyone will examine him, and he will see the secrets of his heart and come to repentance. Then he will prostrate himself and worship God, declaring that "Certainly, God is among you."

Brothers, why is it that when you gather together everyone has a psalm to sing, everyone wants to teach something, everyone has a revelation, everyone wants to speak a different language, everyone wants to translate? Everything you do should be for the benefit of everyone. If people are going to speak in different languages, it should be two or three at most, one at a time, and someone should translate. If there is no one to translate, they should remain silent in the community gathering. He can speak that language to himself and to God. If some are going to preach, two or three should speak, and the others should listen. If someone suddenly decides they have something to say, they should stay silent. You only need one person to preach to all of you so that everyone can learn and be encouraged. If someone is a prophet, they should be able to control themselves. God is not a God of disorder but of peace. This is the way it is in every community of holy ones.

The women of the community should practice silence. They should not be talking when you gather for worship but should be listening and learning. This is what the Torah says. If they want to learn more, they should ask their husbands at home. It is shameful for a woman to be talking in the worship gathering. Has the Word of God departed from you? Are you the only one to receive him? Then why would you be different from every other community? If anyone calls himself a prophet, or a man of the Spirit, he should agree that what I am writing to you are the Lord's commandments. If someone is just ignorant, you should ignore them. Brothers, desire to preach the gospel, and let people speak in different languages, but do everything the right way and in an orderly way.

Brothers, remember the gospel that I preached to you. You received it, you live by it, you are being saved by the Word whom I preached to you, if you hold on to it. If you don't, your faithfulness will have been for nothing. The tradition I passed on to you, which I received, is that the Messiah died for our sins according to the Scriptures. He was buried and was raised from the dead on the third day according to the Scriptures. He appeared to Peter and then to the twelve apostles. Then he appeared to more than five hundred brothers at once, many of whom are still alive, though some have died. Then he appeared to James, and then to all the apostles. Last of all he appeared to me, the miscarriage. I am the lowest of the apostles. I am not even fit to be called an apostle because I persecuted the communities of God. That I am the person I am now is a gift from God, and that gift he gave me has not amounted to nothing. I have worked harder than all of them. Even all this work of mine was really the gift of God as well. Whether you heard me or another apostle, we preach the same gospel, and you are faithful to that gospel.

If we preached to you that the Messiah was raised from the dead, how is it that some of you say that no one rises from the dead? If no one is raised from the dead, then the Messiah hasn't been raised from the dead. But if the Messiah hasn't been raised from the dead, then our preaching is false, and your faithfulness to that preaching is worthless. We would then be lying about God because we testified that God raised up the Messiah. He must not have done that if no one rises from the dead. If no one rises from the dead, then the Messiah has not been raised from the dead. If the Messiah has not risen from the dead, then your faithfulness to him is worthless. You are still under the control of your sins. Also, that would mean that those who have fallen asleep in the Messiah have simply died. If we only have hope in the Messiah right now in this world, then we are more pathetic than any other people in the world.

But the Messiah has been raised from the dead as the beginning of the harvest of those who have fallen asleep. Death began with one man; therefore the resurrection from the dead also begins with one man. Being descended from Adam, everyone dies. Because of the Messiah, everyone will be made alive again. The resurrection will happen in order: First the Messiah, then those who belong to the Messiah when he appears, and then the end of the age will come. Then the Messiah will hand over his kingdom to his God and Father, with all other rule and authority and power being done away with. It is necessary for the Messiah to rule until all his enemies have been put under his feet. The last enemy that he will defeat is death. Obviously, when we say that everything will be put under his authority, we don't mean God the Father, who has put everything under his authority. When everything has been put under the authority of the son, the son will be under the authority of the one who put everything under his authority. Then God will be all in all.

If no one rises from the dead, then why do people take the names of holy ones who have fallen asleep when they are baptized? If they won't be raised from the dead, why be baptized in their name? And why would I put my life in danger over and over again? I could die any day, as you well know, my brothers in the Messiah Jesus our Lord. Why would I face down wild animals in Ephesus? What good would that do me? If no one rises from the dead, then let's eat and drink because we may die tomorrow. Don't be fooled. Keeping company with bad people will end up corrupting you morally. Get sober, purify yourself, and don't sin. Some of you are ignorant about God, and I say that this is shameful.

Someone might ask, "Then, how are the dead raised? What kind of body do they have once theirs has decayed?" Don't be dumb. When you plant a seed, for it to grow the seed must be broken open and destroyed. When you plant a seed, it is a seed, not a full-grown plant, whether it is a grain of wheat or whatever else. Every seed grows into its own plant, as God created it. There are different types of flesh also. Humans have one type of body, animals have another type, birds and fish have other types. Beings in the heavens, like angels, have a different type of body from creatures who live on the earth. What it means for an earthly creature to be fully grown and beautiful and what it means for an angel to be fully grown and beautiful are different. The sun has one type of glory, the moon has a different one, and the stars are different from them and from each other.

This is how to think about the resurrection of the dead. Your body is buried in the ground to decay, but it is raised up again immortal. It is buried in dishonor but rises in glory. It is buried in weakness but rises in power. A natural body made of earth is buried, but it is raised as a body permeated by the Spirit of God. The Scriptures say that when the Spirit entered his body made from the earth, "the first man, Adam, became a living soul." The last Adam, the Messiah, gives us life in and through the Spirit of God. The Spirit didn't come first, but the body made of earth; then the Spirit was breathed into him. The first man was taken from the earth. He was made of dust. The second man came from the heavens. Like Adam, made of dust, all of us are dust. Everyone who belongs to the man from the heavens becomes heavenly like him. We have spent this life in the image of the man made from the earth. In the age to come, we will be like the man from the heavens.

Brothers, let me tell you something. Flesh and blood will not inherit the kingdom of God. Immortality does not inherit decay. Now I will reveal a mystery to you. Not everyone will fall asleep before the day of the Lord, but everyone will be transformed. In a moment, in the blink of an eye, the last trumpet will sound. When that trumpet sounds, the dead will be raised and become immortal, and we who are alive will be changed. The corruptible needs to be clothed with incorruption. The mortal needs to be clothed with immortality. When the corruptible has been clothed with incorruption and the mortal has been clothed with immortality, then, as the Scriptures say, "death has been swallowed by victory." Where is your victory, death? Death, where is your venom? The venom of death is sin. The Torah helps us see sin and its power. Thank God, who gives us victory through our Lord Jesus the Messiah.

Brothers, I love you. Stand firm. Be immovable. Always be doing the works of the Lord. Know that all your work is not for nothing, because of the Lord.

In terms of the collection I am gathering for the holy ones in Jerusalem, as I said to the communities in Galatia so I also say to you: Every Sabbath, each of you should set aside some of what you have received if you have done well financially. Then I won't have to take up the whole collection when I come. When I do arrive, then, we will gather what you collected, and you can designate some people to bring it to Jerusalem. If it makes sense for me to take it to them personally, then I will do that.

I will come to you when I travel through Macedonia, as I am planning to do. I will stay with you for a little while—maybe even the whole winter so that you can help me prepare for wherever I go next. I don't want to just see you briefly. I want to spend some time with you, Lord willing. I am going to stay in Ephesus until Pentecost. There's a door open for me that could bring great things and be very productive, but there are also many people opposing me.

If Timothy comes to visit you, make sure that he is safe with you. He is doing the Lord's work just like me. Don't let anyone look down on him. Supply him in peace with whatever he needs so that he can journey back with me. I am expecting him along with some other brothers.

I encouraged Brother Apollos to come visit with the brothers there. Before that he didn't really want to come, but now he will come when he gets the chance.

Watch, stand firm, and be faithful. Be manly and strong. Do everything you do out of love.

Brothers, I urge you also to assist the household of Stephanas, whom you know. His family is the beginning of the harvest in Achaia, and they are devoted to serving the holy ones of God. Respect and listen to everyone like them who works and labors as we do.

I am glad that Stephanas, Fortunatus, and Achaicus have come there before me; they have gifts that your community has needed. They refreshed my spirit and yours. These are the kind of people you should take note of.

The communities in Asia greet you. They greet you in the Lord, including Aquila and Priscilla and the rest of the community that gathers at their home. All the brothers greet you. Greet each other with a holy kiss.

A greeting with my own hand. Paul.

If anyone does not love the Lord, he is cursed. Come, Lord. The grace of the Lord Jesus be with you, with all my love for you in the Messiah Jesus. Amen.

TO THE

PHILIPPIANS

Paul and Timothy, servants of the Messiah Jesus,

To all the holy ones of the Messiah Jesus in Philippi with your bishops and deacons,

Grace to you and peace from God our Father and the Lord Jesus the Messiah,

I thank my God every time I think of you. You are always in my prayers, and I pray for you with joy. We have been working together to spread the gospel from the first day I arrived there until now. I know that because God has begun to do good works through you, these will continue until the day of the Messiah Jesus. I think it is right for me to feel this way about you because I am always in your heart as well. Even now when I am in chains to defend and confirm the gospel, you are still working together with me. All of you are a gift to me. My God will testify for me, how much I love and care for you in the Messiah Jesus. I pray that your love will grow and grow and that you will also grow in knowledge and discernment. Then you will know and can encourage the things that are excellent and pure and blameless up until the day of the Messiah. On that day, may you be full of good works done through Jesus the Messiah to the glory and praise of God.

Brothers, I want you to know that all the things that have happened to me have allowed the gospel to advance. Even though I am in chains, the Messiah has now become well known to my guards and everyone else whom I encounter. Knowing that this has been the result of my being imprisoned, many of the brothers are now more courageous in speaking about the Word of God without fear. Some of them probably don't have pure motives, but some of them are preaching the Messiah in good faith. Those who are preaching the gospel out of love know that I am here in prison to defend the gospel. Those who are preaching the Messiah for selfish reasons may think that they're causing some kind of trouble for me. They aren't. In every way, whether for bad or good reasons, the Messiah is preached. I rejoice about this, and I always will.

I know that this situation will end up being for my salvation through your prayers and what I receive from the Spirit of Jesus the Messiah. Because of the hope and the expectation that I have for the Messiah appearing in the future, I am never embarrassed by my situation. I am bold now as I always have been that the news of the Messiah will be spread through me, whether through my life or by my death. If I live, I live for the Messiah. If I die, I receive a reward. If I go on living in this world, I will continue to work to bear fruit for Him. Which of these would be better? I don't know. I sometimes desire for myself that I would leave this life and be with the Messiah, which seems better to me. But it may be necessary for me to continue working in this life for your sake. On the whole, I think that this is better, and so I expect to remain and continue working with you as you progress in joyful faithfulness. I will continue to brag about what the Messiah Jesus is doing through you until I am able to come and visit you again.

Live in a way that is worthy of the gospel of the Messiah. Whether I am able to come see you or I remain absent, I want to hear that you are all standing firm and are one in the Spirit. Work together like one person faithfully in the gospel. Do not be afraid of anything threatened by those who oppose you. The fact that they hate you shows that they are on their way to destruction. You are on your way to salvation from God. You have been given the gift not only of being faithful to the Messiah but also to suffer as he did. He was attacked, and you know that I also am being attacked, as you have heard.

If you have encouragement because of the Messiah, if love gives you comfort, if you are in communion with the Spirit of God, if you have any feelings or compassion, fill me with joy by being of the same mind, sharing the same love, being united in soul. Care about the same things. Don't do things based on your own self-interest or according to your own arrogance. Be humble, and think other people are better than you. Don't just look after your own concerns; also help with the concerns of others.

All of you should see things the way the Messiah Jesus did. He existed as God, but he didn't look at equality with his Father as something to which he should cling. Instead, he humbled himself, becoming a servant, looking like a normal man. Looking like nothing more than a man, he humbled himself and was obedient even to the point of death—death by crucifixion. But God lifted him up into the heavens and gave him the name which is above every name. One day, everyone will bow their knees to the name of Jesus, in the heavens and on the earth and in the underworld. All their tongues will then confess that Jesus the Messiah is the Lord, to the glory of God the Father.

I love you. Just as you have always been obedient—not only when I am there but even more now when I am absent—continue working out your salvation with awe and reverence. God is the one who is working in you for you to will and to do his will. Everything you do, do without arguing or grumbling. Then you will be blameless and innocent children of God. You will be pure in a generation that is corrupt and perverted. You will shine like lights in this present world. Hold on to the word of truth so that on the day of the Messiah it will be to my credit, and I will know that I didn't do all my work for nothing. Even if I end up giving my life as a drink offering that is poured out on the sacrifice of your faithfulness, I will be happy and will rejoice with all of you. All of you should also rejoice with me.

I hope in the Lord Jesus to be able to send Timothy to you soon, knowing the good things going on in your community will encourage me. There are not many people who genuinely care about you the way that I do. Not everybody seeks after the Messiah Jesus. You know how valuable Timothy is. He has served with me as if he were my son in the gospel. So, I hope to send him to you, seeing how things are going with me currently. But the Lord has given me confidence that I will soon get to visit you in person.

I also sent you Epaphroditus, my brother, coworker, and fellow soldier. He was a messenger and a minister of my needs to you, and so I sent him. He also wanted to see you. I know that you were worried because you heard that he was sick. He was very sick—he almost died. But God had mercy on him and on me as well, so that I should not have even more sorrow in my life. So, I sent him to you quickly so you could see that he had recovered. Then you could rejoice and stop worrying. Receive him the way you would receive the Lord, with all joy, and honor him for the sake of the work he does for the Messiah. He nearly died because he thought that working with me was more important than his life.

My brothers, finally, rejoice in the Lord. I don't mind writing the same things to you again, because it is a reminder to you. Beware of stray dogs. Beware of those who do evil. Beware of those who present themselves as Jewish but are not. The real Jewish people are those who worship in the Spirit of God and give glory to the Messiah Jesus, not those who are trying to get you to be circumcised. I am circumcised. If someone out there wants to claim to be Jewish just based on external things, I have a better claim. I was circumcised on the eighth day.

I am from the people of Israel, the tribe of Benjamin. I am a Hebrew from a long line of Hebrews. In terms of the Torah, I am a Pharisee. If you want to talk about zeal, I went out and persecuted the communities of the Messiah. If you want to talk about a just life lived according to the Torah, I was blameless.

However much I once thought that these were the important things, because of the Messiah I now consider them unimportant. Compared to the knowledge I now have of the Messiah Jesus my Lord, they seem unimportant. Whatever I had to give up to find the Messiah is garbage by comparison. In him, I have found something greater than the purification I received through the Torah: the purification that comes through the Messiah's faithfulness, God's purification that comes through our faithfulness. Now I know him and the miraculous power of his resurrection. I have come to share in his suffering, and I have shared in his death—all of this so that I can share in his resurrection from the dead.

I am not saying that I have already achieved this or that I am perfect. I am chasing after it and trying to catch it through the Messiah Jesus. Brothers, I don't consider myself to already have it in my hands. The one thing I never forget is to keep moving forward and reaching for the goal. I keep pushing forward toward the reward that God has called me to in the Messiah Jesus. If you are mature, you should think about things in the same way. If you think about this differently, eventually God will show this to you.

Live your lives together following the same rule and with the same mind that leads to this goal. Brothers, imitate me together, and watch those who live in the same way. We are showing you a way of life. Many are living another way, as enemies of the Messiah's cross. I have spoken to you about them before, and I mention them again with tears. They are on their way to destruction. Their god is their own desires. The things they boast about are shameful. They only care about the things of this world. But we are citizens of a kingdom that is in the heavens. We are waiting for our Savior who will come from there, the Lord Jesus the Messiah. He will transform our lives, of which we are ashamed, to be like his life, which is glorious. He is working and empowering us to exercise authority over all things.

My brothers, whom I love and desire to see, you are my joy and my crown. I love you. Stand firm in the Lord.

I encourage you to see things the same way in the Lord with Euodia and Syntyche. If you are truly my coworkers, assist these women who labored with me in the gospel. The same is true for Clement and the rest of my coworkers. All their names are written in the book of life.

Always rejoice in the Lord. I will say it again: Rejoice. Let everyone see how gentle you are. The appearance of the Lord is close. Don't worry about anything, but with prayers and supplications and giving thanks, make all your concerns known to God. Then the peace of God, which is beyond anyone's understanding, will come into your hearts and minds in the Messiah Jesus.

Brothers, finally, whatever is true, whatever is honorable, whatever is right, whatever is pure, whatever is loveable, whatever is admirable— basically anything that is excellent and praiseworthy—these are the things you should think about. What you have learned from me and the traditions you've received—the way you have seen me live—do these things. The God of peace will be with you.

It brought me great joy to know that you still care for me, that you were concerned for me even if you didn't have a chance to help me. I am not destitute. I have learned to be content in whatever situation I find myself. I know how to live in poverty, and I have enjoyed wealth. I have learned the secret of enjoying food and also living in hunger, to succeed and to fail. Whatever happens, I have strength because of the

Messiah who strengthens me. But I thank you for your care and concern for my troubles.

Philippians, you should also know that when I had just begun to preach the gospel when I left Macedonia, you were the only community that partnered with me in terms of support. Even when I was in Thessalonica you sent me assistance more than once. I am not looking for gifts, but I look for the good deeds that result from faithfulness to the gospel, and you are abounding in these. I feel like I have everything I need, that I am full, now that Epaphroditus has told me about your community. Your faithful way of life is a sacrifice that produces a sweet aroma that pleases God. My God will fulfill all your need from his glorious riches in the Messiah Jesus. Glory to God our Father unto the ages of ages. Amen.

Greet all the holy ones in the Messiah Jesus. My brothers who are with me greet you. All the holy ones, especially those from the household of Caesar, greet you.

The grace of the Lord Jesus the Messiah be with you in the Spirit. Amen.

TO THE
COLOSSIANS

Paul, an apostle of the Messiah Jesus by God's will and Brother Timothy,

To the holy ones in Colossae and the faithful brothers in the Messiah,

Grace to you and peace from God our Father,

We give thanks to God the Father of our Lord Jesus the Messiah for you every time we pray. We have heard of your faithfulness to the Messiah Jesus and your love for all the holy ones because of the hope you're waiting for from the heavens. You heard of this hope beforehand in the true word of the gospel. The gospel that you received is also producing results and spreading throughout the whole world, just as it did in your community from the first day that you heard it and received God's true gift. You learned the gospel from Epaphras, who is our fellow servant whom we love. He is a faithful servant of the Messiah and represents us well. He also told us about the love that you share in the Spirit of God.

Having heard this, we never stop praying and asking that you may continue to gain knowledge of his will in wisdom and the understanding of the Spirit. Live in a way that is worthy of the Lord, that pleases him—doing good, bringing forth results, and growing in your knowledge of God. Be empowered with the power of God, who is mighty and glorious, so that you will have endurance, patience, and joy regardless of your circumstances. Give thanks to the Father, the one who has apportioned you a share of the inheritance of the holy ones in light. He has delivered us from the authority of darkness and brought us into the kingdom of his son whom he loves. In him, we are set free by having our sins forgiven.

The son is the image of the invisible God. He has the status of first-born to inherit all of God's creation. In him, everything was created in the heavens and on the earth, the visible world and the invisible world—including the thrones, dominions, rulers, and authorities of the unseen world. Everything was created through him and for him. He exists before anything else, and everything continues to exist because of him. He is the head of his body, the communities of God throughout the world. He is the beginning, the firstborn from the dead. He holds the first place in everything. The fullness of God lives in him so that he could reconcile all things on earth and in the heavens to God in himself, by his blood that he shed on his cross.

In the past, you were not only alienated from God, but your mind was hostile to him as you did evil. Now he has reconciled you within the community through his death. He now presents you as a holy and pure and innocent sacrifice before God, if you continue faithfully. Be established and stand firm. Don't move away from the hope presented in the gospel you heard. The gospel has been proclaimed to all the creation under heaven, and I, Paul, am its minister.

Even though I am currently suffering, I rejoice for you. What is lacking in me, in my sinful flesh, is being healed by the suffering of the Messiah for his body, the communities of God. I am a servant of those communities, appointed to that position by God to bring the Word of God to you. The mystery that was hidden from the ages past and from generation after generation has now been manifested to his holy ones. God wanted to reveal the rich, glorious mystery of the Messiah to all the nations—to you, which is your glorious hope. We preach the Messiah, correcting every person and teaching every person in wisdom so that we can bring every person to maturity in the Messiah. This is why I work and strive, working with God, who is working in me powerfully.

I want you to know how hard I work for you and for those in Laodicea, whom I haven't seen in person. I want your hearts to be encouraged, to be united together in love, and to have full and rich knowledge of the mystery of God, which is the Messiah. In him, all the treasures of wisdom and knowledge are hidden. I say this so that none of you might get fooled by gifted orators. I may be absent from you in the flesh, but I am present with you in the Spirit. I rejoice to see the good order of your community and how strongly committed you are to faithfulness to the Messiah.

You have received the Messiah Jesus the Lord. Continue to live faithfully to him. You were planted in him, and you've grown in him. Continue to be strengthened in your faithful way of life, as we taught you to live. Continually give him thanks. Be careful that none of you gets taken captive by philosophical arguments or empty lies—human traditions that come from the demonic rulers of the world and not from the Messiah. He is God in bodily form. In him, you have everything you need. He is the head of every ruler and authority. In him you were circumcised, not by the hands of a man who removed skin from your body, but in the Messiah's circumcision. When you were baptized, you were buried with him. By the work of God who raised him from the dead, through your faithfulness, you were raised with him. You were dead sinners and uncircumcised. But God made you alive with him, forgiving us all of our sins. He blotted out all the charges against us and took it away, nailing it to the cross. These accusations were the only weapon the demonic rulers and authorities had. He publicly embarrassed them and defeated them at the cross.

Don't let anyone judge you regarding what you eat or what you drink or whether you follow Jewish feasts or Sabbaths. All of these are a shadow of the Messiah who was coming. You are now the Messiah's body. Don't let anyone lead you away with false piety to worship fallen angels. He will tell you stories of the gods. Really, he is arrogant in his mind and in his sinful desires because he won't submit to the head. Because the Messiah is the head, it is he who unites and gives life to all the parts of the body and allows them to grow into the likeness of God. If you died with the Messiah to escape slavery to the gods of this world, why would you follow them again now that you have a new life? Do not use this, do not eat that, do not touch this, etc. All the things of the world are going to decay and pass away. These are all the rules and teachings of humans. They look like they will make you wise through worship and humility and asceticism. You might think they will help you gain control of your sinful desires.

If you have been raised to a new life with the Messiah, you should instead seek after the things from the heavens, where the Messiah is sitting at the right hand of God. Think about the things above, not the things on earth. You have died, and you have a new life that right now is hidden with the Messiah in God. When the Messiah appears, your new life will also appear. Then you will appear with him in glory.

Kill your sinful desires on earth, like sexual immorality, uncleanness, passions, evil desires, and greed, which is idolatry. These things are why the wrath of God is coming on the disobedient. You used to live that way when you were living in the world. But now, you need to cast off all these things. Keep anger, rage, malice, slander, and foul language out of your mouth. Do not lie to each other. Throw off the old person you were and the way he used to live. Become your new self, made new by knowledge, and become the image of the one who created you. This new person you're becoming isn't Greek or Jewish, circumcised or uncircumcised, a barbarian, a Scythian, a slave, or a freeman. Each and every one of you is being conformed to the image of the Messiah.

As those who have been called to this by God, who makes you holy and loves you, gain hearts of compassion, kindness, humility, gentleness, and patience. Bear with each other and forgive each other. If someone has a complaint about someone else, they should forgive that person in the same way that the Lord forgave them. But more than anything, love. Love is the bond of perfect unity. Let the peace that comes from the Messiah rule over your heart. Answer the call to be one as a community. Be thankful. Let the gospel of the Messiah dwell in you and bear fruit. Teach everyone in wisdom. Correct each other when necessary. As you have the gifts, sing psalms, hymns, and odes in the Spirit with your hearts to God. Everything you do and everything you say, do it all in the name of the Lord Jesus. Give thanks to God the Father through him.

Wives, obey your husbands as is appropriate in the Lord. Husbands, love your wives, and never be harsh with them. Children, obey your parents in everything because this pleases the Lord. Fathers, do not anger your children so that they won't become rebellious. Slaves, obey your masters in everything related to the things of this world. Don't do this just outwardly to make them happy, but with sincerity of heart to please the Lord. What you do in terms of your soul, do to serve the Lord and not your human master. You will ultimately receive your inheritance from the Lord. You really serve the Lord Jesus the Messiah. The one who is unjust will be repaid by him for what he has done wrong. He shows no favoritism. Masters, give to your slaves what is right and fair. Remember that you have a master in the heavens whom you serve.

Pray continually. Watch. Give thanks in your prayers. Pray also for us, that God will give us the opportunity to preach the mystery of the Messiah, because of which I am now imprisoned. I am driven to preach it. Live wisely in the sight of those outside your community. Invest your time wisely. You should always speak graciously, seasoned with the salt of the truth, and answer each person carefully who comes to you for answers.

Tychicus, my brother whom I love, and a faithful deacon and fellow servant of the Lord, will let you know how I am doing. I sent him to you for this reason—so that you would know how I am doing and so that he could encourage your hearts. I sent him with Onesimus, another faithful brother whom I love, who is from your community. They will tell you everything.

Aristarchus, my fellow prisoner, greets you. So does Mark, Barnabas's cousin. If Mark comes to visit you, you've received instructions to welcome him. Also Jesus, who is called Justus, who is a Jewish coworker with me for the kingdom of God—he has been a great comfort to me.

Epaphras greets you, who is from your community. He is a servant of the Messiah Jesus who is always diligently praying for you. He prays that you would become mature and fully committed to the will of God. I testify about him that he cares for you deeply and for all those in Laodicea and Hierapolis.

Luke the physician greets you, whom I love. Also Demas.

Greet the brothers in Laodicea and also Nympha and the members of the community that meets in her house.

When you have had this letter read in your community, you should also have it read in the community in Laodicea. You should also get the letter I wrote to Laodicea and have it read to you. Tell Archippus to attend to the ministry that he received in the Lord so that he can fulfill it.

I greet you with my own hand. Paul.
Remember that I am in prison.
Grace be with you. Amen.

TO THE
EPHESIANS

Paul, an apostle sent by the Messiah Jesus according to the will of God,

To the holy ones who are faithful to the Messiah Jesus in Ephesus,

Grace to you and peace from God our Father and the Lord Jesus the Messiah,

Blessed is God the Father of our Lord Jesus the Messiah, who has blessed us with every blessing in the Spirit in the heavens in the Messiah. He called us before he began the creation of the world to be holy and blameless before him. Out of love, he set things in order in advance for us to be adopted as sons of God through Jesus the Messiah, according to his goodwill toward us. Let us praise the gift of glory that he has given us through the Messiah, whom he loves. In the Messiah, we have been set free by his blood through the forgiveness of our sins. So rich is the gift that he has given to us. He has also given us wisdom and understanding by making known to us his will for us, according to his goodwill. When the time was right, he brought everything together in the Messiah, who unites heaven and earth in himself. In him we have obtained an inheritance that was arranged beforehand according to God's purposes. He works all things according to his will. He wants those of us who have already trusted in the

Messiah to one day praise his glory in the age to come. You have heard the true word, the gospel of your salvation. Being faithful to it, you have been sealed with the Holy Spirit for the promises to come. The Spirit of God is the down payment on our inheritance. He sets us free by taking ownership of us for God, until one day we praise his glory in the age to come.

I have heard of the faithfulness of your community to the Lord Jesus and the love that you have toward all the holy ones. I never stop giving thanks for you and mentioning you in my prayers. I pray that the God of our Lord Jesus the Messiah, the Father of glory, will give you the Spirit of wisdom and revelation so that you may know him better. I pray that he will open the eyes of your heart so that you will see the great hope that will come when we answer his call, the riches of his glorious inheritance for the saints. I want you to know just how great the miraculous power of God is toward us who are faithful, who work with his might and strength. He worked this miraculous power in the Messiah when he raised him from the dead and seated him at his right hand in the heavens. The Messiah is enthroned above every angelic and demonic power, including the gods you used to worship. This not only is true now but also will be true in the age to come. He put everything under the Messiah's feet and made the Messiah the head of everything for the communities of God, which are his body. He fills everything.

You were dead in your crimes and sins, in your old way of life in this age, in this world. You followed the authoritarian ruler of the air, the spirit that is still working through the sons of disobedience. All of us once lived to try to fulfill the sinful desires of our flesh, giving our sinful flesh what it wanted. We thought sinful thoughts. We were natural-born children of wrath, just like everyone else. But God, because he has so much mercy and such great love for us, even though we were dead in our sins, he made us alive with the Messiah. Your salvation is a gift.

He raised us up with the Messiah and seated us in the heavens with the Messiah Jesus. In the age to come, he will show us the great riches of his gift given to us in kindness in the Messiah Jesus. Your salvation is a gift, received through your faithfulness. It is not your own doing; God gives it as a gift. You didn't earn it, so no one has a reason to brag. We are his creation, created in the Messiah Jesus to do good works that God arranged in advance for us to do. This is how we now live.

Before, you were descended from the nations. You were called "uncircumcised" by those who have been circumcised by the hands of a man. At that time, you were separated from the Messiah. You were a foreigner to the nation of Israel. You were a stranger to the covenants and the promises to Abraham. You had no hope, and you did not know God. But now, because of the Messiah Jesus, you who were far away have come near through the blood of the Messiah. He is our peace offering. He has made one people from Jews and non-Jews. He has broken down the wall that kept you away from the temple. He has removed the hostility between us through his humanity. The commandments and ordinances of the Torah that kept you away from God have been annulled so that from both groups he could create one new humanity and establish peace. He has reconciled both groups in his one body to God through his death on the cross. With the cross, he killed our enmity. After he rose, he proclaimed the gospel: "Peace be to you." Peace be to those far off, and peace to those who are near. Through him, both groups have access by the one Spirit of God to the Father.

You are no longer strangers and aliens. Now you are fellow citizens with the holy ones and part of God's household. God's household is built on the foundation of the apostles and the prophets. The Messiah Jesus is the cornerstone. In him, the whole building is put together and is consecrated as a holy temple to the Lord. In the Messiah, you are being built into a dwelling place for God's Spirit.

This is the gift that I, Paul, the prisoner for the Messiah Jesus, bring to the nations. You have heard of the position given to me by God, to bring his gift to you. He revealed to me the mystery, just as I have written to you before briefly. If you read it, you will understand my explanation of the mystery of the Messiah. This mystery was not known to humans in previous generations but has now been revealed to the holy apostles and prophets by the Spirit. The nations are coheirs and part of one body regarding the promises to Abraham in the Messiah Jesus through the gospel. I am a servant of the gospel through the gracious gift of God, which was given to me through his miraculous power. I am the very least of all the saints, but I was given this gift, to preach to the nations the inexhaustible riches of the Messiah. I seek to enlighten all people with this mystery that was hidden from the ages in God. The one who created all things is now made known to all the angelic and demonic powers in the heavens through the communities of God on earth. This is the wisdom of God. It has been his plan from ages past. He has accomplished this plan in the Messiah Jesus our Lord. In him we have bold and confident access to God, through his faithfulness. I ask you not to lose heart at my troubles for you. They are your glory.

This is the gift that causes me to bow my knees to the Father of our Lord Jesus the Messiah. Every father of a family in heaven and on earth is named for him. I pray that he might give you the riches of his glory, through his miraculous power. I pray that the Spirit of God will strengthen you, the new person who is forming in you. I pray that through your faithfulness the Messiah will come to dwell in your hearts. Faithfulness is rooted and founded in love. I pray that you will understand, with all the holy ones, how wide and long and high and deep the love of the Messiah is. I pray that you will be filled up full by God. To the one who is able to do all these things that we ask or think through his miraculous power that works in us, to him be glory in the communities and in the Messiah Jesus to every generation and unto the ages of ages. Amen.

I encourage you, as a prisoner in the Lord, to live up to the calling that you have received from God. Be humble and gentle. Patiently bear with each other in love. Work hard to keep the unity of the Spirit and the bond of peace in your community. Be one body and one Spirit. You were called to one hope in all your callings. You have one Lord, one path of faithfulness, and one baptism. One God is the Father of us all, and he is over everyone, creates everything, and is everywhere. Each of us has been given one gift, measured out to us by the Messiah. The Scriptures say, "He ascended on high and took slavery as a slave. He gave gifts to men." The one who ascended is also the one who descended into the underworld at his death. The one who descended into Hades is also the one who ascended above everything and everyone that is in the heavens. He fills all things.

He gave some people the gift of being apostles, others prophets, others to spread the gospel, some shepherds and teachers who serve as leaders in the communities, others for the work of deacons, and all for the building up of the body of the Messiah. This will continue until we all attain unity in faithfulness and the knowledge of the Son of God— until each of us has grown into the likeness of the Messiah. Then we will no longer be infants who are tossed about by waves or blown around by the wind of any new teaching. We won't be deceived by clever human arguments or schemes or deceit. We will speak the truth in love and grow up to be like the one who is the head of all things, the Messiah. Every part of the body is linked together and made alive by being connected to the head. Each part works together to help the body grow and build itself up in love.

I testify to you in the Lord, you should no longer live the way the nations live. Their minds are clouded and useless. Their understanding is darkened because they are separated from the life of God. They are ignorant, and their hearts are hard. They have lost their sensitivity toward God and have given themselves up to the desires of their flesh, to unclean works, and to greediness. This is not how you have learned to live from the Messiah, if you have heard him and have been taught by him in the truth of Jesus. Cast aside your old way of life, the person you used to be, which is corrupt with passions and treachery. Be made new by the Spirit in your mind. Put on the new person that God has created in purity and holiness and truth.

Since you have cast aside lies, tell the truth to each other. We are parts of one body. When you are angry, do not sin. Do not let the sun set on your anger. Do not give the devil an opportunity. If someone was a thief, he must not steal. Instead, he should work hard with his own hands to do good and to have something to share with those in need. Don't let corrupt words leave your mouth. Speak good things that build people up and help with their needs so that those who hear you are given a gift. Do not sadden the Holy Spirit of God, who has sealed you for the day on which you will be set free. Cast away bitterness, rage, anger, and feuding. Cast away all evil. Be kind to one another, tenderhearted. Forgive each other as God in the Messiah forgave you.

Imitate God as children whom he loves. Live in love. Have the same love with which the Messiah loved us, who gave himself for us as a sacrificial offering to God with a sweet-smelling aroma. Don't let sexual immorality or any uncleanness or greed even be referred to in your community. Remember that you are holy ones. Get rid of all filthiness and foolish talk and crude and inappropriate jokes. Instead, use your mouths to give thanks to God. You know that any sexually immoral or unclean or greedy person or an idolater does not have an inheritance in the kingdom of the Messiah and God. Don't let anyone trick you with empty words. The wrath of God is coming to the sons of disobedience because of these things. Don't associate with them.

Before, you were in darkness. Now you are in the light of the Lord. Live as children of light. The fruit produced by a child of the light is goodness and justice and truth. Discern those things that please the

Lord. Don't associate with those whose works are unfruitful, who are still in darkness. Shine the light on them. The things they do in secret are shameful to even talk about. But when you shine a light on them, they become visible. Then they can repent and come to the light. The Scriptures say, "Awake, you who are sleeping, and rise from the dead, and the Messiah will shine on you."

Watch how you live. Do not be foolish but wise. Invest your time wisely because these are evil days. Do not be foolish; learn what the will of the Lord is. Do not be drunk with wine and partying. Be filled with the Spirit. Sing psalms and hymns and odes together in the Spirit. Sing and make melody in your heart to the Lord. Always give thanks for everything in the name of our Lord Jesus the Messiah to God the Father.

Be obedient to one another in reverence toward the Messiah. Wives, be obedient to your husbands, as to the Lord. The husband is the head of the wife as the Messiah is the head of the community. He is the savior of the body. As the communities of God are under the authority of the Messiah, wives are under the authority of their husbands in everything. Husbands, love your wives as the Messiah loves the communities of God and gave himself up for them. He made them holy and purified them with the washing of water by a word. He will present the community of all the holy ones to himself in glory. It will not have a spot or a wrinkle or any blemish. It will be holy and blameless. This is how you who are husbands must love your wives, as if they were your own body. The person who loves his wife loves himself. No one hates his own body. You nourish and protect your body the way the Messiah does the communities. We are all parts of his body. We are bone of his bone and flesh of his flesh. This is why a man will leave his father and mother and be united to his wife, and the two will be one flesh. This is a great mystery. I speak of the Messiah and the united communities of God. But as for each of you, each husband should love his wife as himself, and each wife should respect her husband.

Children, obey your parents in the Lord. This is the right thing to do. Honor your father and your mother. This is the first commandment of the Torah that has a promise attached: "so that it will be good for you, and you will live many years on the earth." Fathers, do not anger your children, but educate them in the knowledge of the Lord. Slaves, obey your masters according to the flesh with awe and reverence and a sincere heart, as if they were the Messiah. Do not just do this outwardly when people can see, but be servants of the Messiah and do the will of God from your soul. Do your work with goodwill as if you are serving the Lord and not people. Know that everyone who serves well will receive a reward from the Lord, whether they are a slave or a freeman. Masters, do the same toward slaves. Do not threaten them with violence, because you know that you have a master in the heavens. He does not show any favoritism.

Be strong in the Lord and in the power of his strength. Put on the whole suit of God's armor so that you will be able to resist the schemes of the devil. We are not struggling against other humans, but against the demonic powers, the cosmic powers of darkness, and the spiritual forces of evil in the heavens and on earth. Put on the whole suit of God's armor so that you can resist when an evil day comes. When you have done all that, you can stand firm. Wear the truth as a belt. Put on justice as a breastplate. Let your feet be ready to move to spread the gospel of peace. Pick up faithfulness as a shield with which you can block all the evil one's flaming arrows that he will shoot at you. Put on salvation as a helmet and the Spirit as a sword. This is God's instruction.

Pray continually at any time and in every season in the Spirit. Watch with perseverance and make intercessions for all the holy ones. Pray also for me, that I may find the right words when I open my mouth, so that I can preach the mystery of the gospel with boldness. I am an ambassador for the gospel in chains. I must speak boldly.

I have sent you Tychicus, my brother whom I love, to tell you everything that is going on with me and everything I am doing. I want him to let you know everything that is going on with me, and I want him to encourage you in your hearts.

Brothers, peace and love with faithfulness be yours from God the Father and the Lord Jesus the Messiah. Grace be with all those who love our Lord Jesus the Messiah without corruption.

TO
PHILEMON

Paul, a prisoner for the Messiah Jesus, and my brother Timothy,

To Philemon, our fellow worker whom I love, and to Apphia our sister, and Archippus our fellow soldier, and the whole community who meets in your house,

Grace to you and peace from God our Father and the Lord Jesus the Messiah,

I thank my God continually as I continually pray for you. I hear of your love and faithfulness to the Lord Jesus the Messiah and to all the holy ones. I pray for your faithful community that you might have every good thing in the Messiah. I have great joy, and I am greatly encouraged by your love because the hearts of the holy ones have been refreshed by you, my brother.

I could write to you very boldly in the name of the Messiah and give you commands. But because of the love that we share, I encourage you as Paul, an old man who is now also a prisoner for the Messiah Jesus. I encourage you on behalf of my child, whom I have begotten by the gospel while in chains, Onesimus. Once he was useless, but now he is very useful to both you and me. I have sent him back to you in person, he who is my heart, even though I wanted to keep him here with me. I sent him so that he could serve you in the chains of the gospel. I didn't want to do anything without your consent, only with your agreement. Maybe he was separated from you for a time so that you would be together in the age to come. He is no longer just a slave. He is more than a slave now; he is a beloved brother to me especially. He should be a much more beloved brother to you, both in this world and in the Lord.

If you and I share a communal bond, then receive him the way you would receive me. If he has wronged you in some way or if he owes you something, charge this to my account instead.

I, Paul, write this with my own hand. I will repay it.

I would never say that you owe me anything. Brother, I have truly profited from you in the Lord. Refresh my heart in the Messiah. Because I know about your obedience, I am writing to you, knowing that you will do far beyond anything I ask. Also, please arrange a place for me to stay. I hope that through your prayers, I will be able to come and visit you.

Epaphras, my follow prisoner in the Messiah Jesus, greets you. So do Mark, Aristarchus, Demas, and Luke, my coworkers.

The grace of the Lord Jesus the Messiah be with your spirit. Amen.

ANOTHER EPISTLE TO THE
CORINTHIANS

Paul, an apostle of the Messiah Jesus by the will of God, and Timothy, my brother,

To the community of God in Corinth and all the holy ones in all of Achaia,

Grace to you and peace from God our Father and the Lord Jesus the Messiah,

Blessed is God, the Father of our Lord Jesus the Messiah. He is the Father of compassion and the God of all comfort. He comforts us in all our troubles so that we can also comfort others in the troubles they face. We are comforted in our own troubles by God. Even though we have suffered a lot for the Messiah, the Messiah has comforted us even more. If we are imprisoned, it is for your comfort and salvation. If we are comforted, it is also for your comfort, so that you can develop endurance when you face the same kind of suffering that we do. But our hope for you is solid. Since we share the same sufferings, we will share the same comfort.

Brothers, we have to be honest that the troubles we faced in Asia were extreme, nearly beyond our power to endure. We were weighed down heavily, and we thought we might end up dead. But even though we felt as though we were under a death sentence, we didn't trust in our own judgment but in God, who raises the dead. He delivered us from death in Asia and will deliver us from death in the future. We have hope that he will continue to deliver us. Please join together with us in prayer so that through many prayers, when God gives his gift, there will be many to give thanks to him for us.

If we were going to brag about something, it would be this: Our conscience is clean. We have lived in the world in holiness and sincerity toward God. We don't live according to human wisdom but by the gift of God. This is especially true of how we lived with you.

We are not writing to you about things that you won't be able to read and understand. I want you now to understand fully some things that you understood only partially in the past. Then on the day of our Lord Jesus, you will give testimony for us, as we will for you.

I was confidently planning to visit you so that I could give you a second gift and then pass through Corinth to Macedonia. Then I would stop and see you again on the way back from Macedonia, and you could have helped prepare me to return to Judea. This was a firm plan that I had in mind. I am not going back and forth and telling you both "yes" and "no." God is faithful, and we have not been noncommittal in our communication with you. We preached the son of God, the Messiah Jesus, to you, Silvanus and Timothy and I. We did not say "yes and no" then, but always "yes" to the Messiah. God gave many promises, and the Messiah is "yes" to all of them. He is the "amen" of God for his glory. God is now establishing you and us in the Messiah by anointing us. He has sealed us and given us the Spirit as a pledge in our hearts.

I can call God as a witness on behalf of my life that I have not come to Corinth yet to spare you. We don't want to lord it over your faithfulness. We are your joyful fellow workers. Stand firm in the faith. I decided not to come to you again in sadness. You make me joyful; I don't want to sadden you. I wrote what I wrote to you so that I wouldn't have to be saddened when I visit. I want to rejoice when I visit. I think that if I am joyful, we all will be. When I wrote to you, I wrote with trouble and sorrow in my heart through tears. I didn't write to hurt you but so that you would know how much I love you.

If anyone has caused pain, he hasn't caused me any. He has really hurt you—not to be mean. He has been punished enough. It would be good for you to forgive him and comfort him so that his sorrow doesn't overwhelm him. Please confirm your love for him. This is another reason I wrote to you, so that I would see how obedient you are. Anyone whom you forgive, I also forgive. Anything that I forgive, I forgive for your sake in the presence of the Messiah so that we don't end up falling prey to Satan. We are aware of how he schemes against us.

When I came to Troas preaching the gospel of the Messiah, I had an opportunity from the Lord. My spirit was restless because I didn't find my brother Titus there. So, I departed to Macedonia.

I give thanks to God, who always leads us in a triumphal parade in the Messiah. The fragrance of the incense of the knowledge of God follows us to every place we travel. We are the sweet aroma of the Messiah to God. To those who are being saved, we are a fragrance of new life. To those who are dying, we are an odor of death. Who could be worthy of this? We are not out there selling the Word of God for a fee, as many people do. We speak sincerely of God, in the presence of God in the Messiah.

Are we trying to promote ourselves? Do we need, like some people do, to get recommendation letters for you or from you? Our letter of recommendation is you, written in our hearts. This letter is available for all people to read. You are a letter from the Messiah, having been ministered to by us, written with the Spirit of God rather than ink. This letter is not written on stone tablets but on human hearts.

Because of the Messiah, we can confidently approach God. We are not worthy of this on our own; God makes us worthy. He has made us the worthy servants of a new covenant, not written on paper but written by the Spirit. The paper kills, and the Spirit gives life. The service of death, engraved in letters on stone tablets, was produced in glory on Mt. Sinai. The sons of Israel were unable to even look at Moses' face because of the glory there, which was slowly fading away. How much more glorious is the ministry of the Spirit? If the ministry of condemnation was glorious, how much more glorious is the ministry of purification? What was once considered glorious no longer looks glorious because something so much more glorious has come. Glory that remains is more glorious than glory that fades.

Because we have hope, we also have great boldness. We don't cover our face with a veil as Moses did because the sons of Israel could not bear to look at the glory that was fading away. Their minds were hardened. Even to this very day, the veil remains for them over the old covenant. They can't bear to look at its glory. In the Messiah, the veil is being removed. But until this very day, when they read Moses, there is a veil over their heart. But if they turn to the Lord, the veil is taken away. The Spirit is the Lord. Where the Spirit of the Lord is, people are free. We have now had the veil removed, and we can look at the face of the Torah. There we see the glory of the Lord, and we are transformed into his image, from one glory to the next, just as the Spirit comes from the Lord.

We received this ministry as a mercy from God. Because we have it, we don't lose heart. We have renounced the hidden, shameful things. We do not walk in deceit or make our own version of the Word of God. We make plain the truth before all people, and this commends us before God. If the gospel we preach is not understandable, it is not understandable to those who are dying. The god of this age has blinded the minds of the faithless so that they won't see the light of the gospel of the glory of the Messiah, who is the image of God. We don't promote ourselves. We preach the Messiah, Jesus the Lord. We are your servants on behalf of Jesus. The same God who says, "Out of darkness, light will shine," shone in our hearts the light of the knowledge of God's glory in the face of Jesus the Messiah.

We have God's treasure in clay pots. This way, you know that the miraculous power is from God and not us. We face all kinds of trouble, but we haven't been broken. We have been beset by confusion, but we haven't given in to despair. We have been attacked, but we have never been forsaken. We have been struck down, but not destroyed. We carry around the death of Jesus in our body all the time so that one day the resurrected life of Jesus will appear in our body. We are alive, but we are constantly facing death for Jesus so that the resurrected life of Jesus may appear in our mortal bodies. Death works in us; life works in you.

We have the same Spirit of faithfulness. The Scriptures say, "I have been faithful, so I have spoken." We are faithful, and we also speak. We know that God, who raised the Lord Jesus, will also raise us from the dead and gather us along with you. Everything is for your sake. Your gifts must increase more and more so that your thanksgiving to the glory of God will also increase. We don't lose heart. The person we are on the outside ages and decays, but the new person inside us is being made new day after day. The troubles that we have in this life can't compare to the incredible glory that awaits us in the age to come. Don't look for things that are easily seen, but for things that haven't been seen yet. The things we see are temporary, but the things we will soon see will last forever.

We know that if our body on this earth, which we dwell in like a tent, is destroyed, we will receive a new house, not made by humans but by God in the age to come in the heavens. We groan because we want to enter into our house that is from the heavens. If we are found in that house, we will not be caught homeless. If we have clothing, we are not naked. We don't want to be naked, but to be clothed. We want our mortal flesh to be swallowed up by immortal life. God is preparing this for us and has given us the Spirit as a deposit. Right now, we are at home in our bodies, but we are not with the Lord. We live faithfully even though we haven't seen our reward. We are confident. We would be pleased to be absent from our body and to be at home with the Lord. Whether we are at home or away from home, we never stop trying to be pleasing to him in our lives. Every one of us will stand before the throne of the Messiah for judgment. Each of us will receive a reward for what we did in our bodies, whether good or evil.

Being reverent toward the Lord, we seek to persuade men. God knows who we are, and I hope that you do also. We are not, again, promoting ourselves to you. But, if someone comes to you boasting about external things and not about the things of the heart, you will have an answer to them from us. We are ecstatic before God, but we are serious concerning you. The love of the Messiah shows us that one died for everyone, and therefore everyone died. He died for everyone so that those who are alive would no longer live selfishly but would live faithfully to the one who died for them and was raised again. Don't look at things from the outside. We once looked at the Messiah from the outside, but we no longer know him that way. Everyone is a new creation in the Messiah. The old person whom he was has passed away. The new person that he will be has been created. All of this is from God, who has reconciled us to himself in the Messiah and has given to us the ministry of reconciling people to God. God has been reconciling the whole world to himself in the Messiah, not keeping record of their sins any longer and giving us the word of reconciliation, the gospel.

We are ambassadors of the Messiah. God calls out through us; we persuade on behalf of the Messiah. Be reconciled to God. He made the one who did not know sin to be a sin offering so that we might be purified before God in him.

Working together with God in this way, we encourage you: Do not let God's gift that you have received amount to nothing. The Scriptures say, "At the right time I listened to you, and in the day of salvation, I helped you." Now is the right time. Today is the day of salvation. We don't put obstacles in people's way that would hinder our ministry. In everything, we seek to be commendable servants of God. We endure trouble, difficulties, beatings, imprisonments, riots, forced labor, being put under guard, and fasting. We endure in purity, knowledge, patience, kindness, in the Holy Spirit, in genuine love, in the word of truth, in the miraculous power of God. We fight with the weapons of purification in our right hand and our left. We endure through glory and dishonor; bad and good reputation; as imposters who are nonetheless true; as unknown, though we are well known; as dying, and yet we live; as being disciplined but not being killed; as those who are sorrowful but are always rejoicing; as poor, and yet we enrich many; as having nothing but possessing everything. We've spoken to you plainly, Corinthians, and our hearts have grown. We are not controlling you; you are controlled by your hearts. I speak to you as children. May your reward grow.

Do not marry someone who is not part of the faithful community. What kind of partnership can justice have with lawlessness? What kind of friendship can light and darkness have? Can the Messiah and Belial live in harmony? Those who are married are one flesh. Can a faithful person have a faithless body part? What agreement is there between the temple of God and idols? We are the living temple of God. God has said, "I will live in them and live among them. I will be their God, and they will be my people. Therefore, come out of them and be separate, says the Lord. Touch nothing unclean, and I will receive you. I will be your Father, and you will be my sons and daughters, says the Lord Almighty."

I love you. We have received the promises to Abraham in the Messiah. We must cleanse ourselves from every uncleanness of flesh and spirit.

We must mature in holiness and reverence toward God. Make room for us in your hearts. We have wronged no one. We have corrupted no one. We have exploited no one. I am not condemning you. You are in our hearts. We die together, and we will live together. I write boldly to you because I am very proud of you. You have encouraged me. I am filled with joy in all our affliction.

When we came to Macedonia, we had no rest for our bodies. We were troubled in every way. From the outside came conflicts. From inside us came fears. But God, who comforts the humble, comforted us through the arrival of Titus. Not only did his company comfort us, but the news he brought to us about you also comforted us. He told me of your mourning and your zeal for me, which made me rejoice even more. If I upset you with my last letter, I don't regret it. I did regret it, but now I see that for a time, that letter upset you. I am not happy that you were upset. I am happy that your being upset led you to repentance. You were saddened in a godly way, so the letter did you no harm. This kind of godly sadness produces repentance that leads to salvation without regret. Worldly sadness only leads to death.

Look at what this godly sadness has produced. You have become dedicated, you give a reasoned defense, you are indignant, you are reverent, you have longing and zeal, you are vindicated. Through all of these, you have rendered yourself innocent. I didn't write to you for the one who did wrong. I didn't write to you for the one who suffered the wrong. Rather, I wrote to you to reveal this dedication of yours before God in repentance. This brought us great comfort. Beyond our comfort, we also rejoiced at Titus's joy. He was refreshed in the Spirit by your community. You lived up to everything I told him about you. Everything we had said to Titus turned out to be true. He has great affection for you and remembers all your obedience and how you received him with honor and reverence. I rejoice that my confidence in you was not misplaced.

Brothers, I have given you the gift of God that was also given to the communities in Macedonia. They have faced great difficulties with an abundance of joy. Despite their deep poverty, they have been richly generous. I can testify that they gave of themselves even beyond what they were able. They begged us for the gift and community of serving among the holy ones. Beyond what we hoped, they gave first to the Lord and then also to us by the will of God. We encouraged Titus that as he had made a beginning with you, he should continue with this gift. You have many great gifts: faithfulness, speaking, knowledge, dedication, and the love that we share. I want you to receive this gift, supporting the ministry, as well. I am not giving you an order, but seeing the dedication of others, I hope that you will prove that your love is real.

You know the gift of our Lord Jesus the Messiah. For your sake he became poor even though he had been rich, so that you would be made rich by his poverty. I will give my opinion in this. I think it would be good for you. You began to do this and to desire it a year ago. Now you should follow through. Bring your goodwill into action by giving from what you have. If you have the desire, you should give according to what you have, not what you don't have. I am not trying to make things easier on others but more difficult on you. Now, your abundance can help those who are in need. Maybe some of their abundance can help your own needs, and then all needs will be met. The Scriptures say, "He who has much does not have too much, and the one who has little does not lack anything."

I thank God that he put the same dedication to you in Titus that I have. He accepted our comfort, but being very dedicated, he decided himself to return to you. We sent a brother with him who is famous in all the communities for preaching the gospel. He was chosen by the communities to travel with us and share in our gift of ministry. We sent him for the glory of the Lord and to show our goodwill. We don't want anyone to think that we are selfish or arrogant about this ministry that has been entrusted to us. We want to have a clear conscience before God and other people. We also sent our brother with them who has proven how dedicated he is, often and in many things. Now he is even more dedicated to you. Regarding Titus, he is my partner and coworker for you. As for our brothers, they are sent by the communities for the glory of the Messiah. Show them the proof of your love and of all that we've said about you. By showing this to them, you will show it to all the other communities of the faithful.

There is no reason for me to write to you about the ministry to the holy ones. I know your commitment, and I have told the Macedonians that Achaia has been ready to help for a year. Your zeal has been encouraging a great number of Macedonians to participate. I have sent you the brothers so that what we have said about you will not prove to be false. They will make sure that you are committed, as you told me. Otherwise, if some Macedonians came with me and you were unprepared, we would be embarrassed. You would be embarrassed, too, for all of my confidence in you. So, I encouraged the brothers to go to you first so that they could bring you this blessing, just as we spoke of a year ago. When you are ready, it will be a free gift, not a question of greed.

The one who sows stingily will also reap stingily. The one who sows blessings will reap blessings. Each person should give from the heart, not out of sadness or guilt. God loves a cheerful giver. God is able to give all abundant gifts to you so that in every way you will always have what you need to do every good work. As the Scriptures say, "He has scattered seed widely. He has given to the poor. His justice remains unto the age to come." God provides seed to the one who sows and gives bread for food. He will supply and multiply your seed, and he will increase the just yield of your harvest. In every way, he will enrich you so that you can be generous. This generosity causes us to give thanks to God. The service of this ministry is not just meeting all the needs of the holy ones. It overflows into thanks and praise to God. Those who receive this ministry will glorify God for what you have given, because you confessed the gospel of the Messiah. They will give thanks for the communal generosity that you have toward everyone. They will care for you and pray for you because of the gift that God has given through you. Thank God for his incredible gift.

I, Paul, encourage you by the meekness and gentleness of the Messiah. When I was with you, I was humble. Now that I am absent from you, I am bold. When I am there again, I don't want to have to be bold in confronting some people who have been saying that we live according to our sinful desires. We are alive in the body, but we fight against our sinful desires. The weapons of our warfare are not fleshly desires. We use the miraculous power of God, which can destroy the enemies' strongholds. We crush arguments and any other proud attempt to counter the true knowledge of God. We seek to make every thought that comes into our minds a captive and make it obey the Messiah. If we have to, we will deal with disobedience, but we would rather see your complete obedience.

Don't just look at how things appear from the outside. If anyone is confident that he is a follower of the Messiah, he should think again. If he is a follower of the Messiah, he should know that so are we. I may go on too much about our authority, but it was given to us by the Lord to build you up, not to tear you down. I am not embarrassed. I don't write letters to scare you. I know people say that my letters are heavy and powerful, but in person I am weak and don't speak well. They should know that what we say in letters when we are absent, we do when we are there in person.

We are not going to compare ourselves with people who go around promoting themselves. They measure themselves and compare themselves to each other, competing for your attention. They don't understand. We are not here to promote ourselves. We measure ourselves by the ministry assigned to us by God, a ministry that touches you. I am not overreaching to say that it touches you because we came to you preaching the gospel of the Messiah. We are not going to promote ourselves based on the work of others. We have hope that your faithfulness will continue to grow, which will greatly increase our reach. We want to continue the work in a land past yours, not brag about what has already been done. If someone is going to brag, let him brag about the Lord. Anyone who promotes himself is not approved. The one whom God promotes is approved.

Please bear with a little foolishness on my part. Please bear with me. I am jealous for you the way God is jealous. I betrothed you to one husband so that as a pure virgin you could be presented to the Messiah on your wedding day. But I am afraid that, as when the serpent tricked Eve with his deceit, your minds might also be corrupted and lose the simple purity that you have in the Messiah. If someone comes to you preaching another Jesus—not him whom we proclaimed to you—or if you receive a spirit other than the Spirit you received when we came, or a gospel different from the one you accepted from us, then you will hear that person out. I am not inferior to these very important apostles. My speech may be a little unskilled, but I don't lack in knowledge. I have been completely open to you in everything.

Did I do wrong when I humbled myself so that you might be lifted up when I preached the gospel of God to you without charge? I robbed other communities. I received support from them that I used to minister to you. When I was with you, even though I was in need, I didn't burden anyone. The brothers who came from Macedonia filled all my needs. I made sure that I was never a burden to you. I didn't burden you, and I won't burden you. By the truth of the Messiah in me, this is known in all of Achaia. Why? Because I don't love you? God knows that I do.

I am going to continue to operate this way so that none of these false teachers will be able to say that they work the same way we do. These are false apostles, treacherous workers. They disguise themselves as apostles of the Messiah. No wonder—Satan himself disguises himself as an angel of light. You shouldn't be surprised that his servants disguise themselves as just servants. They will receive the rewards of their evil deeds.

No one should think that I am a fool. But allow me to play the fool for a moment so I can speak about myself. I am not now speaking on behalf of the Lord but as a fool. Since these people like to brag about their bona fides, allow me. You seem to like to listen to fools, though you are very wise. If one of them comes to enslave you or devour you or take advantage of you or boast about themselves or slap you in the face, you are fine with it. I am a little embarrassed that we were too weak to do any of that when we were there.

Whatever those fools brag about, I can also brag about as a fool. Are they Hebrews? Me too. Are they Israelites? Me too. Are they descendants of Abraham? Me too. Are they servants of the Messiah? Now here's the thing. I am a servant of the Messiah, but I have worked harder, spent more time in prison, been beaten more, faced death more often than they have. Five times from the synagogue I have received the forty lashes minus one. Three times I was beaten with rods. Once I was stoned. Three times I was shipwrecked. Once I spent a night and a day floating in the sea. I travel continually, facing roaring rivers, robbers, opposition from the Jewish people and from people among the nations, trouble in the city, trouble in the desert, trouble at sea, and betrayal by false brothers. I work and I toil. I stay up late into the night. I am hungry and thirsty. I fast continually. I have shivered in the cold, naked. All these things are just my external struggles. Inwardly, I face the stress of my care for communities spread throughout the world. When the brothers are weak, I am weak. When my brothers fall into sin, I burn inside.

If I have to brag, I will brag about all these weaknesses of mine. The God and Father of the Lord Jesus, who is blessed unto ages of ages, knows I am not lying. In Damascus, the governor who served King

Aretas was guarding the city when the Damascenes arrested me. I was let down through the city wall out a window in a basket, and I escaped.

If I still need to brag, though it isn't really helpful, we can talk about visions and revelations of the Lord. I know a person in the Messiah who, fourteen years ago, either in or out of the body, was caught up to the third heaven. God knows if it was inside or outside of the body. I know that this man, whether it was in the body or outside of the body—I don't know—was taken into Paradise, and he heard things there that no human can repeat. I would boast about someone like that, but I would never brag about myself—other than about my weaknesses. If I were to brag, I wouldn't be foolish. I could just speak the truth, but I won't because I don't want anyone to think too much of me. In order to keep me from becoming arrogant because of the revelations, God gave me a thorn in my flesh, an angel of Satan, that would vex me so I wouldn't become arrogant. Three times I asked the Lord to take it away from me. Each time he said to me, "My gift is enough for you. My miraculous power is manifested fully in your weakness." This is why I'm happy to brag about my weaknesses: they show the power of the Messiah. I take pleasure in my weaknesses, in being insulted, in facing difficulties, in being attacked, and in struggles for the Messiah. When I am weak, I am actually the most powerful.

Look, now I am a fool, and you drove me to it. You should have vouched for me. There is no way in which I am inferior to those very important apostles, even though I am nothing. The signs that I was sent by God appeared when I was with you in my perseverance, and in signs, wonders, and miracles. How were you any worse off than any of the other communities of the Messiah? Is it because I didn't burden you financially? Forgive me for doing that to you.

I am ready to come to you a third time, and I will not burden you this time either. I'm not coming for the things that belong to you; I'm coming for you. Children shouldn't save up for their parents; parents should leave an inheritance for their children. I will gladly spend and even be spent to save your souls. If I love you more, why would you love me less? Do you think that because I didn't burden you financially, I was being clever and tricked you somehow? Did anyone I sent to you later take advantage of you? Did Titus take advantage of you? Do we not live by the same Spirit? Do we not share a way of life?

Don't think that this letter is defending ourselves to you. I love you. All of this is written to help build you in the Messiah before God. I am worried that when I come there, I will find that you are not how I want you to be, or that I will not be who you want me to be. I am worried there will be arguments, jealousy, anger, disagreements, slander, gossip, arrogance, and general disorder. I am worried that when I come, my God will humble me, and I will have to weep over many of you who have sinned before and have not repented of the uncleanness, sexual immorality, and sensuality that you have lived in.

When I come to you this third time, we will establish everything with two or three witnesses. I have warned you before, and I'll warn you now—like when I was there the second time—that if when I return, those who sinned before and all the rest of them, if they have not repented, I will spare no one. If you want proof that the Messiah speaks through me, see how he is not weak as I am, but he is powerful among you. He was crucified in weakness, but he lives by God's miraculous power. We are weak in him now, but we will live again with him by the miraculous power of God that already works in you. Examine yourselves, whether you are faithful. Test yourselves. Do you not realize that Jesus the Messiah is in you unless you fail this test? I hope by now you know that we have passed the test. We now pray to God that you do nothing wrong—not so that we can receive credit but so that you will do what is right. We may receive no credit.

We don't have any miraculous power against the truth, but only for the truth. We rejoice when we are weak but when you are strong. We pray for you to become mature. I write these things to you while I am absent so that when I am there, I won't have to use the authority that the Lord has given me harshly. I would rather use that authority to build you up than to tear you down.

Brothers, finally, rejoice. Come to maturity, be encouraged, be of the same mind, and be at peace. The God of love and peace will be with you.

Greet each other with a holy kiss. All the holy ones greet you.

The grace of the Lord Jesus the Messiah and the love of God and communion in the Holy Spirit be with all of you. Amen.

TO THE

HEBREWS

In many times and places and many ways, God spoke to our fathers in the prophets. In these last days, he has spoken to us in his son, whom he has made the heir of everything and through whom he made the ages. He is the radiance of God's glory and the perfect image of his person. He supports everything with the word of his miraculous power. He made purification for sins and then sat down at the right hand of the highest majesty. He has become greater than any angel and has inherited the name more majestic than theirs.

To what angel did God ever say, "You are my son. Today I have given birth to you"? Or "I will be his Father and he will be my son"? And also, when he brings his firstborn into the world, he says, "Let all the angels of God worship him." What he says about the angels is, "He makes his angels spirits and his ministers flames of fire." To the son he says, "Your throne, O God, is unto ages of ages. The scepter of justice is the scepter of your kingdom. You have loved purity and hated lawlessness. So, God, your God, has anointed you with the oil of joy beyond all your friends." Also, to the son he says, "Lord, in the beginning you laid the foundations of the earth, and the heavens are the work of your hands. They will be destroyed, but you will remain. All created things will grow old like a piece of clothing. You will roll them up like a robe. You will roll them up and change them like clothes. But you are the same, and there will be no end to your years." To what angel did God say, "Sit at my right hand until I make your enemies a footstool for you"? Aren't all the spirits ministers who are sent out by God to serve him? He sends them to minister to those who will inherit salvation.

This means we need to hold on tightly to the things we have been taught so that we don't drift away from them. The Torah was given through angels, and it is unalterable. Every sin and disobedience have a corresponding punishment. How will we fare if we neglect the salvation that has been declared to us by the Lord himself? What we teach was confirmed to us by those who heard him. What he taught was accompanied by signs, wonders, and miraculous powers. He distributed the Holy Spirit as he willed.

God did not place angels in the administration of the world to come, about which we taught you. But someone somewhere testified, "What is a human, that you are mindful of him, or a son of Adam, that you watch over him? You made him slightly inferior to the angels, but then you crowned him with glory and honor. You appointed him to govern your creation. You put everything under his authority." In putting everything under his authority, he left nothing outside of his authority. Right now, we don't see everything under his authority.

We see Jesus who, for a little while, was below the angels because of his suffering and death. After this, he was crowned with glory and honor. God's gift is that Jesus tastes death for everyone. It was appropriate that the one for whom everything was created and by whom everything was created bring many sons to glory. He is the archetype of their salvation. He brought their salvation to completion through his suffering. The one who makes them holy and those who are being made holy are all one. So he is not ashamed to call them brothers when he says, "I will declare your name to my brothers. In the midst of the council I will sing praises to you." Also, "I will trust in him." And "I and the children whom God has given me." The children are flesh and blood, and so he also shared their flesh and blood so that through his death he could destroy the one who holds the power of death, the devil. He has set free all of those who have spent their whole life afraid of death. That fear made them slaves. He did not come to help the angels. He came to help the descendants of Abraham. He needed to become like his brothers so that he could be a merciful and faithful high priest to God to make purification offerings for the sins of the people. Because he suffered and was tested, he is able to help those being tested.

Holy brothers who share in our heavenly calling, think of Jesus. He is the one sent for us to be the high priest of our confession. He is faithful to the one who appointed him, as was Moses in the tabernacle of the Lord. But Jesus is worthy of even greater glory than Moses. The one who builds a house is more honorable than the house itself. Every house is built by someone. This house is built by God. Moses was a faithful servant in God's house and spoke as a testimony to God. But the Messiah is the son in his house, and we are a part of that household if we remain committed to our hope firmly until the end.

The Holy Spirit says, "Today if you hear his voice, do not make your hearts hard as you did when you rebelled when you were tested in the wilderness. There, your fathers tested me, and they saw my works for forty years. I was angry with that generation, and I said, 'Their hearts are always wandering. They do not know my ways.' So, I swore in my wrath that they would not enter the place of my rest." Brothers, watch so that you never have an evil and faithless heart. Do not fall away from the living God. Encourage each other every day, for as long as your days last, so that none of you will grow hard in sinful lies. You are sharers with the Messiah if you hold on to your commitment from the beginning to the end.

As was said, "Today, if you hear his voice, do not make your hearts hard as you did when you rebelled." Those who heard then rebelled. But hadn't all of them come out of Egypt led by Moses? He was angry for forty years with those who had sinned. Their bodies fell in the desert. Those who were disobedient he vowed would never enter into the place of his rest. They were not able to enter the land because of their faithlessness.

We must be wary then, because the promise of entering God's rest remains, and none of us wants to fall short. We have had the gospel preached to us just as they did. Their hearing of it did them no good, because they were not faithful to what they heard. We who are faithful will enter into his rest. The Scriptures say, "So I swore in my wrath, 'They shall not enter the place of my rest.'" But his works have been finished since the creation of the world. He has said somewhere about the seventh day, "God rested on the seventh day from all his works." Remember, "They shall not enter the place of my rest." Some will still enter into the place of his rest, but not those who heard the gospel then. They did not enter because of their disobedience.

Remember, he calls a certain day "today" through David when he says a long time later, "Today, if you hear his voice, do not make your hearts hard." If Joshua had brought them into his rest, then David would not have still needed to say this many years later. So, there is still a Sabbath rest that awaits God's people. The one who has entered his rest rests from all his works just as God did from his works. We must remain dedicated to entering into that rest so that no one falls because of disobedience the way they did then.

The Word of God is alive and at work. He is sharper than any two-edged sword. He is so sharp that he cuts between soul and spirit, between joints and marrow. He can judge the thoughts and motivations of the heart. No creature is hidden from him. Everything is uncovered and stripped away before his eyes. He is the one we must please.

We have a great high priest who has gone through the heavens, Jesus, the son of God. We should keep hold of what we have said together.

We don't have a high priest who can't sympathize with our weakness. We have a high priest who has been tested in every way but hasn't sinned. We should come with boldness before the throne of God in the holy place so that we can receive mercy and grace to help us in our time of need.

High priests who are taken from among the people are appointed to represent people before God. They offer sacrifices for sins, and they exercise patience with those who are ignorant and wandering because they are also beset by weakness. A high priest must offer sin offerings not only for the people, but also for himself. No one decides themselves to be a high priest, but God calls them, as he did with Aaron.

The Messiah did not make himself a high priest. The one who says to him, "You are my son; today I have given birth to you" also says, "You are a priest unto the age to come, following the pattern of Melchizedek." During his life, he offered prayers and intercessions to the one who was able to save him from death. He offered them up with crying and tears. He was heard because of his reverence, but as a son, he learned from his sufferings what it means to come under authority. When he had completed this, he became the cause of salvation in the age to come to all those who are obedient to him. He was appointed as high priest by God after the pattern of Melchizedek.

There is a lot to say about this, and it is difficult to interpret, especially since you are getting tired of listening. You really ought to be teachers by now yourselves, but you still need someone to teach you the basic, beginning principles of the things of God. You are like infants who need milk rather than solid food. If you only drink milk, you will not gain knowledge of the word of purification, because you are still an infant. Someone mature can have solid food. These people use their senses constantly and train to be able to discern what is good and what is evil.

Having moved on from the beginnings of the teaching of the Messiah, we must move on toward maturity. We can't keep laying the same foundation over and over by only talking about repenting from works that lead to death, faithfulness to God, baptism, and catechesis, the laying on of hands for ordination, the resurrection of the dead, and the judgment of the age to come. We will move on and build on this foundation, if God allows. It is not possible once someone has been enlightened by baptism—having tasted of the heavenly gift in the eucharist, having received the Holy Spirit, and received the word of God that carries the miraculous power of the age to come—if they fall away, for them to repent and return. They would need to crucify the son of God again and expose him to public shame. Land that has received frequent rainfall will grow crops useful for the farmer. This is the blessing of God. Land that brings forth thorns and thistles is worthless and cursed. It is good for nothing but burning.

We love you, and we think better of you. Even though we need to speak this way, we seek your salvation. God is not unjust. He will not forget your work and the love that you've shown toward his name. You have ministered to the holy ones, and you are still ministering. We want each of you to show the same dedication and confidence in our hope until the end. Do not be lazy. Imitate those who have inherited the promises through faithfulness and patient endurance.

God gave his promises to Abraham. He had no one greater than himself to swear by, so he swore by himself: "I will surely bless you and multiply you." He endured patiently for years, and then he obtained the promise. People swear by someone greater than them. They use an oath to end any dispute. God used this to show to the heirs of the promise that his purpose would not change. He guaranteed it with an oath. He swore by two unchangeable things. It is impossible for God to lie. Be strongly encouraged. We have fled to God for refuge, and he has given us hope. We have an anchor for our soul that is solid and unshakable. Jesus has entered in behind the veil, going ahead of us.

He has become a high priest after the pattern of Melchizedek to the age to come.

Melchizedek was the king of Salem and the priest of God Most High. He met Abraham when Abraham was returning from the slaughter of the northern kings, and he blessed him. Abraham tithed to Melchizedek a tenth of everything. Melchizedek's name can be translated as "king of justice" and also "king of Salem," meaning "king of peace." His father and mother aren't named. He has no genealogy. Genesis says nothing about his birth or his death. Like the son of God, he remains a priest forever.

How great is Melchizedek, that the patriarch Abraham would give him a tenth of his finest possessions? The Levites, who later received the priesthood, received a tithe of a tenth of the people's goods according to the Torah from their brothers. Levi was the great-grandson of Abraham. Melchizedek is in no way related to them but received a tithe from Abraham. Melchizedek blessed the one who received God's promises. It should be past the point of argument that a superior blesses an inferior. The Levites who received tithes are mortal men, but Melchizedek lives on. Because he is a descendant of Abraham, Levi himself pays the tithe to Melchizedek in Abraham. Levi was in Abraham's loins when Abraham met Melchizedek.

If the Levitical priesthood was perfect, and the people received that priesthood with the Torah, why would there need to be another priesthood like Melchizedek's that would come, rather than a descendant of Aaron? For the priesthood to change, that would mean a change in the Torah. The person we've been speaking about, Jesus, is from a tribe that didn't serve at the altar. Our Lord comes from the tribe of Judah. Moses says nothing about any priests from the tribe of Judah. The priesthood that arises patterned after Melchizedek is not based on a commandment of the Torah. It is also not based on a succession of generations but on an immortal life. The Scriptures testify that "You are a priest to the age to come according to the pattern of Melchizedek."

The earlier of the commandments regarding the priesthood are superseded because that priesthood proved weak and ineffectual. The Torah brought nothing to completion because there was a stronger hope coming that brings us closer to God. Like the promises to Abraham, this priesthood is sealed with an oath, because no one becomes a priest without an oath. He swears an oath when he says, "The Lord has sworn and will not change his mind. You are a priest to the age to come." Jesus has become the guarantee of a stronger covenant.

There have been many generations of priests because death prevents them from continuing. Because he remains to the age to come, his priesthood is permanent. He can completely save all those who draw near to God through him. He will live forever to intercede for them. He is a fitting high priest for us. He is holy, innocent, and undefiled. He has been separated from sinners and ascended higher than the heavens. He does not need to offer a sin offering every day for his own sins as the Levitical high priests do before making an offering for the sins of the people. He offered himself up once and for all. The Torah makes men high priests. They have weaknesses. After the Torah, a son has been perfected unto the age to come.

To sum things up, we have a high priest who sat down at the right hand of the throne of the highest majesty in the heavens. He ministers in the holy of holies of the true tabernacle, which was set up by the Lord, not by humans. Every high priest is appointed to offer gifts and sacrifices. It was necessary also for this high priest to make an offering. On earth, he was not a priest. Here, there are those who offer the sacrifices according to the Torah. They serve in a copy and a shadow of the heavenly sanctuary. We were taught this by Moses when he was about to complete the tabernacle. "Make everything according to the pattern that was shown to you on the mountain." Now, Jesus has obtained a greater ministry. It is as much better as the covenant of which he is a mediator, which has enacted the promises in a better way.

If the first covenant had been perfect, then there would have been no place for a second one. But finding fault with Israel, he says, "The days are coming, says the Lord, when I will cut with the house of Israel and the house of Judah a new covenant. It will not be like the covenant I made with their fathers on the day that I took them by the hand and led them out of Egypt. They did not continue in my covenant, and I disregarded them, says the Lord. This is the covenant that I will make with the house of Israel after those days, says the Lord. I will put my Torah into their mind, and I will write it upon their hearts. I will be their God, and they will be my people. No one will teach his neighbor or his brother saying, 'Know the Lord.' Everyone will know me, from the least of them to the greatest. I will be merciful toward their injustice, and I will no longer remember their sins." In saying that there will be a new covenant, he shows that the first one was imperfect. It is growing old and will eventually vanish.

The Torah contains regulations for worship and describes the sanctuary in this world. A tabernacle was made. In the first room were a lampstand and the table and the prothesis table, where the bread was kept. This room was called the holy place. Behind the second veil of the tabernacle was a place called the holy of holies. It had the golden altar of incense and the ark of the covenant, which was also covered all over with gold. There also were the golden jar containing the manna, Aaron's staff that had budded, and the tablets of the covenant. Over the ark were the glorious cherubim overshadowing the cover of the ark.

Once these things were built, the priests entered the first chamber every day to serve the daily services. The high priest entered the second chamber only once a year and not without blood that he offered for himself and the ignorant sins of the people. The Holy Spirit shows by this that the way was not open into the second chamber while the first chamber was still in use, pointing to our present age. The gifts and sacrifices that were offered in the first chamber were not able to make the worshippers perfect. These were the offering of food and drink and various ritual washings that were a means of controlling sinful desires until the time came for transformation in the Messiah.

The Messiah has appeared as the high priest of the good things that have now come. He has entered the greater and perfect tabernacle that was not made by human hands. It is not a part of the creation. He does not bring the blood of bulls or calves but his own blood. He entered once and for all into the holy of holies and gained us freedom for the age to come. If the blood of goats and bulls and the ashes of a heifer when sprinkled on something defiled made them holy for purification from the effects of sin, how much more will the blood of the Messiah, who offered himself unblemished to God through the Spirit of the age to come, clean our conscience from the works that lead to death and free us to serve the living God.

He is the mediator of a new covenant. He died to set us free from the violations of the first covenant so that we who have been called might receive the promise of the eternal inheritance. When a will is written, the one who made it must die in order for it to take effect. A will is affirmed after the person's death. It is not enforced while the person who made it is still alive. The first covenant was not made without blood. When Moses had spoken every commandment of the Torah to all the people, he took the blood of calves and goats with water and scarlet wool and hyssop. He sprinkled the book of the covenant and all the people, saying, "This is the blood of the covenant, which God has given to you." He sprinkled the tabernacle and all the vessels used for the services in it with blood. Almost everything was purified with blood in the Torah, and without shedding blood there was no purification.

Since the copies of the heavenly sanctuary were purified in this way, the heavenly sanctuary itself required a greater sacrifice than these. The Messiah has not entered the holy of holies made by human hands, the copy of the true one, but into the heavens themselves. He appears in the presence of God for us. He does not offer himself up for us repeatedly, as the high priest enters the holy of holies every year with another animal's blood. Otherwise, Jesus would have had to suffer and die over and over again since the world began. Instead, once, at the end of the ages, to get rid of sin once and for all, he has entered by his own sacrifice. People die once, and then they face judgment. So also, the Messiah offered himself once and bore the sins of many. He will appear a second time, with sin now taken care of, to those who are waiting for salvation.

The Torah contains a shadow of the good things that are coming. It does not contain the things themselves. Each year they offer the same sacrifices continuously, which are not able to make those who approach perfect. Otherwise, they would not still need to be offered, because everyone's consciences would have been cleansed of sins once by those serving. But there is a reminder of sins every year on the day of atonement. The blood of bulls and goats can't do away with sin. As he was coming into the world, he says, "Sacrifice and offerings you don't want. You have prepared a body for me. You do not delight in burnt offerings or sin offerings. Then I said, 'I have come to do your will, O God, as it is written about me in the scroll of the book.'" When he says, "You don't desire or delight in sacrifices and offerings and whole burnt offerings and sin offerings," he means the offerings of the Torah. Then he says, "I have come to do your will." He takes away the offerings of the first covenant to make the offering for the new covenant. We have been made holy through the offering of the body of Jesus the Messiah once and for all.

Every priest stands every day ministering and offering the same repeated sacrifices. They are never able to do away with sin. The one who offered himself as a sacrifice for sins in perpetuity sat down at the right hand of God. He now waits until his enemies are made his footstool. By one offering, he has made perfect for all time those who are being made holy. The Holy Spirit testifies to us about this by saying, "This is the covenant that I will make with them after those days, says the Lord. I will put my laws in their hearts, and I will write them in their minds." And "Their sins and their lawlessness I will not remember any more." Where there has been purification, there is no longer an offering for sin.

Brothers, we now have the confidence to enter the holy of holies through the blood of Jesus. He has created a new way of life that leads through the veil that is his flesh. We have a great high priest over the house of God. We should draw near with an honest heart, assured by our faithfulness. Our hearts have been sprinkled and made clean from an evil conscience. Our body has been washed with pure water. We should hold firmly to the hope that we profess because the one who gave the promises is faithful. We should think of one another, stirring each other up to love and good works. Do not forsake gathering with the community for worship as some do. Encourage one another, especially as you see the day of the Lord coming closer.

If we sin deliberately after we know the truth, then there is no longer a sacrifice for our sins. All that is left at that point is the expectation of judgment, fire, and fury that will devour the adversaries of God. In the Torah, Moses says that anyone will be executed on the testimony of two or three witnesses. How much worse will the son of God punish the one who tramples on the blood of the covenant, thinking it is something common? By that blood he was sanctified. This insults the Spirit of grace. We know that God said, "Vengeance is mine. I will repay" and "The Lord will judge his people." It is a frightening thing to fall into the hands of the living God.

Remember in the past when, after you were baptized, you endured conflict and suffering? You were slandered and faced trouble. You were made a spectacle. You are now part of a community that has also dealt with these things. You sympathized with prisoners. You let your own possessions be stolen and accepted it with joy. You knew that you had better possessions and a dwelling place in the age to come. Do not abandon your boldness; it has a great reward. You need endurance so that, having done the will of God in this life, you may receive the promises.

In a little while, the one who is coming will come without delay. The one purified through faithfulness will live. If he abandons his faithfulness, then my soul isn't pleased with him. We are not those who leave faithfulness for destruction. We are those who faithfully preserve our souls.

Faithfulness gives substance to the things we hope for and gives us confidence in things that we haven't seen. The elders received good testimony for this. Through our faithfulness, we know that the world was formed by God speaking. From things that didn't exist, he made all the things that we see. Because of his faithfulness, Abel offered a better sacrifice to God than Cain did. Because of this, it was testified that he was in the right; his sacrifice bore witness to his faithfulness to God. Though Abel died, he still speaks. Because of his faithfulness, Enoch was removed from the world so that he would not see death. He was not found on earth because he had been taken up to God. Before he was taken, it is said that he pleased God. Without faithfulness, it is impossible to please God. Faithfulness requires someone to draw near to God. They must know he is there, and they must seek after him to receive a reward. Noah was faithful to the instructions he received from God concerning things he hadn't seen yet. Piously, he built an ark for the salvation of his household. His faithfulness condemned the rest of the world. He became an heir of the purification that comes through faithfulness.

When Abraham was called, he faithfully obeyed and went out to a place where he was told he would receive an inheritance. He left, not knowing where he was going. He sojourned faithfully in the land that had been promised to him. He dwelt in tents in a foreign country with Isaac and Jacob, the coheirs of the same promise. He was waiting for the foundation of the city whose architect and builder is God. Sarah, though barren, was faithful and by miraculous power conceived a son. This happened well beyond the age in which it should be possible, because the one who made the promise saw her faithfulness. From one elderly man whose body was nearly dead were born children as numberless as the stars of heaven or the sand at the seashore. Generations lived and died faithfully without receiving the promises. They saw them at a distance, and they embraced them. They considered themselves strangers and wanderers on the earth. That they said those things revealed that they were seeking their own country. They weren't thinking of where they came from. They could have returned. They yearned for a better country in the heavens. God is not ashamed to be called their God. He has prepared a city for them.

Abraham faithfully offered Isaac as a sacrifice when he was tested. He was even willing to offer his unique son, the one who had received the promises. It was said to him, "Through Isaac your line will be reckoned." Abraham knew that God was able to raise the dead, having seen a child come from a dead womb. Isaac blessed Jacob and Esau faithfully because of the things that were coming. Jacob faithfully blessed each of the sons of Joseph as he was dying, and he offered worship as the head of his clan. When he was dying, Joseph faithfully remembered the exodus of the sons of Israel and gave instructions concerning his bones.

Faithfully, Moses' parents hid him for three months after he was born because they saw he was a beautiful child, and they did not fear the edict of the king. Moses, when he was grown, because of his faithfulness refused to be called the son of Pharaoh's daughter. Instead, he chose to suffer along with the people of God rather than to enjoy sin. He saw that the suffering of the Messiah is a greater treasure than all the wealth of Egypt. He looked forward to his reward. Faithfully, he left Egypt not because he feared the king; he persevered before the eyes of God. Faithfully, Moses kept the Passover and sprinkled the blood so that the destroyer of the firstborn would not touch them. Faithfully, the Israelites passed through the Red Sea as though on dry land. When the Egyptians tried it, they were swallowed up. After the Israelites faithfully circled the city of Jericho for seven days, the walls fell. Rahab the prostitute because of her faithfulness did not die with those who were disobedient. She received the spies in peace.

What more can I say? There is not enough time to talk about Gideon, Barak, Samson, Jephthah, David, Samuel, and all the prophets. Faithfully they conquered kingdoms, administered justice, obtained the promises, shut the mouths of lions, quenched powerful fires, escaped the mouth of the sword, became strong in weakness, became mighty in war; they put to flight armies of foreigners. Women received their dead back by resurrection. Others were tortured and did not accept release, in order to obtain a better resurrection. Others were mocked and scourged and put on trial. They were imprisoned in chains. They were stoned, they were sawn in two, they were slaughtered with the sword. They wandered the earth in sheep and goat skins. They were destitute, oppressed, and mistreated. The world was not worthy of them. They wandered in deserts and mountains and caves and holes in the ground.

The faithfulness of all these is witnessed to, but they did not ultimately receive the promise. God had something better planned, so they were not made perfect before us. Since we are surrounded by a cloud of witnesses like these, let us lay aside everything that weighs us down and the sin that will ensnare us. With endurance, we should run the race that stretches out before us. We should look to the initiator and perfecter of our faithfulness, Jesus. Because of the joy that was in front of him, he endured the cross, rejected its shamefulness, and sat down at the right hand of the throne of God. Think of him—how he endured so much hostility from sinners—so that you don't grow weary, and your souls don't faint.

You are struggling with sin, but you have not yet had to shed your blood. You have forgotten the encouragement that is addressed to you as sons: "My son, do not take the Lord's discipline lightly. Do not faint when he corrects you. The Lord disciplines every son whom he loves and corrects every son whom he receives." When you endure discipline, God is treating you as his sons. What son is not disciplined by his father? If you never share in discipline, then you are illegitimate children and not sons. Our human fathers corrected us, and we respected them. How much more should we be obedient to the Father of spirits so that we will live? For a short time, they disciplined us as best they could. God disciplines us for our benefit to share his holiness with us. When you are being disciplined, it is painful, not joyful. Afterward, however, discipline can bear good fruit. To those who have been taught by it, discipline produces purification through repentance. Lift those with drooping hands and wobbling knees. Make the paths straight for your feet so that those who can't walk will be healed rather than suffer.

Seek peace with everyone. Seek holiness. Without holiness, no one will see the Lord. Watch that no one falls away from the gift of God. Do not let any root of bitterness spring up within you. By bitterness, many people can be made unclean. Do not be sexually immoral or profane like Esau, who sold his firstborn status for a meal. Later, when he wanted to inherit the blessing, he was rejected. He did not receive it despite his repentance with tears.

You have not come to Mt. Sinai that cannot be touched, which is kindled with fire and covered in darkness, gloom, and the storm. There was the sound of a trumpet and a voice speaking words that, when they heard it, they begged that they not hear God speak to them directly. They could not bear his commands. If even an animal touched that mountain, it was stoned to death. The mountain was so fearsome that Moses said, "I am greatly afraid and trembling." Instead, you have come to Mt. Zion, the city of the living God, the heavenly Jerusalem. You have come to myriads of angels, the assembly and gathering of the firstborn, whose names are written in the heavens. You have come to God, the judge of all, and to pure spirits that have been made perfect. You have come to Jesus, the mediator of a new covenant. The sprinkling of his blood speaks better things for us than the blood of Abel.

Pay attention that you don't reject the one who is speaking to you. They did not escape on the earth when they refused Moses' instruction. How much less will we escape if we turn away from the one in the heavens. His voice shook the earth at Sinai. He has promised, "One more time I will shake not only the earth but also the heavens." This "once more" shows that the things being shaken are being removed. They are all created, but after the shaking, the things not shaken will remain. We are receiving a kingdom that will never be shaken. We have a gift that lets us worship in a way that is pleasing to God, with reverence and awe. Our God is a consuming fire.

Continue to love each other as brothers. Do not forget hospitality, because some have entertained angels without realizing it. Remember those in prison as if you were in chains with them. Remember those who are mistreated as if you shared a body with them. Let marriage be honored by everyone, and let the marriage bed not be defiled. God will judge the sexually immoral and adulterers. Live your life without greed. Be satisfied with what you presently have. He himself has said, "I will never leave you or abandon you." We are so confident that we are able to say, "The Lord helps me, so I have no fear of what people might do to me."

Remember your leaders, who spoke to you of the Word of God. Look at their way of life and its results. Imitate their faithfulness. Jesus the Messiah is the same yesterday and today and to the ages. Don't be carried away by various strange teachings. It is good for your heart to be strengthened by grace and not with food that doesn't benefit those dedicated to it. We have an altar from which those who serve in the tabernacle have no authority to eat. The blood of animals is brought to their high priest, and he brings it into the holy of holies. The bodies of those sacrifices are burned outside the camp. Jesus also, so that his blood could make the people holy, suffered outside the city gate. We should go out to him, outside the camp, and share in the insults hurled at him. Here we have no city that will remain. We look for the city that is coming.

Through him, we offer the sacrifice of praise for everything to God. We offer the fruit of our lips, confessing his name. Do not forget to do good and to share. God is pleased with these sacrifices. Obey your leaders, and be obedient. They watch over your souls, and they will have to give an account for you to God. Let them do this with joy and not grumbling. Otherwise, it will not be beneficial for you.

Pray for us. We have a good conscience about everything and want to conduct ourselves well. Continue to do this, and as soon as possible I will visit you again.

May the God of peace, who brought back from the dead the great shepherd of the sheep, by the blood of the covenant of the age to come, our Lord Jesus, equip you in everything good. Then you will do his will. His will works in us to do the things that are pleasing to him through Jesus the Messiah, to whom be glory unto the ages of ages. Amen.

Brothers, I encourage you to accept this word of encouragement. I have written to you in a few words. You know that our brother Timothy has been released. I will come with him to see you if he arrives soon.

Greet all your leaders and all the holy ones. Greet those who are from Italy.

Grace be with all of you. Amen.

TWO LETTERS TO
TIMOTHY

The First Letter to Timothy

Paul, an apostle of the Messiah Jesus sent at the command of God our Savior and the Messiah Jesus, our hope,

To Timothy, my son to whom I gave birth in faithfulness,

Grace, mercy, and peace from God the Father and the Messiah Jesus our Lord,

Remember when I encouraged you to stay in Ephesus when I went to Macedonia. I wanted you to give certain people a warning not to teach strange things or to hold on to myths or endless genealogies of spiritual beings. These are the subject of unending speculation, but they don't produce faithful servants of God. What we teach produces love from a pure heart and a good conscience and sincere faithfulness. Some people have not achieved these things because they got distracted by idle talk and speculation. They want to be Torah teachers, but they don't understand what they are saying, despite how confidently they make assertions.

We know that the Torah is good if one interprets it properly. The Torah is not for the person who is pure; it is to correct people who are lawless, insubordinate, ungodly, and sinful. It judges what is unholy and profane: people who would murder their fathers and mothers, murderers, the sexually immoral, men who have sex with men, slavers, liars, perjurers, and those who do anything else that is opposed to correct teaching—sound teaching like the gospel of the blessed glory of God with which I was entrusted.

I am thankful for the one who strengthened me, namely, the Messiah Jesus our Lord. He considered me faithful, and he appointed me to ministry even though I used to be a blasphemer, a persecutor, and rebellious. He had mercy on me because I was ignorant. I did what I did faithlessly. Since then, the gift of our Lord to me has only increased with the faithfulness and love of the Messiah Jesus. It is a trustworthy statement that you should hold to: "The Messiah Jesus came into the world to save sinners. First of all, me." I was shown mercy so that Jesus the Messiah could show his patience with humanity through me, the worst sinner. He made me a pattern for those who would become his faithful followers on the way to the life of the age to come. To the king of all ages who is immortal, invisible, and the only God be honor and glory unto ages of ages. Amen.

I give you this directive, Timothy my son. Learn the Scriptures written by the prophets who came before us. Knowing them, you will be able to fight well in the warfare that we face. Remain faithful and keep a good conscience. Some people have lost these things and shipwrecked, like Hymenaeus and Alexander. I removed them from the community so that by suffering at the hands of Satan they will learn not to blaspheme.

I encourage you, first, to make requests, prayers, intercessions, and offer thanks to God for every person. Especially pray for kings and those who hold positions of authority, so that we can lead a peaceful and quiet life in piety and holiness. This is a good thing that pleases our Savior, God. God desires that every person would find salvation and come to know the truth. There is one God, and there is one mediator between God and humanity, the man, the Messiah Jesus. He gave himself to free everyone. This was witnessed when it happened, at the appropriate time. I was appointed to announce, and sent as an apostle, to tell this truth. I am not lying. I teach the nations faithfulness and truth. I want men everywhere to pray, to lift up their hands, without anger and disagreement.

Women in the community should wear respectable clothing, be modest and self-controlled. They don't need to ornament themselves with elaborately braided hair or gold or jewelry or expensive clothes. If a woman is reverent toward God, she should ornament herself by doing good. A woman should learn in the community by gathering in humility and practicing silence. I do not allow a woman to teach or exercise authority over a man. She should learn in silence. Adam was formed first and then Eve. Adam was not deceived, but his wife was, and sin came into the world. She will be saved by the birth of the Messiah, as will women who maintain faithfulness, love, holiness, and self-control.

Here is another saying you should accept: If someone aspires to be a bishop, he wants a good thing. A bishop needs to be above reproach. He must have only one wife and must be sober, self-controlled, respectable, hospitable, and able to teach others. He must not be a drunk or a brawler but gentle, peaceful, and not greedy. He must manage his own family responsibilities well, having humble and dignified children. If he can't manage his own household, he can't be given additional responsibilities to manage the community of God. He cannot have joined the community only recently. If so, he might become proud, and the devil may tempt him into condemnation. He should have a good reputation outside the community so that he won't fall into the devil's trap through accusations.

Deacons should also be dignified, not two-faced, not given to drunkenness or greed. They should hold faithfully to the mystery of the gospel with a clear conscience. These men must first be tested and then allowed to serve when they are seen to be blameless. Deaconesses ought also to be dignified, not slanderers, clear-headed, and faithful in everything. Deacons must be the husband of only one wife and manage their children and families well. Deacons who serve well have a good standing before God and a confident faithfulness to the Messiah Jesus.

I am writing these things to you because I am hoping to come to see you soon. If I get delayed, I want you to know how someone should conduct themselves as a leader in God's household, which is the gathered communities of the living. These communities are the pillar and base that supports the truth. We must admit, our piety is a great mystery. The Messiah was revealed in the flesh, purified in the Spirit, seen by angels, preached among the nations, faithfully followed in the world, and taken up to the heavens in glory.

The Spirit has said clearly that in these last times before the Messiah appears, some will abandon faithfulness. Instead, they will follow lying spirits and the teachings of demons. They are hypocrites, liars; their conscience is scarred over from burns. They don't want people to get married; they tell people not to eat food that God created for the faithful, who know the truth, to eat with thanksgiving. Everything God created is good, and nothing should be rejected. Everything should be received by giving thanks to God for it. Everything is made holy by the Word of God through prayer.

If you explain these things to the brothers, you will be a good servant of the Messiah Jesus. They will be fed with the faithful words and good teaching that you follow. Reject silly and useless fables. Train yourself in piety. Bodily exercise has some value, but piety is valuable in every way. Piety brings the promise of life now and in the age to come. Here is another saying that you should accept: "We work and struggle because we have hope in the living God. He is the savior of all humans, especially the faithful."

Command and teach these things. Don't let anyone look down on you because you are young. Let your life be a pattern for the faithful in speech, conduct, love, faithfulness, and purity. Until I get there, listen to the Scriptures when they are read publicly and to the preaching and teaching that you receive. Don't neglect your own gift of preaching, for which you were set aside by the laying on of hands by the presbyters. Think about these things and focus on them so that you will continue to make progress for everyone's benefit. Know yourself and what you teach. If you continue this way, you will save yourself and those who hear you.

Don't publicly correct a presbyter of the community. Encourage him as if he were your father. Treat younger men as your brothers, older women as if they were your mother, and younger women as if they were your sisters in purity. Care for widows who are truly alone. If a widow has children or grandchildren, those children need to learn to be pious and to honor their parents. This is what pleases God. A widow who is truly left alone in the world has hope in God and can pray continually night and day. If she lives in a self-indulgent way, she is already dead, even while she is still alive. Teach them so they will be above reproach. If someone doesn't provide for themselves, or especially if they don't provide for their own family, he has rejected faithfulness and is worse than the faithless outside the community.

A widow should assist in the community if she is over sixty years old, has been the wife of one husband, is known for doing good works, has brought up children well, has entertained strangers, has shown humility toward others and comforted the troubled, and if she has been faithful in every good work. Younger widows should not be given leadership positions like this, because they may, because of the desires of the flesh, decide to remarry. If someone in a leadership position remarries, this will bring judgment because they have set aside their faithfulness to God in favor of something else. Younger women in these positions may also fall into laziness, gossip, and going from house to house being busybodies and stirring up trouble. A young widow should just marry again, have children, manage her household, and not give anyone cause to make an accusation. Some who were given leadership positions too soon have turned aside to follow Satan. If a faithful woman has a widow in her family, she should take care of her if she can, rather than making the community responsible. This way widows who are truly alone will get the care they need.

You should give twice as much honor to presbyters who govern their communities well. This is especially true of presbyters who work hard in studying and teaching. The Scriptures say, "You will not muzzle an ox while it treads out your grain." They also say, "The worker deserves his wages." Do not listen to an accusation made against a presbyter unless there are two or three witnesses. Those who are sinning should be corrected publicly so that everyone else will have reverence.

I testify before God and the Messiah Jesus and the chosen angels that you should do these things with no favoritism. Do nothing out of partiality. Do not make anyone a leader too hastily. Do not share in other people's sins. Keep yourself pure. Don't drink only water. Drink a little wine. It will help with your stomach and your health issues.

Some people's sins are obvious and public, so they are judged. Some people's sins are hidden and will appear only on the day of the Lord. Some good works are obvious and public, but those that aren't will be revealed.

Those of you who are currently enslaved should honor your masters so that the name of God and the teaching of the gospel won't be blasphemed by outsiders. If your masters are faithful to the Messiah, do not be disrespectful to them, because they are your brother. Rather, serve them because they are faithful and God loves them. They will be helped by your good service. Teach these things and encourage them.

If someone comes teaching something else and won't hear the words of our Lord Jesus, the Messiah, and pious teaching, he is arrogant and knows nothing. All he wants are unhealthy controversies and a war of words. Nothing comes out of this but jealousy, strife, slander, suspicion, and evil. Being constantly involved in disputes will corrupt a person's mind and leave them not knowing the truth. They think piety is a way to make money. Stay away from people like this.

There is a lot to gain from piety if you are content. We brought nothing with us when we were born into the world. We will not be able to carry anything out with us when we leave it. But if we have food and clothes, we can be content with that. People who want to be rich fall into a trap and give in to temptations. Greed will plunge people into ruin and destruction through foolish and harmful desires. The love of money is the root of all kinds of evil deeds. Some people who grasp for wealth have been seduced away from faithfulness. They have been pierced with sorrows like many arrows.

You are a man of God. You must run away from these things and chase after purification, piety, faith, love, endurance, and gentleness. Fight the good fight faithfully. Grasp for the life of the age to come. You were called to it, and you have made a good confession before many witnesses. I command you before God, who gives life to all things, and the Messiah Jesus, who stood before Pontius Pilate and gave a good confession, to keep the commandments without stain. Be above reproach until our Lord Jesus the Messiah appears. When the time is right, he will display the only blessed ruler, the king of kings and Lord of lords. He alone has immortality and dwells in unapproachable light. No human has seen him or is able to. To him be honor and might unto the ages. Amen.

Command those who are rich in this present age not to be proud or to put their trust in uncertain riches. They should place their trust in God, who provides all things richly for our enjoyment. They should do good. They should be rich in good works. They should be generous and ready to share what they have. With their wealth, they can lay themselves a good foundation in the age to come that they can use to take hold of life in that age.

Timothy, guard the deposit that was given to you. Avoid profane, empty, and endless arguments about what is not truly knowledge. Some people, in professing those things, have wandered from faithfulness. Grace be with you all. Amen.

The Second Letter to Timothy

Paul, an apostle of the Messiah Jesus sent by the will of God with the promise of life in the Messiah Jesus,

To Timothy my son, whom I love.

Grace, mercy, and peace from God the Father and the Messiah Jesus our Lord,

I thank the God of my fathers, whom I serve with a pure conscience for you in my prayers both by night and by day. I want to see you because I remember your tears, and I want to be filled with joy. I remember your sincere faithfulness. You inherited it from your grandmother Lois and your mother, Eunice. I know that their faithfulness lives on in you.

I want to remind you of the gift that God gave you when I laid hands on you to assign you to ministry. God has not given us a Spirit of cowardice, but a Spirit of miraculous power, of love, and of self-control. Do not be embarrassed to testify about our Lord or about me, his prisoner. Suffer with me for the gospel, which is the miraculous power of

God. God has saved us and called us to ministry not because of something we did, but for his own reasons, as a gift that has been given to us in the Messiah Jesus before the first age of time. Now this ministry has appeared because our Savior, the Messiah Jesus, has appeared. He has abolished death and brought us life and immortality through the gospel. I have been called to preach this gospel, and I was sent to teach it. This is why I suffer with all the things that have happened to me. I am not embarrassed. I know the one to whom I am faithful. I am confident that he will guard the deposit that I have entrusted to him until the day of the Lord.

Keep to the words of teaching that you heard from me in faithfulness and love, in the Messiah Jesus. Guard the deposit that I entrusted to you through the Holy Spirit, who dwells in us. You know that everyone in Asia abandoned me, among whom are Phygelus and Hermogenes. May the Lord have mercy on Onesiphoros and his family because they often helped me, and he was not embarrassed of me. When he arrived in Rome, he tracked me down and found me. May the Lord grant him mercy on the day of the Lord. You know how much help he was to me in Ephesus as well.

But you, my son, be strong in the gift you received from the Messiah Jesus. The things that you have heard me preach publicly, entrust them to faithful men who are able to teach others. Deal with hardship the way a good soldier in the Messiah Jesus does. No one who is serving as a soldier gets involved in worldly affairs while he is serving. He waits until after his term of service. He wants to please his superior officers. Someone who competes doesn't get the trophy unless he competes according to the rules. A farmer who has worked hard will need to eat the firstfruits of his farming. Think about the things that I say, and the Lord will help you understand everything.

Remember that Jesus the Messiah has been raised from the dead. He is the seed of David. All of this is in the gospel that I preach. I am suffering for that gospel. I am held in chains like a criminal. But the Word of God is not imprisoned. I am willing to endure everything for those called by God so that they may achieve salvation in the Messiah Jesus and obtain glory in the age to come. Here is a saying that you should hold to: "If we have died with him, we will also live with him. If we endure, we will reign with him. If we deny him, he will deny us. If we are faithless, he remains faithful. He is not able to deny himself."

Remind them of these things. Charge them before God not to argue about words. This is worthless and doesn't help those who hear it. Work yourself so that when you are presented to God as a workman, you will not be embarrassed. Handle the word of truth correctly. Don't get involved in empty, worldly babbling. It only leads to more ungodliness. This kind of talk spreads like gangrene. Hymenaeus and Philetus, who have wandered from the truth, are like this. They say that the resurrection has already happened. Their teachings are destroying the faithfulness of some people. The foundation that God has laid is still there. This is its seal: "The Lord knows who belongs to him," and "Everyone who worships the Lord must leave behind injustice."

In a large household there are some vessels made of gold and silver. There are also vessels made from wood and clay. Some of these are used for honorable purposes, and some of them are used for dishonorable purposes. Any of these vessels, if they are cleaned, can be used for honorable, even holy, purposes by the master of the house. Washing will make it ready for any good purpose it might be used for. Flee from the sinful desires of your youth. Pursue purification, faithfulness, love, and peace with those who worship the Lord with a pure heart. Reject foolish and ignorant speculations, because they only give birth to arguments. A servant of the Lord shouldn't pick fights. He should be gentle toward everyone, teaching them, being patient with them, and discipling them gently. Then God may give them repentance and knowledge of the truth. Then they might come to their senses and escape the devil's trap. They have been captured by him to do his will.

Know this: these last days will be difficult times. People will love themselves; they will love money; they will be boastful, proud, blasphemers, disobedient to their parents, ungrateful, unholy, unloving, merciless, slanderous, out of control, savage, lacking love for what is good, treacherous, reckless, pleasure loving rather than God loving. They have a kind of piety, but it has no miraculous power. Stay away from these people. These are the kind of men who enter houses and take weaker women hostage, heavy with their sins. They are led away to chase all kinds of sinful desires. They seem to always be learning, but they never actually learn the truth. Just like Jannes and Jambres opposed Moses, these depraved men oppose the truth. They are disqualified from faithfulness. They will not go on for much longer. Soon everyone will realize they are fools, just like Jannes and Jambres were.

You have followed my teaching, my way of life, my sense of purpose, my patience, my love, my endurance, the attacks against me, and everything that I suffered in Antioch, Iconium, and Lystra. I suffered all kinds of attacks, but the Lord saved me from all of them. Everyone who wants a pious life in the Messiah Jesus will be attacked. Evil men and phonies will go from bad to worse, deceiving others and being deceived themselves. Keep with the things that you have learned and that you know. You know from whom you learned them. You have known the Scriptures from your childhood. They can make you wise and bring about your salvation through faithfulness to the Messiah Jesus. All the Scriptures are spoken by God and are valuable for teaching, for convicting, for correction, for training in purification. Knowing the Scriptures will make you a mature man of God who is prepared for all kinds of good work.

I testify before God and the Messiah Jesus, who is coming to judge the living and the dead, and by his appearing and his kingdom: Preach the Word. Be ready in good times and in bad times. Convict, rebuke, and exhort with patience as you teach. A time is coming when they won't tolerate true teaching. They will gather teachers for themselves who will tell them what they want to hear and allow them to indulge their sinful desires. They will reject hearing the truth, and they will chase after myths. But you, be sober. Endure all kinds of suffering. Do the work of spreading the gospel, and carry out your ministry.

I am about to be poured out as a drink offering. Soon I will leave this world. I have fought the good fight. I have finished the race. I have remained faithful. What remains for me is the crown of justice, the Lord's reward for me on the day in which he judges justly. It is not only my reward, but the reward of everyone who loves his appearing.

Please come to me quickly. Demas has deserted me because he loves the present age and has gone back to Thessalonica. Crescens went back to Galatia. Titus went to Dalmatia. Luke is the only one here with me. Get Mark and bring him with you, because he is helpful to me in my ministry. I sent Tychicus to Ephesus. Bring the cloak I left with Carpus in Troas with you when you come. Also bring the books, especially the parchments. Alexander the coppersmith hurt me badly. The Lord will repay him for his deeds. Beware of him. He is violently opposed to what we preach.

During my first trial, no one stood with me. Everyone abandoned me. Do not blame them for it. The Lord stood by me and strengthened me so that my preaching would be complete and all the nations would hear it. I was saved from a lion's mouth. The Lord will deliver me from every evil deed and will save me in his kingdom in the heavens. To him be glory unto the ages of ages. Amen.

Greet Priscilla and Aquila and the household of Onesiphoros. Erastus remained in Corinth. I left Trophimus in Miletus because he was sick. Try to come before winter. Eubulus greets you and Pudens and Linus and Claudia and all the brothers.

The Lord be with your spirit. Grace be with you all. Amen.

TO

TITUS

Paul, a servant of God, an apostle sent by Jesus the Messiah for the faithfulness of those called by God and to spread the knowledge of the truth, which is piety, in the hope of the life of the age to come that was promised by God before the first age of time. God cannot lie. At his own time, he revealed his Word. I have been entrusted with preaching him according to the commandment of God our Savior.

To Titus, my son to whom I gave birth through our common faithfulness,

Grace and peace from God the Father and the Messiah Jesus our Savior,

I left you in Crete so that you could put things into good order and appoint presbyters in every city, as I directed you. If a man is blameless, the husband of only one wife, has faithful children, is not accused of loose living or being insubordinate, he can become a presbyter. A bishop must be blameless because he serves as the master of God's house. He should not be selfish, angry, drunk, a brawler, or greedy. He should be hospitable, a lover of good things, self-controlled, just, holy, and self-disciplined. He must be faithful to the teaching of the Word so that he will be able to encourage those with correct teaching and to correct those who contradict it.

There are many who are insubordinate, babblers, and liars, especially among the Jewish members of the community. If they aren't publicly corrected and prevented from teaching, they will lead whole households astray. They teach to make money. One of their own prophets said that all Cretans are liars, bestial, gluttons, and lazy. This testimony is true. You need to publicly correct them so that they may become faithful to God. Don't get involved in the fine details of Jewish traditions and commandments added by men that turn away from the truth. Everything is pure to those who are pure. Nothing is pure to a person who is faithless and unclean in their mind and their conscience. They claim that they know God, but they deny him by what they do. They are wicked and disobedient and unworthy to do any good work.

You should speak the things consistent with correct teaching. Older men should be sober, dignified, self-controlled, and stable in their faithfulness, love, and endurance. Older women, similarly, should behave piously; they should not slander or drink too much, which will make them slaves. They should teach what is good so that they can educate the young women. They should love their husbands and their children. They should be self-controlled and pure. They should govern their homes kindly and be obedient to their husbands so that no one criticizes the Word of God based on their behavior.

Young men should be exhorted to exercise self-control. You need to set a good example in everything you do. Teach with integrity, dignity, and reasoned arguments, and be above reproach. This way anyone who opposes you will be ashamed because they have nothing evil to say concerning us. Slaves should obey their masters and do everything they do well, without arguing. Don't steal, but faithfully show goodness so that the teaching of our Savior God may beautify everything.

The Messiah has appeared as the gift of God to bring salvation to all people. He teaches us that by rejecting ungodliness and the sinful desires of this world, we should live in the present age with wisdom, purity, and piety. We await the blessed hope, the appearance of the glory of our Great God and Savior, the Messiah Jesus. He gave himself for us to free us from all lawlessness and to purify a people for himself. He called us to zealously pursue good works. Teach and encourage these things, and rebuke those who oppose this teaching with all your authority. Do not let anyone look down on you.

Remind them that they should be obedient to the rulers and civil authorities. Be ready for every good work when the opportunity presents itself. No one should speak evil. Be peaceful and gentle. Show humility to everyone. Once we were foolish and disobedient. We were deceived and served the lusts and desires of sin. We lived in malice and jealousy. We were hateful; we hated each other. Then God our Savior's kindness and love for humanity was shown, not in some pure works that we did, but through his mercy. He saved us by giving us the washing of a new birth and renewing us in the Holy Spirit that he poured out on us through Jesus the Messiah, our Savior. Having been purified by that gift, we have become heirs of the hope of the life of the age to come. What we've just said is reliable, and I want you to affirm these things strongly in your preaching. That way those who are faithful to God will become devoted to doing good works. Pursuing good works is good and valuable for all people.

Avoid controversies and intricate arguments and infighting about the Torah. These arguments are not worth it and are not helpful. After correcting him twice, expel a man from the community who causes arguments and divisions. This kind of person is corrupt. They are sinning and will condemn themselves.

When I send Artemas to you or Tychicus, be sure to come to me in Nicopolis. I have decided to spend the winter there. Do everything you can to provide for Zenas the lawyer and Apollos whatever they need. Let all our people learn to pursue good works and meet each other's needs so that they won't be unfruitful.

All those who are with me greet you. Greet those faithful who love us. Grace be with all of you. Amen.

Index

This index only covers the first part of this book; the interpretive translation of St. Paul's epistles is not indexed. Maps are indicated by page numbers in italics.

We hope you have enjoyed and benefited from this book. Your financial support makes it possible to continue our nonprofit ministry both in print and online. Because the proceeds from our book sales only partially cover the costs of operating **Ancient Faith Publishing** and **Ancient Faith Radio**, we greatly appreciate the generosity of our readers and listeners. Donations are tax deductible and can be made at **www.ancientfaith.com.**

To view our other publications,
please visit our wesite:
store.ancientfaith.com

Bringing you Orthodox Christian music, readings, prayers, teaching, and podcasts 24 hours a day since 2004 at **www.ancientfaith.com**

www.ingramcontent.com/pod-product-compliance
Lightning Source LLC
Chambersburg PA
CBHW021701120626
46545CB00004B/1345